JAPANESE AMERICANS AND THE RACIAL UNIFORM

Japanese Americans and the Racial Uniform

Citizenship, Belonging, and the Limits of Assimilation

Dana Y. Nakano

NEW YORK UNIVERSITY PRESS

New York

NEW YORK UNIVERSITY PRESS
New York
www.nyupress.org

© 2023 by New York University
All rights reserved

Please contact the Library of Congress for Cataloging-in-Publication data.
ISBN: 9781479816361 (hardback)
ISBN: 9781479816378 (paperback)
ISBN: 9781479816408 (library ebook)
ISBN: 9781479816392 (consumer ebook)

This book is printed on acid-free paper, and its binding materials are chosen for strength and durability. We strive to use environmentally responsible suppliers and materials to the greatest extent possible in publishing our books. Manufactured in the United States of America.

10 9 8 7 6 5 4 3 2 1

Also available as an ebook

To my mother,

Sheri Nakano

And in loving memory of my father,

Gary Nakano

They are the reason for this book.

CONTENTS

I Was Born to Write This Book

I exist because of a place called Japanese Village and Deer Park. Deer Park—as it is affectionately remembered—was a small amusement park and orientalist fantasy open for less than a decade in Orange County, California. As Southern California attractions go, Deer Park is easily overshadowed by the fame and longevity of its closest neighbors, Knott's Berry Farm and Disneyland. Seemingly forgotten in the annals of Southern California history, Deer Park and the community it spawned were deeply familiar to me long before I embarked on this study. Deer Park is where my parents met. And not just my parents, but many of my aunts and uncles worked and met their spouses at Deer Park. Beyond family, so many of my parents' friends while I was growing up seemed to be Japanese American, and nearly all these life-long friendships stemmed from Deer Park. As a kid, it would often happen that when I made a new Japanese American friend at school or through a sports team, my parents already knew their parents because of Deer Park. Throughout my life, my parents' house has been filled with a surprising amount of Japanese art, dishware, tea sets, and other ornamentation for people who had never been to Japan. Save for a few family heirlooms, most of these objects were from Deer Park. These trinkets were part of my first and formative exposure to Japanese—or perhaps Japanese American—culture. Unquestionably, my life—biological, social, and cultural—has been shaped by Deer Park.

That I found myself part of the fourth generation of Japanese Americans that owes its very existence to Deer Park is sheer luck of the genetic draw. That I have come to write this book is no accident. If not for my parents, I may not even have known Deer Park existed, but my life and experiences have developed in me unique knowledge and insight to understand Deer Park as a peculiar and unintentional space where the

Japanese American community continued and thrived. I was born to tell this story.

To fulfill this calling, I needed to accrue the tools that would allow me to tell this story effectively. While Deer Park is the origin of this book and an important story in its own right, I wanted to show that it is part of a larger pattern of a concerted persistence of Japanese American identity and community. For this reason, I decided to pursue my doctorate in sociology. Not only would this education provide me with the methodological tools necessary to complete this study, but it also reinforced my need to tell this story. This is a lesson I learned early.

In the first quarter of my doctoral program, my cohort was required to attend a proseminar course that introduced us to the various opportunities, resources, and faculty within the department. One hour a week, a revolving door of faculty members representing the various subject-area strengths of our department would stop by and tell us about their past and future research. I was most interested to hear from the immigration scholars. When the day came, the two faculty members, both white, who joined us in the proseminar spoke about their research on the incorporation of Mexican immigrants in the United States. I listened patiently, and finally my classmate asked the question that was circulating in my own head: "Do you study other groups as well?" One of the faculty members made a passing comment that they had supervised a thesis on Asian Americans, so perhaps they could say they studied that. Red flag number one.

Both faculty members then began to defend their focus on the Mexican-origin immigrant population. Given our location in Southern California and the proximity to the US-Mexico border, the focus made sense. Mexico has long been the country sending the largest number of immigrants to the US; fair enough. As they continued their defense, one of the faculty members stated that Mexican Americans are also one of the oldest immigrant-origin communities in terms of generations. The other faculty member added, "Japanese Americans have also been here a long time." The first faculty member—the same one who claimed to have studied Asian Americans after advising a thesis—quickly shot back, "Well, some groups are so assimilated, you wouldn't be able to find them"—as if I was not sitting right there in the classroom. Red flag number two.

To be clear, I do not assume that these two faculty members had any ill intent. While their words rendered me invisible—or perhaps just racially white—they were simply speaking from their research expertise and towing the sociological line. This was an early—and, I would learn, frequent—reminder of how Japanese Americans and Asian Americans more broadly have come to be understood in the sociological imagination. Sociology and I have very different perspectives on the contemporary Japanese American experience.

These two personal anecdotes reveal why I wrote this book. This book makes substantial and well-researched claims that I hope will impact the disciplines of sociology and ethnic studies, but it is also deeply personal. In revealing these personal connections to my subject matter, I do not mean to centralize myself. The words and experiences shared in the pages of this book are not mine, and I have made every honest effort to maintain the integrity of my participants' voices. But as sociologist Eve Ewing (2018) succinctly states, "Indeed, the story is not an objective one; I am not an objective observer, nor do I aspire to be" (7). Notwithstanding debates on the existence of objectivity, I want to be honest about my positionality as it relates to my subject. My connection to Deer Park, my personal political commitments to productive, intersectional anti-racist discourse, and my experiences as part of Japanese American communities are central to my interpretation of the Japanese American experience, which I argue is misunderstood and described inadequately in terms of race, particularly in the discipline of sociology. While flaws may exist within the design and implementation of this research project, my honesty on this point and the elevation of Japanese American voices on this subject do not make my scholarship any less valid or less reliable. Ewing continues, "The experiential knowledge of people of color not only is a legitimate source of evidence, but it is critical to understanding the function of racism as a fundamental American social structure" (8). This may seem a banal point to ethnic studies scholars, but it remains an important one in the face of sociology and the sociological description of the Japanese American experience.

Growing up as a fourth-generation Japanese American—yonsei—in Southern California, I cannot understand the argument that Japanese Americans are "so assimilated you wouldn't be able to find them." Such sociological arguments do not reflect the rich Japanese American community I grew up with. Such sociological arguments do not reflect the persistent racialization and racism I experience as an Asian-appearing person in the US—an Asian racial uniform. I recognize that not all Japanese Americans grew up with Deer Park or in environments similar to the Southern California suburbs, but my own unease with the sociological arguments about my experience is also not aberrant. It is my insider status that provides an important alternative perspective and allows me invaluable insights and reflections on the persistence and racialization of the Japanese American community that is so quickly dismissed in the mainstream sociological literature.

To say that it is hard to move a discipline is an understatement. I am under no delusions that a single monograph from an unknown scholar at the margins of the discipline can move mountains. But any effort to shift a conversation must begin with the language we use and the vocabulary at our disposal. As I tell my students at the beginning of each term of my Race and Ethnic Relations course, we need to build a better vocabulary and fluency in race, ethnicity, and racism if we are to bring about meaningful justice and liberation. Despite living in a world that functions so deeply on the logics of race, the hegemonic powers within our society have intentionally left us ill prepared and uncomfortable in conversation on these topics. Our public discourse lacks the critical language to have productive exchanges that work toward intersectional solutions for racial inequities. Without a shared vocabulary, it is difficult to actively work for change. Without a shared vocabulary, we can only repeat hegemonic language and further entrench hegemonic ideas.

From my childhood in the afterlife of Deer Park to my doctoral disciplining, my experiences have shown me that the sociological imagination as applied to Japanese Americans is limited by its vocabulary and narrow conceptualizations of its own key concepts. There is an awareness that key terms like assimilation, race, and racism can have multiple manifestations within different populations and are context dependent. But this amounts to lip service, as its implementation continues to be sparse and selective. Assimilation continues to be too often defined by the classic quantitative measures of parity with non-Hispanic whites. Assimilation is not a one-size-fits-all process where you can simply swap out "Mexican American" and "Asian American" and claim expertise. In terms of race and racism, there is a continuing reliance on a Black-white paradigm. Understanding and centralizing anti-Blackness is important and foundational work, to be sure, but it is not a perfect fit for understanding the racism faced by Asian Americans. And so I write this book in hopes of building a more expansive and nuanced racial vocabulary exploring the question, How does race—particularly in its specific Asian American manifestation—continue to limit the full integration of later-generation Japanese Americans? While the ideas and concepts shared in this book are not the only ways of discussing the Japanese American experience—or racialized immigrant experiences more generally—I hope the ideas and concepts shared here are points of departure to expand our vocabulary and the ways we discuss, analyze, and imagine society, its processes, and its outcomes.

1

Race, Belonging, and
the Affective Dimensions of Citizenship

1970. Driving north on the Santa Ana (5) Freeway heading from the urban sprawl of Orange County toward downtown Los Angeles, a revolving sign emerges on the south side of the highway at Knott Avenue in Buena Park (figure 1.1). The lone sign, reading "Japanese Deer Park," is clearly visible as it rises above the mundane suburban landscape of wide streets lined with an endless series of strip malls, low-rise office buildings, and residential neighborhood tracts. The sign marks the entrance to the amusement park—Japanese Village and Deer Park, a tourist escape into an exotic oasis touting the cuisine, entertainment, architecture, and landscaping of ancient Japan within the comforts of America's lily-white suburbia. From 1967 to 1974, Japanese Village and Deer Park opened its gates in Southern California as part of the Orange County entertainment corridor, anchored by Disneyland and Knott's

Figure 1.1. The main signage for Japanese Village and Deer Park could be seen from the I-5. Courtesy of Gary and Sheri Nakano.

Berry Farm. As a short-lived product of capitalist consumer culture, Japanese Village and Deer Park is a seemingly peculiar and narrow place to begin a discussion on the broad topics of race and citizenship. However, on closer inspection, the peculiarities of this amusement park provide invaluable insights into the local and mundane impacts of much larger social forces on everyday life.

"Deer Park," as it is affectionately remembered by former employees, was the brainchild of Allen Parkinson, a white entrepreneur and inventor of Sleep-Eze, an over-the-counter sleep-aid medication. He proclaimed his unique addition to Orange County tourism as "America's only authentic Japanese village" (figure 1.2). In the beginning, the park was little more than an enclosed pen with a small herd of sika deer, similar to those found in the famous parks and temples of Nara, Japan, gifted to Parkinson by business associates after a trip there. Attracting the attention of passersby, the deer pen was soon joined by teahouse eateries, gift shops, and a dove pavilion. Upon entering the new park, patrons were greeted by kimono-clad hostesses while walking under a torii gate and over a bridge spanning a koi-filled lagoon. Deer Park also offered shows, including tea ceremony, dance, and martial arts, exposing the largely white middle-class patrons to a visage of Japan and Japanese culture. Such cultural shows, as well as the architecture, landscaping,

Figure 1.2. The architecture and built landscaping of Japanese Village and DeerPark circa 1970. Courtesy of Karen Yoshikawa.

and food, offered some semblance of authenticity, as Japan-trained performers, chefs, architects, and gardeners helped create the ambiance and
entertainment. As Lisa, a former Deer Park employee, recalled:

> [Deer Park] was a beautiful place because it was very authentic, and
> they were careful to keep it authentic. So most of the building materials
> and everything came in from Japan. . . . As you walked through, every-
> thing was very beautiful, very authentic. Authentic Japanese gardens, the
> woods, the fabrics, the landscaping, everything in there was pretty much
> from Japan.

Similar to the park's entertainment and built environment, the proprietors of Deer Park sought a staff that was in keeping with the authentic
façade and "enchantment of old Japan." They found a ready workforce
among high school and college-aged sansei—third-generation Japanese
Americans, the grandchildren of Japanese immigrants—from the
surrounding Orange County and Los Angeles suburbs. Deer Park management sought to exploit the racial uniform of sansei—their visual
embodiment of a racially coded phenotype—as part of their work uniform. As an amusement park intending to showcase the spectacle of
ancient Japan through displays of visual culture, Deer Park's employment
of young Japanese Americans played into the superficial authenticity of
the park by providing a match between "oriental" faces and Japanese
costume, landscape, and architecture.

While it is unsurprising that the proprietors would want a staff who
appeared racially Japanese, it is less obvious why sansei youth flocked to
the employment opportunity. Sansei employees certainly fit the part in
terms of appearance and added to the façade of authenticity. However,
given their third-generation status, these youth, having grown up in the
new suburban communities in Orange County and south Los Angeles
County, were largely unfamiliar with Japanese language and culture and
otherwise thought of themselves as all-American kids. Further underscoring the peculiarity of sansei seeking employment at Deer Park is
the significant distance they had to travel. For these local youth who
might have more easily worked at the corner diner or shopping mall,
working at Deer Park was clearly a conscious choice. Commutes of fifteen to twenty miles to this minimum-wage, part-time job were not

uncommon and demonstrated the considerable effort undertaken by sansei to work there.

The commute was worth the effort for these young sansei because of what they found at Deer Park, something that would not be found working at a gas station or a movie theater closer to home. Deer Park provided a sense of community and belonging that was often missing for sansei in the middle-class, overwhelmingly white suburbs of Orange County and south Los Angeles County where they grew up. Deer Park was the first time many of them associated with a large number of Japanese Americans of their own age. Donna, a former employee and sansei, stated:

> Deer Park was a chance to meet Japanese Americans. It was a good experience to see all different kinds of Japanese with different backgrounds and everything and a big group of them. Because in high school, the few Asians that were in my class, there were like maybe three Japanese boys and that wasn't really a good experience of three Japanese boys because they were not cool. But at Deer Park . . . there was such a broad range of them. The ones in my high school, they weren't very good examples of what Japanese Americans could be like. So this gave me the opportunity to kind of see all the different kinds of people that were in Orange County or who worked at Deer Park.

At Deer Park, sansei were exposed to a critical mass of other sansei with a diverse set of interests and personalities. The connection among sansei, however, went beyond common interests and superficial judgements of "cool." Growing up in isolation from other Japanese Americans, and Asian Americans more broadly, former employees of Deer Park shared a lingering and unshakable sense of being different from their white peers despite their third-generation American status, interracial friendships, and active participation in school and local community institutions, such as sports leagues, Boy and Girl Scouts, and student government. Common experiences of racial marginalization amplified sanseis' ability to relate to each other and laid a foundation for building the sense of local belonging at Deer Park. Brenda and Jack, a married sansei couple who met while working at Deer Park, elaborated this point:

JACK: It's amazing how similar everybody was [at Deer Park]. The way they think and how they acted. So you kind of fit in really easily.

BRENDA: I mean, our backgrounds are the same. Our parents kind of all have similar experiences. You know, the war and the prejudice.

JACK: You just feel actually comfortable with people.

BRENDA: You know, with *hakujins* [white people], it's just a little bit of a—

JACK: They're different. I mean, you don't realize they're different until you meet a lot of Japanese people and then think, "Oh my gosh! They're like me!"

BRENDA: Yeah, I mean there were certain times growing up and just feeling a little bit the odd ball out. . . . They were little instances that would happen. I don't know what it was, an odd feeling. So once you get to [Deer Park], it's like, oh you weren't odd at all. It's just, it's because you're Japanese, you know. You didn't realize that you felt this way.

The commonality found among sansei at Deer Park was not simply based in ethnicity or shared hobbies. Prior to Deer Park, sansei employees may not have thought of their lives in explicitly racialized terms. However, as Deer Park brought sansei into contact with each other, they came to recognize the ways in which race was central in their marginalization within their local communities—even as they may not have used this precise vocabulary. Ironically, experiences of isolation and marginalization became a basis for connection and community building that would ultimately allow sansei to find a local community at Deer Park that recognized their membership and belonging. While ethnic affinity for Deer Park's Japanese cultural theme certainly played a role in attracting young sansei to the employment opportunity, nearly all former employees explicitly stated that knowing they would meet a critical mass of sansei their own age enhanced Deer Park as a desired workplace. It was the sansei community and social life that led employees to continue working at Deer Park year after year. Like Brenda and Jack, sansei often felt denied full membership and belonging within the local, predominately white neighborhoods and schools of their childhoods. Deer Park provided an important alternative form of belonging and community that, while ethnic, was no less local or American. Importantly, sansei recognized each other's experiences of racial marginalization in explicitly American terms. Their marginalization and othering were dependent on the local social milieu of Southern California, and their minority status was contextualized by the US racial landscape. Within the ethnic and racialized local community of Deer Park in the Southern California suburbs, common racialized experiences were exposed and helped sansei feel less alone and gain a sense of belonging and recognized membership within local surroundings despite the persistent denial of that full sense of belonging in their neighborhoods and schools.

Despite being narrowly defined by a specific time and space, Deer Park proves itself a microcosm for the broader arguments and themes of this book. Deer Park was a racialized space that simultaneously highlights the persistence of "assimilated" third-generation Japanese American racial difference and created the possibility for continued—and uniquely American—ethnic community formation. This book brings together conceptions of race, community, and, ultimately, citizenship to ask about and provide insight into a simple but fundamental question: Who is American? Certainly, this question is related to those posed within the sociological literature on assimilation, which examines the convergences and divergences of immigrant-origin communities within their "host" societies. However, the question of who is American requires a rethinking of traditional frameworks of assimilation. As ethnic studies scholar Catherine S. Ramírez (2020) notes, this question highlights "the gap between assimilation and citizenship" (14). Assimilation, as the word implies, requires progress toward increasing similarity between immigrant-origin individuals and communities and their host society. A focus on community and citizenship has no such explicit requirement. Rather, a sociological understanding of community membership and citizenship might require only the recognition of belonging by others present in the community (Glenn 2002). Questioning who is American and how such an identity is claimed and recognized casts doubt on sociology's adherence to acculturation and parity of socioeconomic achievement—assimilation—as the metric by which integration success is determined for a multiracial, multiethnic society.

Segmented assimilation theory (Portes and Zhou 1993) is offered as an expanded framework for immigrant incorporation and expressly views immigrants as assimilating into a society variegated by race and class. In their original formation of segmented assimilation, Portes and Zhou (1993) posit three trajectories: integration into a white-dominated middle class, selective acculturation with strategic retention of immigrant culture and community, and downward assimilation into a racialized underclass. This framework added tremendously to the literature by examining immigrant integration pathways outside the narrow prescription of upward mobility. But even here, there is no account of how the particular racial experience of Asian Americans that differs from Black, Indigenous, and other people of color may impact integration outcomes. Rather, model minority Asian Americans, and Japanese Americans more specifically, are placed in the upward mobility path within the segmented assimilation paradigm, which more or less mimics straight-line assimilation theory. Selective acculturation is also an ill fit to describe the Japanese American case. While it would appear that Japanese American socioeconomic success is tied to their maintenance of ethnic community ties—a hallmark of the selective acculturation path—I find that the causal link is reversed. When we examine Japanese American mobility through an explicitly racialized lens, we uncover a clear, concerted effort among sansei and yonsei to seek out racial and ethnic spaces of belonging as a result of their assimilated position within predominately white suburban neighborhoods. The selectivity of this acculturation is not a strategic decision in pursuit of socioeconomic upward mobility but rather a reaction to the racial marginalization experienced in ostensibly integrated spaces.

Furthermore, despite such attempts by various sociologists to address how racially diverse immigrants integrate into a class-stratified host society through the logics of segmented assimilation (Portes and Zhou 1993), the critiques of assimilation scholarship's colorblind assumptions persist (Jung 2009; Kim 2007; Ramírez 2020; Romero 2008; Saenz and Douglas 2015). In telling a race story, this book joins these critiques and looks to provide answers to questions of Americanness that do not fit squarely into the standard sociological frameworks of assimilation, which too often evaluate success via specific, often quantitative, socioeconomic and cultural measures that ultimately converge with the dominant group over time and across generations. Particularly in the US context, this parity has been inextricably tied to whiteness. Asking "Who is American?" forces a more direct grappling with the racialization of American identity and its alignment with whiteness, notwithstanding other associated hegemonic statuses. Thus, there are several related queries that underly the simple question. How is American identity popularly defined, recognized, and understood? Who belongs, and how do we belong? What are the possibilities of claiming an American identity decoupled from whiteness? This book is concerned ultimately with how the persistent recognition of racial markers—the racial body as a visible, ever-present uniform—continues to impact how Japanese Americans claim and have recognized their American identity and citizenship.

If we look back at some of the earliest works on assimilation in American sociology, racial othering and the impact of non-white status were very much part of the analysis. The title of this book, *Japanese Americans and the Racial Uniform*, is taken from one such early work about Japanese Americans by much debated Chicago school sociologist Robert Ezra Park:[1]

> The trouble is not with the Japanese mind but with the Japanese skin. The Jap is not the right color. The fact that the Japanese bears in his features a distinctive racial hallmark, that he wears, so to speak, a *racial uniform*, classifies him. He cannot become a mere individual, indistinguishable in the cosmopolitan mass of the population, as is true, for example, of the Irish, and to a lesser extent, of some of the other immigrant races. The Japanese, like the Negro, is condemned to remain among us an abstraction, a symbol, and a symbol not merely of his own race, but of the Orient and that vague, ill-defined menace we sometimes refer to as the "yellow peril" (1914, 611).

In choosing the title of this book, I am cognizant of Park's problematic legacy, and I do not wish to recuperate his image. However, this early recognition of the enduring role of race in the processes of integration is difficult to ignore. Park's bleak observation is more than one hundred years old, but I argue that the intervening century has not made the metaphor of the racial uniform less apt. In Park's original construction, the racial uniform particularly references "skin" and "color" as "distinctive racial hallmarks." Racial meanings, valuations, and difference hinge on visually based assumptions. Park extends the metaphor to note the simultaneous loss of individuality for those who don a uniform at the same time that a uniform makes individuals identifiable and distinct from the general (white) public. Park notes that the uniform transforms the individual into a symbol imbued with meanings not always of the wearer's own choosing. Taking the metaphor further than Park explicitly stated, uniforms are generally a compulsory form of conformity—externally defined, required, and enforced. Uniforms are tools of control. Similarly, the racial uniform is not optional for structurally disempowered racial groups. The racial uniform confines expectations of status, behavior, and interaction, all of which are constructed and policed by a white-supremacist system and the elites it empowers. The uniform makes deviance easier to identify and punish.

As with all metaphors, race and uniform do not constitute a perfect comparison. If uniforms most often reference required garments for members of a particular institution (the military, sports teams, workspaces), those garments are removed at the end of the day or when the individual leaves the physical confines of the institution. In our private lives, the uniform is no longer required. Of course, as the racial uniform is the body itself, it cannot be put on and taken off. The racial uniform is ever present, ever visible. Although it cannot be removed, the racial uniform can take on different signification in different contexts. W. E. B. Du Bois is instructive on this point. In his conceptualization of double consciousness, Du Bois uses the metaphor of the veil as the separation between Black and white consciousnesses as well as Black and white spaces—"two worlds within and without the Veil" (1903, 155). The veil, as a sheer covering fabric, is a protective physical division but one that does not totally obscure vision or passage through. The impacts and interpretations of Blackness—another racial uniform—on either side of the veil is distinct. Black spaces provide some respite from the direct scrutiny of the white gaze—thanks to the veil. Viewed through a Du Boisian lens, the racial uniform is the color line manifested on the body. While the racial uniform cannot be fully removed, passing through the veil changes the meaning of the racial uniform within each context. Ultimately, racial uniform is a pithy, but meaningful, way to highlight the continued visibility and centrality of race in the daily lives of Japanese Americans. Japanese Americans continue to be defined by their racial uniform, an externally enforced, structural barrier to their sense and recognition of belongingness within their local communities and the nation. And as demonstrated at Deer Park, it is race and the marginalization it brings that continues to shape the boundaries of belonging and community negotiated by later-generation Japanese Americans.

It is the presence and concerted effort of sansei as employees in a racialized space promoting the fantasy of ancient Japan that makes Deer Park a remarkable reference point for this study. The very existence of Deer Park, its hiring practices, and the experiences of the employees illustrate the persistence and social impact of the Japanese American racial uniform. Starting with Deer Park and extended throughout the pages of this book, I call attention to the racial limits of assimilationist interpretations of the Japanese American experience. Certainly, the physical site of Deer Park in the Orange County suburbs and the employment of local, residentially integrated sansei seems to edify assimilationist claims, as upwardly mobile Japanese Americans participated in the postwar phenomenon of white flight from the urban residential core (Brooks 2009; Kurashige 2007). Working part time at an amusement park further marks a particularly middle-class adolescent and young adult experience. Generally speaking, the sansei employees of Deer Park—and Japanese Americans more broadly—achieved high scores on nearly all assimilation benchmarks (e.g., socioeconomic upward mobility, acculturation, educational attainment, intermarriage, residential integration). The sociological story of Japanese Americans as assimilated subjects seems complete with fairytale ending: happily American ever after. However, the easy consumption of Japanese American bodies as foreign objects within the context of Deer Park, the denial of belonging within their local communities, and the subsequent ethnic community-seeking practices of sansei point to the shortcomings of assimilation theory's ability to explain how integration experiences and processes are racialized. This is the racial uniform at play in the lives of Japanese Americans at Deer Park and beyond.

I do not refute the quantitatively measured assimilation of Japanese Americans as defined by the sociological literature. However, in this book, I challenge the asserted assimilation success of "happily American ever after" based on such measures. On its own, assimilation success implies a lack of discrimination and prejudice against Japanese Americans. With this implicit—and sometimes, explicit—bias, assimilationist scholars focusing on quantitative measures of socioeconomic attainment and acculturation miss the trees for the forest. In focusing on broad measures of assimilation success, scholars overlook the persistent impact of the racial uniform on Japanese Americans' daily lived experiences and sense of belonging within their local communities—what should be a fundamental end goal of assimilation. Just because an individual or group achieves socioeconomic success, recognized membership and belonging does not automatically follow. Racialized xenophobia can and does continue to exist. As is clear from the memories of former Deer Park employees, Japanese Americans continued to feel racially marginalized well into the 1970s and the third generation, despite living among predominantly white peers within their residentially integrated suburban neighborhoods. Within an assimilation framework that privileges the achievements of socioeconomic attainments, residential integration, and intermarriage, Japanese Americans may be heralded as the model minority of model minorities, but it is important not to lose sight of the fact that they remain visible and marginalized as racial minorities, nonetheless. Their racial uniform persists. Race continues to shape lived experiences despite achievement of assimilationist goals of acculturation and socioeconomic parity. As such, an understanding of integration and its achievement cannot simply rely on measures of acculturation or socioeconomic parity. Rather, a full integration that takes seriously the persistent and pernicious impact of race must also include a sense of membership and belonging—citizenship—recognized by other members of the community and the nation.

The ethnic and racial motivations for seeking employment at Deer Park and the racialized experiences shared by former employees bely a more complex social process than existing assimilation frameworks can explain. As their membership and belonging remained unrecognized in their own neighborhoods and schools by predominantly white peers, sansei sought out such recognition elsewhere, particularly within ethnic communities. Furthermore, while Deer Park served as an unintended vehicle for sansei community formation, Deer Park's strategy to enhance its visual authenticity by hiring sansei implicitly enhanced the personal feelings and external perceptions of employees as "forever foreign" in their own backyard. While "playing" Japanese at Deer Park, sansei employees were readily recognized and accepted by the management and white middle-class patrons of Deer Park as foreign objects capitalizing on the forever-foreigner racialization of Japanese Americans—regardless of place of birth, generation, acculturation, or socioeconomic status. The favored measures of assimilation scholars remain important measures of progress and potential inequality. However, such feelings of marginalization and maintained importance of ethnicity, so readily shared by Deer Park sansei, demonstrate the inadequacy of such measures in determining integration and full American membership.

Scholars in ethnic and cultural studies have conceptualized Asian American marginalization and incomplete integration, more broadly, in psychoanalytic terms, as racial melancholy—feelings of unresolved grief inherent in processes of integration and a false pursuit of the American Dream for people of color (Cheng 2000)—and national abjection—the necessary and simultaneous inclusion of Asian Americans within the national imaginary but racially differentiated and marginalized as foreign in order to illuminate the boundaries of national membership (Shimakawa 2002). Such states of abjection and melancholy call attention to a membership that is systemically denied, perhaps even unattainable, to Asian Americans as forever foreigners despite formal inclusion as citizens. Relating these psychoanalytical concepts back to sociological frameworks, full assimilation is a false pursuit for Japanese Americans whose membership continues to be constrained by their racial uniform. While not utilizing psychoanalytical terminologies, Park's usage of the uniform metaphor names race as a key mechanism inevitably leading to the ever-present, but often unnamed, afflictions of melancholy and national abjection.

The racial uniform is clearly at play within the confines of Deer Park as a workplace. However, the racial uniform is also at play in the daily lives and local communities informing the visibility of Japanese Americans—or lack thereof—within the broader suburban racial landscape of Southern California, and perhaps beyond. Sansei employees are certainly visible to white patrons within the context of Deer Park as foreigners, residents of a fictitious Japanese village. However, to these same patrons, many of whom were residents of the same neighborhoods, sansei employees went unrecognized as local residents, classmates, and members of the suburban communities they called home. Beyond Deer Park, both physically and temporally, later-generation Japanese

Americans remain invisible as members of their own neighborhoods, their sense of belonging within those communities denied.

In highlighting the persistent racialization and marginalization of later-generation Japanese Americans, I do not mean to paint my respondents, or Japanese Americans more broadly, as passive victims of social marginalization. In illuminating the role of race and the persistence of ethnic community, I demonstrate that Japanese Americans are active participants and agents in their own negotiated claims of belonging. Anthropologists provide a useful foundation for understanding such negotiated claims of belonging by marginalized populations in developing the concept of cultural citizenship. Seminally, Renato Rosaldo (1994) defines cultural citizenship as simply "the right to be different in terms of race, ethnicity, and native language" and the substantive action taken by minoritized and marginalized populations to claim this right (57). More recently, Takeyuki Tsuda (2016) examines Japanese American racial citizenship as an assertion of national belonging and rights. On multiple scales, Japanese Americans challenge the racially narrow conceptions of US citizenship calling for a recognition of their racial and ethnic difference as part of the nation (Tsuda 2016).[2] Sansei and yonsei interviewed here offer similar insights to those found in these earlier anthropological studies. In addition to calls for a more racially inclusive definition of citizenship, this book focuses on the ways in which later-generation Japanese Americans assert and navigate their own forms of belonging in their everyday lives at the local and national levels that rely upon membership in ethnic and racial communities. In this way, sansei and yonsei claim belonging and citizenship because of their racial and ethnic difference, not in spite of it. While assimilation scholars often paint racial and ethnic community maintenance as detrimental to integration, sansei and yonsei across my study, at Deer Park and beyond, express a genuine interest and enjoyment in interacting with other Japanese Americans, demonstrating that ethnic community is a key component in Japanese American claims of local and national belonging.[3]

The Affective Dimensions of Citizenship: A Racial Critique of Assimilation

Feelings of invisibility and marginalization and the community-seeking practices they produce are exemplified by the Deer Park experience and highlight a shortcoming in assimilation theories—the persistent impact of race on daily lived experience. However, the existence of such feelings and practices also illuminates an alternative and more broadly applicable framework for understanding the process of integration as racialized and multigenerational. Rather than quantitative measures of socioeconomic parity and cultural mimicry, I focus on a sociopolitical and affective conception of citizenship that requires broad and reciprocal recognition of membership and belonging as a desired and necessary social outcome of integration. Such a framework moves beyond the gates of Deer Park to reveal the integration of later-generation Japanese Americans—and perhaps Black, Indigenous, and other communities of color generally—as incomplete. While citizenship is most often thought of as a legal status providing an equally and universally granted set of rights and privileges within a sovereign state, *Japanese Americans and the Racial Uniform* expands beyond the conception of citizenship as a liberal legal designation. Citizenship is, in fact, not an egalitarian legal status where all citizens hold the same rights and privileges regardless of their differences along other social axes (Cohen 2009; Smith 1997). The assumption of universalism and its connection to narrow legal definitions of citizenship fails to recognize the social life of citizenship—the legal, material, and social inequalities and incongruities that continue to exist among citizens, impact abilities to access truly equal lives, and beget particular social practices and structures (Cohen 2009; Glenn 2002). In this sociopolitical conception, citizenship is a set of experiences and practices built on differential recognition and feelings of belonging shaped simultaneously by multiple axes of social difference.

Given fallback assumptions of universalism and equality under the law, the stratification and incongruities of citizenship are perhaps most evident in the localized, day-to-day lived experiences of citizens as they interact with the state, local institutions, and other citizens and residents. This is a particularly sociological approach to citizenship. Evelyn Nakano Glenn, in her 2010 presidential address to the American Sociological

Association, called for an approach to citizenship not as a mere legal designation but "a matter of belonging, which requires the recognition by other members of the community" (Glenn 2011, 3). Citizenship is not only constructed by the state but is given life and meaning "through face-to-face interactions and through place-specific practices that occur within larger structural contexts" (2). The local and place-specific focus on the experiences and practices within Deer Park—and the broader Japanese American community in the surrounding Southern California suburbs—provides an ideal cite for exploring a sociological framework of citizenship that emphasizes the impact of micro-level interactions and lived experiences on feelings and recognitions of belonging. The sense of racial marginalization felt by Deer Park sansei, despite markers of assimilation, is a manifestation of the unequal citizenship of Japanese Americans experienced and identified through every day, local relationships. Centralizing citizenship as a social process—and the recognized belonging and membership it entails—enables a vision of inequality and integration as unfolding lived experiences rather than as mere outcomes. In particular, an examination of Japanese American citizenship and sense of belonging exposes the persistent, entrenched, and insidious impact of race in the everyday experiences of Japanese Americans and provides an understanding of their incomplete integration left unexplained by traditional, deracialized assimilation metrics.

Understanding citizenship as an externally validated sense of belonging and membership rather than as a set of rights or material outcomes points toward an affective dimension of citizenship. Marginalization and belonging are things that are felt: affects. Affect theory, then, is useful in shaping an understanding of citizenship as a more robust and racially accountable framework for integration. More than emotion, affect encompasses a body's inventory and negotiation of contact with the social world. Most often, a sense of belonging—or not belonging—exists "in-excess of consciousness," a fact of everyday life that is not immediately recognizable or named but is nonetheless registered and impactful for affected individuals or communities (Clough 2007, 2). For sansei employees, as shared by Jack's and Brenda's earlier quotations, Deer Park provided an essential and catalytic space for bringing their lifelong sense of non-belonging into consciousness. Before Deer Park, such racial marginalization and lack of belonging were always felt but never named or recognized.

Certainly, from a sociological standpoint, affect is difficult to measure, and unsurprisingly, assimilation scholars have paid it little attention. However, while feelings of belonging may be less verbally articulated by research respondents, such feelings nonetheless shape how individuals interact within society and negotiate their own communities of belonging. For this reason, affect theory requires us to look beyond the mere fact or origin of belonging—or non-belonging—and instead explore its performative effect (Sedgwick 2003). Affect theory does not ask why, or even how, Japanese Americans do not belong to local and national communities but rather how Japanese Americans negotiate and cope with their feelings of non-belonging—the performative effect of non-belonging. To uncover performative effect, affect theory emphasizes lived everyday experiences and the local and contingent nature of knowledge (Sedgwick 2003; Seigworth and Gregg 2010). In this way, affect theory mirrors Glenn's call for a sociology of citizenship that focuses on belonging as a product of local, everyday practices, interactions, and struggles (Glenn 2011).

From the standpoint of both sociological considerations of citizenship and affect theory, Deer Park, as a highly localized space, becomes less peculiar as a reference point for a study on Japanese American integration. The hyperlocal site of Deer Park and the concerted efforts by sansei to work there focus attention on the particular ways in which racialized affect, manifested as a sense of non-belonging, impacts the citizenship of Japanese Americans and leaves their assimilation incomplete despite integrated suburban residence, community involvement, and middle-class status. The space of Deer Park and the high levels of cross-racial interaction that took place there leverage affect theory's focus on performative effect and the local, contingent nature of experience and knowledge. Recall former Deer Park employee Brenda's statement quoted earlier: "There were certain times growing up and just feeling a little bit the odd ball out. They were little instances that would happen. I don't know what it was, an odd feeling." This "odd feeling"—"feeling a little bit the odd ball out"—exemplifies racialized affect. Brenda is describing a melancholic sense of non-belonging within the suburban Southern California community where she was born and raised, as were her parents. Brenda does not speak of these feelings in terms of affect—reflecting the methodological challenge of affect theory.

However, Brenda's experiences of racial marginalization and active seeking out of Deer Park as a place to meet other sansei are performative effects of the affect of non-belonging. If integration scholarship and traditional assimilation theories rely too heavily on quantitative socioeconomic outcomes and parity, Brenda's experience and her sense of non-belonging and unfulfilled integration go unnoticed. However, they are central within a framework of citizenship that takes into account its extralegal, mundane, and affective dimensions.

In response to their daily encounters with racial marginalization, sansei actively sought out Deer Park—and the critical mass of Japanese American youth it drew—to find a community where their belonging and membership would be readily recognized. While sansei found belonging at Deer Park, the existence of such sansei negotiations for recognized membership is a demonstration that their integration within local communities and as part of the nation remained incomplete. They continued to be racially marginalized as foreign, and their membership went unrecognized in broader society. Counter to predictions of ethnic attenuation by standard sociological assimilation theories, communities of belonging based in ethnicity become important foundations for people of color to cope with their racial marginalization and claim their place within their local communities and the national fabric.

Given that Deer Park is part of a bygone era, opened from 1967 to 1974, it may be easy to brush aside the persistent racial marginalization described by former sansei employees, who were well into the third generation, as a simple case of delayed assimilation.[4] By the turn of the twenty-first century, Japanese Americans, now in the fourth and fifth generation, surely must have shed the stigma of their perceived racial uniform and gained full recognition of their citizenship and belonging. However, the experiences of sansei at Deer Park, which exemplify the racial dimensions of affective citizenship, are not limited to this finite place and time and continue to impact sansei lives beyond Deer Park, as well as the lives of fourth- and fifth-generation Japanese Americans—yonsei and gosei, respectively. This book demonstrates that Japanese American racial marginalization persists for sansei and yonsei in particular well into the present day. The framework of citizenship helps illuminate the affective and racialized integration of Japanese Americans in both historical and contemporary analyses.

The Practices of Affective Citizenship: Performative Effect and Minority Cultures of Mobility

While *Japanese Americans and the Racial Uniform* makes important interventions into abstract and generalizable conceptualizations of integration through a race- and affect-focused framework of citizenship, it does so through a focus on the mundanity of these abstractions—how they play themselves out and are negotiated and practiced in the daily lives of citizens. As previously mentioned, Glenn's formative call for a sociology of citizenship and affect theory's focus on the performative effect of marginalization reinforce citizenship as a set of fundamentally local and everyday negotiations and practices. This book reveals how the affective dimensions of citizenship—a sense of belonging—have practical real-world impacts, affect's performative effect.

As the title of this book suggests, race holds a central role in shaping the lived experiences and sense of belonging of otherwise "assimilated" later-generation Japanese Americans. It is not, however, the only impactful status. As alluded to in the Deer Park anecdotes, middle-class and suburban upbringings were common for sansei in the postwar period, and this trend continued among the yonsei in the closing decades of the twentieth century. Middle-class status and suburban location have a profound impact on the contours and content of Japanese American community, culture, and practices, reflecting particularly "minority cultures of mobility." Neckerman and colleagues (1999) introduce the concept of minority cultures of mobility as an expansion upon segmented assimilation (Portes and Zhou 1993). While segmented assimilation theory expanded our vision of possible assimilation pathways and outcomes by introducing selective acculturation and downward assimilation, minority cultures of mobility provides an alternative way of understanding the practices of middle-class minorities that "draw upon available symbols, idioms, and practices to respond to distinctive problems of being middle class and minority" (Neckerman, Carter, and Lee 1999, 949). In the continuing context of racial discrimination and socioeconomic inequality, Neckerman and colleagues argue that middle class minorities are faced with two problems: increased interracial interactions, particularly with whites, in public settings, and inter-class interactions within their own ethnic-minority community. Minority cultures of mobility represent strategies for negotiating such problems present in middle-class minorities' daily lives.

Looking at the case of middle-class African Americans, Neckerman and colleagues find that entry into the middle class—or even a long-standing presence—does not negate stigmas attached to race. Rather, being a middle-class minority gives rise to experiences that are distinct from co-ethnics from other class backgrounds as well as from middle-class whites. Over time, these experiential differences produce cultural practices distinguishable from both the white middle class and co-ethnics of other class backgrounds. In a quintessentially intersectional approach, minority cultures of mobility highlight the ways in which middle-class status fundamentally changes how race and ethnicity are lived and negotiated on a daily basis and vice versa. To borrow phrasing from Evelyn Nakano Glenn (2002), class is raced, race is classed.

This book's focus on local and everyday practices and negotiations of belonging highlights the experiences of a minority middle-class group in a suburban setting and demonstrates how racialized minorities navigate upward mobility in ways that differ from a white racial norm.[5] Here, I assert explicitly that local and everyday practices of citizenship as performative effect are minority cultures of mobility. As racialized and middle-class subjects, Japanese Americans create particular demonstrations and negotiations of their membership and belonging within their local communities and the nation. In the case of the sansei and yonsei studied here, I explore the practices of ethnic community and identity formation—simultaneously performative effects and minority cultures of mobility—that enable a sense of belonging and alternative claim on an American identity that is not reliant on whiteness or the white gaze. Rather, Japanese Americans come to a sense and recognition of belonging on their own terms. I establish where and how Japanese Americans perceive and establish their sense of belonging through their commentaries on levels of comfort within varying racialized spaces, their access to which is impacted by class. Seeking out or even creating particular types of communities along racial and ethnic lines reveals how later-generation Japanese Americans negotiate the affective dimensions of citizenship. Such paths are navigated within the context of middle-class suburbia and in reaction to the lack of recognition of Japanese American belonging by broader US public sentiment, which still holds all Asian

Americans as forever foreigners. In looking toward ethnic and racial communities as locations of recognition, Japanese Americans are actively rejecting the equations of whiteness, American, and belonging.

Japanese Americans also represent a particularly interesting case for the exploration of minority cultures of mobility that differs from previous studies of the minority middle class. These previous studies have examined racial and ethnic minority groups that have heterogeneous or bimodal distributions by socioeconomic class (Lacy 2007; Lee and Zhou 2015; Neckerman, Carter, and Lee 1999; Pattillo 1999; Vallejo 2012). In comparison, Japanese Americans are rather homogenous with regard to class. Japanese Americans are more concentrated in the middle class than the US population as a whole. According to traditional measures of socioeconomic class—educational attainment and household income—Japanese Americans are more heavily represented in the middle and upper segments. Compared to under 30 percent of the total US population, over 50 percent of Japanese Americans held a bachelor's degree or higher in 2017 (US Census Bureau 2017). Seventy-two percent of Japanese Americans households earned more than $40,000 in 2015, and nearly 50 percent earned over $75,000. Meanwhile, in the total US population in 2015, 62 percent earned more than $40,000, and only 36 percent earned above $75,000 (US Census Bureau 2017). Certainly, Japanese Americans also exist in the lower segments of household income and educational attainment. Such class diversity is evident in the recollection of Deer Park employees who recalled the greater affluence of some of their friends and coworkers. Regardless of class diversity, however, the co-location and community building that occurred at Deer Park, a space of primarily part-time employment, demonstrates the impact of middle-class habitus on sansei regardless of individual class status. Even sansei coming from lower socioeconomic backgrounds, who sought out Deer Park in large part to connect with other Japanese Americans, could do so only in a space that was not just racialized but also classed. In this way, the concentration of Japanese Americans in middle- and upper middle-classes has important influence and even dominates the structuring of the institutional spaces and norms of the Japanese American community. As such, and regardless of class, Japanese Americans who wish to participate in and connect with Japanese American community most often do so on middle-class terms.

Method and Data

Uncovering the affective dimension of citizenship—a social fact that is often "in excess of consciousness"—may seem to present a methodological problem. How do you measure "feeling," often ephemeral and difficult to put into words? As previously discussed, the observable evidence of affect is often found in its performative effect. Performative effect is how affect reveals itself through its impact on mundane, everyday social behaviors, processes, and interactions. Still, performative effect is difficult to capture via the standard quantitative measures of assimilation. To uncover performative effects and move beyond the quantitative focus of assimilation theory, this study takes a multi-method, qualitative examination of Japanese American lived experiences. This study relies mainly on in-depth, semi-structured interviews conducted with ninety-three later-generation Japanese Americans who grew up in the Orange County and Los Angeles County region but also leverages an original archive of over four hundred visual records.

The interview data were accrued via snowball sampling through two distinct, although often intertwining, paths. Just as the narrative of this book began with Deer Park, so too does the sampling methodology. Deer Park and its former employees are the starting point for my sample. Employees were identified from a memory book published with personal mailing addresses as part of a reunion held in 1986. Individuals were sent study information and interview requests via US mail. As individuals responded to requests for interviews, I asked them to put me in touch with other friends and family who also worked at Deer Park. From this sample of former sansei employees, I was also able to begin accruing yonsei—fourth-generation—research participants by asking former sansei employees to put me in contact with their yonsei children. In sum, former Deer Park employees account for forty-one sansei respondents. An additional seventeen yonsei respondents are the children of former employees.

In addition to participating in interviews, former Deer Park employees also provided a second source of data: visual archival material. Private and promotional photographs from their Deer Park days, official press releases, souvenirs, and other memorabilia from the personal collections of former employees were aggregated in original or digital form as part of an original archive of Japanese Village and Deer Park. Most important for this study are the 404 unique personal photographs and promotional material. These images form the basis of data for chapter 4 of this book. More information on the analytical methodology used on the visual images can be found in that chapter.

The second snowball sample path originated from Japanese Americans previously known by the researcher or other non-Japanese American acquaintances. I took special care to avoid recruitment from Japanese American or Asian American organizations and focused mainly on Japanese American individuals who were known through non-Japanese American or non-Asian American specific sites.[6] I felt that this was important to avoid sampling on the dependent variable as much as possible (Lee and Bean 2010). It would not be surprising to find evidence of a persistent ethnic community if I recruited from an institution with an identity and mission so closely tied to ethnicity. As such, I attempted to recruit individuals who were least likely to have a sense of community with other Japanese Americans. The second sample path resulted in eleven sansei respondents and twenty-one yonsei respondents. My full yonsei sample also includes individuals of multiethnic and multiracial backgrounds in addition to non-mixed Japanese Americans.[7] I intentionally sought multiethnic and multiracial respondents, as they form a sizeable portion of the contemporary Japanese American populations and are an increasingly important part of an ever-evolving ethnic story. My final sample includes eleven multiracial and two multiethnic yonsei.

Interviews took place in personal homes and offices, public spaces, or over the phone depending on the preference and location of the respondent. Most interviews were conducted one on one; in a few cases, interviews were completed with two respondents simultaneously. All interviews were transcribed and analyzed through an iterative coding schema. This schema began with open coding to establish relevant and common themes and topics across all interviews. Upon completion of this first round of coding and consolidation of codes, a second round of coding was completed on all transcripts to ensure that all themes were coded for across all data.

My final sample included fifty-four sansei and thirty-nine yonsei individuals. The average age of my sansei respondents was sixty-one;

the average of age of my yonsei respondents was twenty-nine. Growing up in suburban Southern California, all respondents readily identified as middle class based on residential location, occupation, level of education, and social networks. All sansei respondents were monoracial, monoethnic Japanese Americans. Thirteen of the yonsei respondents had multiracial or multiethnic backgrounds. Multiracial individuals are those who self-identify as Japanese American and one or more other races. Among the eleven multiracial yonsei included in my sample, all were mixed with white, except for one who was Mexican American. Multiethnic individuals are those who self-identify as Japanese American and one or more other Asian ethnicities but not any other racial category. Of the two multiethnic respondents, one was mixed Korean American and the other Chinese American.

As noted in the preface, I have a deep and personal connection to the topic of this study. As a fourth-generation Japanese American born and raised in Orange County, the child of two former Deer Park employees, my execution of this project might rightly be labeled "me-search." While this term for self-interested research is most often used to disparage the work of marginalized scholars studying their own communities, I do not use this term as a diminutive. However, I would be remiss not to acknowledge the ways in which my positionality may have impacted my data collection and analysis. My connection to Deer Park and my ethnic insider status were overall assets in the recruitment of participants. Individuals were by and large excited and interested to discuss and explain their racial and ethnic identities and experiences.[8] Conversations with my respondents often began with a back and forth about family backgrounds, childhood experiences, and possible overlaps in social networks. Among former Deer Park employees, respondents would often ask me how my parents or other family members were doing. During the interviews, my insider knowledge was also beneficial, as my familiarity with the topics and colloquial vocabulary created a greater ease of conversation. I was often able to empathize and share similar experiences of my own in the course of our dialogue.

Although I view my insider status as a positive asset, in reality it is just a matter of fact. It would be difficult, if not impossible, to have approached this study in any other way. But this would be true of any researcher. The position of any researcher in relation to the research topic and subjects—insider, outsider, or something in-between—will always impact all facets of the research process in ways unique to that relationship.

A Note on Disciplines: Sociology versus Ethnic Studies

I would like to preempt two broad disciplinary critiques of this book, one from sociology and the other from Asian American studies. *Japanese Americans and the Racial Uniform* is itself a critique of the sociological approach to the question of assimilation, calling out the lack of attention paid to the long-term impacts of race on integration processes. Some may respond to this critique by calling it a straw-man argument that misses the nuance embedded within the broad and diverse literature in the sociology of immigration. I do not claim to be the first to make this critique, and I fully recognize that even the scholarship I have cited in this book is only a fraction of the scholarly attempts to understand assimilation as a racialized process. However, there is a distinction to be made between claiming the existence of some scholarship that takes seriously the role of race and claiming that such scholarship represents the disciplinary mainstream. My critique is of the established orthodoxy of assimilation that continues to marginalize race-focused studies within the sociology of immigration. To brush aside this critique is to ignore the persistent and problematic hegemony of the assimilation orthodoxy. This is academic gaslighting. In this book, I ask how we might conceptualize the process and outcomes of assimilation differently if we were to place racial experiences outside of whiteness at the center of our analyses.

Before I was disciplined in sociology, I was trained in Asian American studies, and I have always felt the mutual tension between these two fields. Sociology, as with many "traditional" disciplines, largely dismisses ethnic studies as less rigorous or too narrowly focused. As one of my sociology professors once said, ethnic studies is "basically a journalism degree."[9] This is institutional racism showing its face in academia. Within Asian American studies, I have witnessed a disciplinary shift toward the humanities and cultural studies alongside a growing skepticism toward sociology and the social sciences more broadly. Fewer and fewer attendees of the Association of Asian American Studies annual meeting hail from social science disciplines, a trend that sparked the creation of a social science caucus in 2017. Ethnic studies' mistrust of the social sciences is not without provocation, and rather than fight for a seat at the sociological table, many Asian Americanists have developed distinct literatures that bypass standard sociological frameworks in the study of race, ethnicity, and immigrant status, among others. This fact was highlighted for me when my Asian American studies advisor urged me not to use the term *assimilation* in my writing, because ethnic studies had "moved beyond" the term.

Divergent intellectual movements are understandable and are often the basis for distinct disciplines in the first place. However, in the case of sociology and Asian American studies—particularly regarding race, immigration, and assimilation—the disciplines seem to run in parallel. They are on different tracks focused on different metrics and outcomes to explain similar phenomena, rarely intersecting or coming into meaningful conversation with each other. Despite discussing many of the same topics, these two disciplines talk past each other and dismiss the ideas of the other. Asian American studies' aversion to the term *assimilation* is one example of this. Don't get me wrong; I am no cheerleader for assimilation as a goal or a framework. However, I believe that to avoid the word is to leave the shortcomings of assimilation unaddressed and at risk of being replicated under new names. This is unhelpful in expanding a broader understanding of the Asian American experience and goes against the interdisciplinary foundations of ethnic studies. Because sociology is often seen as a more legitimate academic discipline, Asian American studies does itself few favors by denying the potential for intellectual crosspollination. The fact remains that sociologists still use and develop assimilation theory. In continuing to leverage the language of assimilation, I attempt to bring an ethnic studies lens and critique more directly to bear on the sociological concept. I assert that the best way to accomplish this goal is to unpack and dismantle sociological understandings by simultaneously using sociological terminology (e.g., assimilation) and pushing sociology to examine sociological problems through an expanded lens. Again, this is not to say there are not tremendous scholars doing work at the intersection of Asian American studies and sociology. It is to say that such scholarship is too often marginalized in both disciplines.

Of course, as Audre Lorde (1984) cautions, "The master's tools will never dismantle the master's house." This might well be true. Yet I believe using sociological language—the master's tool—to expose the racial blind spots embedded within assimilation's favored metrics and limited recognition of racialized lived experiences in assimilation analyses is a first step and will have one of two outcomes: either we will see a change in the orthodoxy of sociological approaches to the study of so-called assimilation, or sociology will have to admit that the orthodoxy does not exist as is by accident. Assimilation is an intentionally racist framework. We move forward from there.

On the Centering and Decentering of Whiteness

Notwithstanding my critiques of Asian American studies and sociology, I begrudgingly position myself and this book within both. Asian American studies is, of course, ethnic studies. An essential part of the ethnic studies project—with which I align myself and this book without reservation—is the decentering of whiteness and the centering of the perspectives of historically excluded populations in our narratives. As noted, this is very much at odds with the sociological conception and operationalization of assimilation. Given both the demographic and political history of the United States, the scholarly literature and popular understandings of assimilation and boundaries of American identity have been inextricably bound to whiteness as its ideal type. After all, Park's original conceptualization of the racial uniform was as a physical demarcation of Japanese Americans vis-à-vis white people. While this book is premised on a critique of assimilation and the role of white supremacy in erasing the racialized reality of integration experiences for communities of color, I also recognize white supremacy for its embeddedness in our cultural and political history and discourse. In many ways, Japanese Americans' everyday understanding and navigation of their own racial positioning—as in other marginalized communities— does not consistently adhere to the tenets of ethnic studies. That is to say, their racial self-reflection is often made in reference to whiteness.

This book sits in the tension between the anti-racist imperative and desire to decenter whiteness and the grounded reality of how our white-supremacist system continues to center whiteness in innumerable ways.

As products of US society and as demonstrated in the white gaze evident in places like Deer Park, sansei and yonsei are deeply impacted by public discourses that continue to use whiteness as the default category and the focus of comparison. Their perceptions of their everyday interactions, personal identities, and community bonds are fundamentally shaped by the omnipresent structures of white supremacy. For this reason, the specter of whiteness remains present in this book and must be acknowledged.

This acknowledgment of the inescapable presence of whiteness in the interview responses, however, does not negate the many instances shared by sansei and yonsei that demonstrate a decentering of whiteness in their everyday lives. Comparisons, distancing, and community building practices are frequently employed by Japanese Americans vis-à-vis other Asian American ethnic communities and individuals. Such behaviors and orientations are also notable in the persistent seeking of Japanese American ethnic connections and community among sansei and yonsei. Both examples that decenter whiteness are simultaneously the result of and resistance to the marginalization felt by Japanese Americans at the hands of white supremacy. In demonstrating the ways in which sansei and yonsei negotiate identity and community formation through observable behaviors and practices that both center and decenter whiteness, this book offers insight into how white supremacy continues to operate in the lives of the so-called model minority— whether they recognize it or not.

Scope and Organization of the Book

Japanese Americans and the Racial Uniform builds on and brings together in a unique way three distinct and interdisciplinary literatures: assimilation, citizenship, and affect. Previous works in assimilation have lauded later-generation Japanese Americans as model minorities, proof of assimilation's ability to cross the color line (Alba and Nee 2003; Petersen 1971). Such studies, however, fail to address why "California's Japanese Americans still suffer from discrimination and prejudice four generations after their ancestors arrived here" (Gans 2005, 19). To remedy this oversight, this book draws on Evelyn Nakano Glenn's call for a sociology of citizenship (2011), which understands citizenship beyond a mere legal status. Rather, citizenship is best understood as a feeling and sense of belonging. A focus on belonging, rather than assimilation's focus on socioeconomic parity and social distance, is better able to account for the persistent impact of race in the daily lives of otherwise assimilated Japanese Americans. As something felt, citizenship and the belonging it promises introduces the literature on affect. I find overlap between affect theory's focus on performative effect and a sociological approach to citizenship, both of which require focus on the local and interactional constructions and recognitions of belonging and membership. In sum, critiquing the colorblind logic of sociology's quantitative measures of assimilation, this book develops a framework of citizenship as affect—a sense of belonging and recognized membership, or lack thereof—to centralize the role of race in the community-building efforts, mundane social practices, and general lives of suburban third- and fourth-generation Japanese Americans.

The chapters that follow unfold through an examination of citizenship's performative effect—the lived everyday experiences and social behaviors of sansei and yonsei in the Southern California suburbs of Los Angeles and Orange Counties. Despite their seeming assimilation success, their lived experiences and behaviors are highly impacted by their racial difference. In the next chapter, "Contextualizing Japanese America," I provide an overview of the shifting demographic context of Southern California since the 1950s. The development of suburban sprawl and changes in immigration law in the second half of the twentieth century had a significant impact on the shape of the Japanese American population and the terrain on which they sought to maintain and build community. This chapter also highlights the shortcomings of data available on the Japanese American population. The incomplete demographic picture of Japanese America underscores the data-driven limitations of assimilation theory to accurately account for Japanese American integration.

Chapter 3, "The False Promise of Assimilation," extends the critique of assimilation theory by calling attention to the paradox it presents for later-generation Japanese Americans. Demographic realities of upward mobility, middle-class status, and residential dispersal of sansei and yonsei from the time of Deer Park through the turn of the twenty-first century are at odds with the persistent racial marginalization and othering of Japanese Americans, demonstrated through the experiences shared by my interview respondents. In this chapter, the paradox of Japanese American assimilation is made evident through an unpacking of the model minority myth and the selective and assimilationist rendering of the Japanese American ethnic narrative.

The remainder of the book defines particular performative effects of Japanese Americans' sense of non-belonging—citizenship as affect—and its impacts on practices of particular minority cultures of mobility. Such practices have implications for both local and national senses of belonging, and the chapters progress along these expanding boundaries of membership. "How to Be Cool at Deer Park" (chapter 4) returns to the peculiar origin of this study. This chapter expands on the themes of racialized workplace interactions and community formation practices introduced in this introduction but also pushes further to examine Deer Park as a hyperlocal space that reveals citizenship and communities of belonging are not only racial constructs but also gendered and often signaled through material visual culture. In leveraging the visual culture constructed by Deer Park as well as by sansei for themselves, this chapter explores the ways and moments in which sansei become visible and invisible to white middle-class park patrons—who often lived in the same local communities—as well as to other sansei. Such visual analysis, combined with the recollections of former Deer Park employees, illuminates particular citizenship practices and behaviors—performative effects and cultures of mobility—leveraged and negotiated by sansei in their daily lives in and around Deer Park.

Chapter 5, "The Racial Replenishment of Ethnicity," examines how sansei and yonsei come to define their own identities and their communities along ethnic and racial lines. Such definitions shape the citizenship practices of sansei and yonsei—how and where they seek belonging. I assert that such community and identity definitions have been particularly impacted by the demographic shifts associated with post-1965 waves of immigration, which dramatically increased the size and ethnic diversity of the Asian American population. Conversely, immigration from Japan has been minimal in the post-WWII period. The lack of contemporary Japanese immigration, but large influx of similarly racialized immigrants from Asia generally, has a direct and simultaneous impact on the persistence of ethnic identity and community formations among sansei and yonsei, as well as on the construction of a racial consciousness shared with other Asian Americans. This process constitutes what I term a *racial replenishment of ethnicity*. This process and the communities of belonging it helps construct are particularly impacted not only by immigration patterns but also by the middle-class positioning of Japanese Americans. The racial replenishment of ethnicity sets the groundwork on which Japanese Americans live as both racial and ethnic subjects within the complex and stratified structure of US citizenship and belonging.

Chapter 6, "Have Ethnicity, Will Travel," focuses attention on the geographic context of suburban Los Angeles and Orange Counties, where sansei and yonsei grew up and made their homes from the 1960s into the 2000s. This chapter makes explicit critiques of structural assimilation—the integration of immigrants into mainstream (predominately white) social groups and institutions (Gordon 1964)—and spatial assimilation—the residential integration of immigrants into more affluent (predominantly white) cities and neighborhoods as their own socioeconomic status rises (Massey and Denton 1993). As residents of suburban Southern California, sansei and yonsei seem to have achieved the desired forms of integration outlined by both structural and spatial assimilation. However, within these predominantly white—or, at times, racially mixed—neighborhoods, Japanese Americans maintain concerted ethnic community-seeking practices. Despite access and participation in local neighborhood activities and institutions, sansei and yonsei, in childhood and adulthood, traveled significant and often inconvenient distances within the suburban communities of Los Angeles and Orange Counties to participate in ethnic-specific activities and organizations. They did so to find community and a sense of belonging among co-ethnics they found lacking within their immediate, predominantly white, vicinities. Such intentional ethnic community-seeking practices—a search for recognized citizenship—provide another example of the performative effect of the affective dimensions of citizenship.

The preceding chapters establish how sansei and yonsei negotiate, define, and find local communities of belonging through racialized and ethnic-specific paths. The final empirical chapter, "Ethnic History as American History" (chapter 7), asserts that negotiations of belonging and citizenship also operate on a broader national stage. Chapter 7 argues that sansei and yonsei work to construct a sense of national belonging and citizenship through claims of ethnic-specific historical presence and participation in broader US history. Establishing such historical presence and participation forces other Americans to recognize Japanese Americans as part of a broader national citizenry and fabric.

The concluding chapter begins by underscoring the central role of race in shaping the citizenship—as affect and lived experience—of third- and fourth-generation Japanese Americans. The chapter continues with a discussion of the broader implications of this research by demonstrating how the Japanese American case exemplifies the present and future racial predicaments faced by many contemporary immigrant-origin communities, which are predominantly non-white, as they seek to claim citizenship and belonging in the US. In addition, this chapter provides a summary of the major theoretical contributions of the book and also offers insight into possible future directions of research on Japanese Americans as well as racial and ethnic formations more broadly.

While this introductory chapter refers to a space that no longer exists—Deer Park—and to a century-old observation by yet another dead white man—Robert Park—the issues and concerns raised and analyzed through this text are not artifacts of a bygone era. Our recent history and continuing struggle with US and global anti-Asian racism underscore that Deer Park and Park's reference are familiar episodes in an unfortunate and recurring history of the Japanese American— and broader Asian American—racial uniform. In 1982, Vincent Chin was brutally murdered in Detroit, Michigan, at the hands of two white American auto workers, one of whom had just been laid off as a result of the growing competition from Japanese automakers. Detroit and the rest of the nation were in the throes of growing anti-Japanese animosities exacerbated by growing global economic tensions. Chin, a Chinese American, was mistaken for Japanese. In further confirmation of the systemic nature of anti-Asian bias, after pleading guilty, Chin's murderers served no jail time and paid only a minimal fine for taking his life. In 2020, as the world struggled against the COVID-19 pandemic, anti-Asian sentiment and violence were once again on the rise. Given the origins of the virus in China and the dangerous, racist rhetoric emerging from news media, elected officials, and the Trump White House, Asian Americans—and the broader global Asian diaspora—found themselves being attacked regardless of their ethnic background. In 2021, a white gunman opened fire at two massage parlors in the Atlanta, Georgia area, killing eight people, six of whom were Asian American women. The gunman struggled with sex addiction and saw these locations and the women employed there as dangerous racialized and sexual temptations. These tragic events, coupled with the long history of anti-Asian racism in the US, demonstrate the continued need to understand the complex and nuanced way that the racial uniform operates in the everyday lives of Asian Americans regardless of model minority accolades and acclamations of assimilation success.

Lastly, the implications of this study are by no means limited to later-generation Japanese Americans or even Asian Americans. Rather, this book spotlights the ways in which race continues to impact a more generalized experience of non-white immigrants, across multiple generations, even as they progress positively in other aspects of integration. The Japanese American case opens a theoretical door for exploring how issues of race, lack of belonging, and citizenship claims arise in other ethnic and racial minority communities, immigrant and non-immigrant. The racial uniform continues to impact the recognition of full membership, regardless of legal citizenship status. Understanding this racial impact requires a critical examination of the continuing assumed relationship between whiteness and an American national identity, even as the multiracial composition of the United States population is tacitly recognized in our public discourse. The later-generation Japanese American case explored in this book pushes a rethinking of who is American and a reexamination of the distinct, racialized pathways to belonging.

2

Contextualizing Japanese America

Do we really need yet another book about Asian Americans in California? Arguably, no. But Deer Park is a particular and important point of departure for clarifying dynamics of race, ethnicity, and integration, and it is difficult to imagine Deer Park as it was existing anywhere outside of Southern California. If it were located anywhere else (except perhaps Hawaiʻi), Deer Park would not have been able to bring together such a sizable ethnically Japanese staff. The amusement park infrastructure of Southern California helped to make the region a more dynamic, family-friendly national and international tourist destination. Deer Park certainly benefited. California, positioned on the Pacific coast, is linked to the global markets of the Pacific Rim, driving business connections as well as cultural interest in Japan. This fact helped make Deer Park a viable venture—if only briefly. Without question, Deer Park is uniquely Californian.

While acknowledging the need for greater geographic diversity in Asian American scholarship (Sumida 1998), the California focus within the broader scholarship is not without warrant. California has long been a diverse racial crucible, bringing white, Black, Latine, Asian, and Indigenous populations into direct contact and pushing society and scholars to think beyond a Black-white racial binary (Almaguer 1994). While racial diversity has been present across California since the westward expansion of US settler colonialism and has impacted the region's institutional landscape, white racial status remained demographically and ideologically dominant in Los Angeles and Orange Counties through the latter half of the twentieth century. As shown in table 2.1, Los Angeles County did not officially become a racial plurality until 1990, and Orange County joined shortly after the turn of the century. Both demographic shifts were driven by significant growth among Latine and Asian American populations.

TABLE 2.1. Population Change from 1950 to 2010 in Los Angeles and Orange Counties, California, by Race and Asian Ethnicity (US decennial census)

County Populations by Race and Ethnicity: United States Census—1950–2010

Los Angeles County	1950	1960	1970	1980	1990	2000	2010
Total Population	4,151,687	6,039,771	7,032,075	7,477,503	8,863,164	9,519,338	9,818,605
White	3,877,944	5,453,866	6,006,499	5,073,617	5,035,103	4,637,062	4,936,599
Non-Hispanic				3,985,022	3,618,850	2,959,614	2,728,321
Black	217,881	461,546	762,844	943,968	992,974	930,957	856,874
American Indian, Alaska Native[1]	1,671	8,109	24,509	48,120	45,508	76,988	72,828
Native Hawaiian, Pacific Islander				17,641	28,924	27,053	26,094
Asian	45,948	550,982	178,335	417,209	925,561	1,137,500	1,346,865
Chinese	9,187	461,546	40,798	93,747	245,033	294,178	350,119
Japanese[3]	36,761	77,314	104,078	116,543	129,878	111,349	102,287
Filipino		12,122	33,459	99,043	219,653	260,158	322,110
Korean				60,618	145,431	186,350	216,501
Asian Indian				18,562	43,829	60,268	79,169
Vietnamese				28,696	62,594	78,102	87,,468
Cambodian					27,819	28,226	32,125
Hmong					359	651	660
Laotian					3,742	2,763	28,47
Thai					19,016	20,040	25,014
Bangladeshi					681	1,689	4,550
Indonesian					6,490	6,648	8,804
Malaysian					745	660	883
Pakistani					4,580	4,981	9,530
Sri Lankan					1,921	2,979	4,680
Taiwanese[2]						35,174	40,336
Burmese					1,105		4,375
Nepalese							1,104
Bhutanese							40
All Other Asian					12,685	43,284	54,263
Other Race	8,243	6,528	59,888	976,948	1,835,094	2,239,997	2,140,632
Two or More Races						469,781	438,713
Hispanic, Latino, Spanish Origin				2,066,103	3,351,242	4,242,213	4,687,889

TABLE 2.1. (*cont.*)

County Populations by Race and Ethnicity: United States Census—1950–2010

Orange County	1950	1960	1970	1980	1990	2000	2010
Total Population	216,224	703,925	1,420,386	1,932,709	2,410,556	2,846,289	3,010,232
White	105,112	694,354	1,381,742	1,669,314	1,894,593	1,844,652	1,830,758
Non-Hispanic				1,515,887	1,554,501	1,458,978	1,328,499
Black	469	3,171	10,179	25,287	42,681	47,649	50,744
American Indian, Alaska Native[1]	145	730	3,920	12,782	12,165	19,906	18,132
Hawaiian & Pacific Islander				3,195	8,489	8,938	9,354
Asian	1303	5081	16,618	81,674	240,703	386,785	537,804
Chinese	117	444	2,832	14,210	41,403	50,217	65,923
Japanese[3]	1,186	3,890	10,645	20,886	29,741	31,283	32,276
Filipino		747	3,141	10,934	30,356	48,946	71,060
Korean				11,339	35,919	55,573	87,697
Asian Indian				4,972	15,212	27,197	40,732
Vietnamese				19,333	718,22	135,548	183,766
Cambodian					3,979	4,517	5,718
Hmong					575	986	1,102
Laotian					2,893	2,711	2,554
Thai					2,227	3,022	4,015
Bangladeshi					113	311	863
Indonesian					1,395	1,903	2,631
Malaysian					107	168	270
Pakistani					1,508	2,636	5,318
Sri Lankan					314	709	1,385
Taiwanese[2]						9,500	13,159
Burmese					223		655
Nepalese							274
Bhutanese							1
All Other Asian					2,916	11,558	18,405
Other Race	1,014	589	7,927	140,457	211,925	421,208	435,641
Two or More Races						117,151	127,799
Hispanic, Latino, Spanish Origin					286,339	564,828	875,579	1,012,973

[1] 1950, 1960, 1970—recorded as "Indian"; 1980, 1990—recorded as "American Indian, Eskimo, & Aleut"
[2] Prior to 2000, Taiwanese was included in the count for Chinese
[3] Inclusive of Okinawan

The multiracial history and shifting demography of the Southland provides important context for the community and identity formations of sansei and yonsei. In my conversations with sansei and yonsei about their lived experiences and about making sense of their own racial and ethnic identities, they were most likely to reflect on intraracial, rather than interracial, dynamics. This is not to say that interracial relationships and interactions did not impact the identity and community formation strategies and choices of Southern California sansei and yonsei. Certainly, whiteness continues to loom large in sansei and yonsei racial consciousness. Nonetheless, sansei and yonsei referenced relationships and juxtaposed their experiences far more often with other Asian Americans than they did with other individuals and communities of color.

California and the greater LA region are home to some of the largest and most diverse Asian American populations. In the postwar, post-1965 period, the Southern California growth in Asian American ethnic diversity is among the highest of any region in the US. As shown in table 2.1, this diversity grew from only three census-enumerated categories in 1950 to twenty in 2010. Southern California is not just broadly diverse; it is also home to the largest communities for many Asian American ethnic groups—Cambodian, Filipino, Indonesian, Korean, Thai, and Vietnamese (Pew Research 2021). For Japanese Americans, the Los Angeles metropolitan area has the largest community on the US mainland. Even into their fourth—even fifth—generations, California Japanese Americans are among the most regionally concentrated of all US ethnic groups (Portes and Rumbaut 2014). According to the 2010 census, 71 percent of all Japanese Americans reside in the western region, and a higher percentage of Japanese Americans live in California (approximately 33 percent) than in the next two states, Hawai'i and Washington, combined (Hoefell et al. 2012). The highly concentrated—but still minoritized—population of Japanese Americans and the sizeable communities of so many other Asian American ethnic groups begins to explain why comparisons and relationships with other Asian Americans looms large in racial sense-making of sansei and yonsei in Los Angeles and Orange Counties. Such co-location sets the stage for micro-level interaction and makes the Southland ideal for exploring the intraracial—but interethnic—dynamics and formation of Asian American racial consciousness, identity, and community.

While the ethnic and racial diversity of Los Angeles and Orange Counties is fundamental in understanding the community and identity formations of sansei and yonsei, inter- and intraracial interactions are also shaped by its unique development and infrastructure. The trajectory of American sociology and its interest in the impact of urban infrastructure on social interaction moved its attention westward from its origin at the Chicago School. Los Angeles provided a new laboratory for Chicago-trained sociologists to explore urban space and social relations. The postmodern construction and layout of the region and the emergence of sprawling, semiautonomous suburban communities was a stark contrast to the urban core paradigm of Chicago and East Coast cities. Building community within what Kling, Olin, and Poster (1991) would term the "postsuburbs" complicates our understanding of Japanese American assimilation and mundane manifestations of citizenship and belonging. It is the postsuburbs of Southern California, along with the unique structural and demographic characteristics of Los Angeles and Orange Counties, that provide the landscape on which Japanese American history and community formations unfold.

Barred from Belonging: Japanese American Immigration and Exclusions

Japanese immigration to California began in earnest in the 1880s after the 1882 passage of the Chinese Exclusion Act, which banned the entry of Chinese laborers. While this law solved the West Coast's "Chinese Problem," it did not solve California's need for cheap labor for a growing agricultural industry. Japanese immigrants were quickly recruited to fill the labor shortage (Chan 1991; Takaki 1998). Following the pattern of many labor migrants, early Japanese immigrants were mostly young, unattached men. Without women, however, the ability to extend the community beyond a single generation through the formation of families was severely limited. This pattern was especially limiting for immigrants from Asia whose family formation difficulties were compounded by sexual racism and anti-miscegenation statutes. Even before the Chinese Exclusion Act, Chinese women were effectively banned from entering the US as a result of the Page Act of 1875.[1] Similarly, early Filipino immigrants arriving in the 1920s and 1930s were predominantly male and could move within the US empire without restriction. In the Filipino case, the gender imbalance was caused by the global economic hardships related to the Great Depression and capitalist labor interests that would pay transport for male laborers only (Chan 1991; España-Maram 2006; Takaki 1998). The present-day communities of Chinese, Filipino, and all other Asian Americans—except Japanese Americans—largely do not extend unbroken from these early waves of immigration, having grown instead from arrivals that occurred after the comprehensive reopening of US borders to Asian immigrants with the passage of the Immigration and Naturalization Act of 1965.

Japanese American immigration history follows a different trajectory. While immigration from Japan remained formally open until 1924, Japanese immigration was significantly limited by the Gentleman's Agreement of 1908. As an act of diplomacy rather than of congressional legislation like the Chinese Exclusion Act, the United States recognized the emerging strength of Japan as a world economic and military power. In this agreement, the Japanese government agreed to stop the emigration of laborers; in return, the United States agreed to promote a hospitable environment for Japanese immigrants already in the United States and also allowed immigrants already present to bring over their wives, children, and parents. By allowing the migration of women and children, the Gentleman's Agreement enabled an early formation of family units and multigenerational communities that were not possible for other Asian American groups.[2]

Despite such diplomatic overtures, Japanese immigrants ultimately met the same legislative fate as other Asian immigrants, with their full and legal exclusion enacted with the passage of the racist 1924 National Origins Act.[3] While immigrants from southern and eastern Europe were provided a nominal quota of 2 percent of each national origin group's population size in 1890, Japanese immigrants were completely excluded by name (Daniels 1962; Takaki 1998).

As the fate of Japanese immigration and future generations was being decided at the federal level, the local daily lives of Japanese Americans already in California continued. While San Francisco was the main port of entry for Japanese immigrants around the turn of the twentieth century, the Great Earthquake of 1906 pushed many Japanese Americans south to Los Angeles. By 1910, Los Angeles would be home to the largest mainland population and the locus of Japanese America (Kurashige 2002; Nishi 1958). Despite limitations placed on Japanese immigration, the Japanese American population in Los Angeles County alone grew to nearly 37,000 by 1930 as a result of internal migrations and the entry of wives and families allowed by the Gentlemen's Agreement (Nishi 1958).

Alongside immigration exclusion and internal migration, this early period of Japanese American history is marked by profound racism and discrimination. In the state of California, the anti-miscegenation statute was expanded in 1905 to ban the marriage between a white person and a person of Asian descent (Volpp 2012). In 1913, California targeted Japanese Americans by enacting the first of its alien land laws, which prohibited immigrants from owning or leasing land (Daniels 1962). Such laws sent a clear message that Japanese Americans were not welcome in California, their social and legal membership unrecognized. This marginal status was further underscored by the US Supreme Court, which heard nine different cases concerning Japanese immigrant eligibility for naturalization beginning in 1894 (Lopez 1996). Without exception, each decision denied Japanese immigrants the right to naturalize and placed them in the same racial exclusion category as Chinese immigrants. The final and definitive ruling came in 1922 with *Ozawa v. the United States* (Ichioka 1988; Lopez 1996). While Japanese Americans retained jus soli citizenship rights, Japanese immigrants immediately became aliens ineligible for naturalization.

World War II Removal, Mass Incarceration, and Postwar Reform

From their earliest appearance in the US, Japanese immigrants have been drawn outside the legal and social boundaries of national membership. The denial of naturalization rights, based on the perception of unassimilability, and outright exclusion sends a clear message of undesirability and non-belonging. While Japanese immigrants faced ineligibility and eventual exclusion, their American-born children, the nisei, maintained their birthright citizenship. This birthright provided legal membership but fell short of providing the sense of belonging necessary for full citizenship. Nothing makes this lack of recognition clearer than the mass removal and incarceration of Japanese Americans from the mainland West Coast during the Second World War, which stripped

Japanese Americans, citizens and non-citizens, of their legal rights and membership (Carbado 2005). Ushered in by President Franklin D. Roosevelt's signing of Executive Order 9066 in 1942, wartime incarceration reiterated non-belonging as Japanese Americans—with as little as one-sixteenth Japanese ancestry—were reclassified from citizens and permanent residents to enemy aliens, physically removed from their local communities, and incarcerated in makeshift concentration camps within the nation's interior (Carbado 2005; Weglyn 1996). Following the concerted effort to marginalize and oust Japanese Americans for over half a century, local communities and federal officials questioned Japanese Americans' loyalty to the US. No verified act of espionage by a Japanese American has ever been found.

The majority of Los Angeles County and Orange County Japanese Americans were removed to Manzanar in California, Poston and Gila River in Arizona, Granada/Amache in Colorado, Heart Mountain in Wyoming, and Jerome and Rohwer in Arkansas (Los Angeles Historic Resources Survey 2018). In total, approximately thirty-eight thousand Japanese Americans—citizens and non-citizens—were removed and incarcerated from the Los Angeles and Orange County region (Los Angeles Historic Resources Survey 2018). Japanese American incarcerees were finally allowed to return to the West Coast in January 1945, and all camps but Tule Lake would close down by the end of that year (Weglyn 1996). Despite having been allowed to leave the camps and return home to Los Angeles and Orange Counties for almost a year, many incarcerees opted to remain in the camps until they were forced to leave. Many feared what was waiting for them in their home communities after being outcasted and vilified (Weglyn 1996).

As Japanese Americans began to slowly return to the West Coast and local communities recovered from the devastation of WWII mass incarceration, the rise of the Cold War geopolitics in the immediate postwar period gave rise to significant progressive changes in federal and state-level policies. Despite its root as a global conflict against the spread of communism, the Cold War marks a significant turning point in domestic race relations broadly as well as a particular shift in the racial positioning of Asian Americans. Dudziak (2000) insightfully connects Cold War politics and the passage of the Civil Rights Act of 1964, Voting Rights Act of 1965, Immigration and Naturalization Act of 1965, and

Fair Housing Act of 1968. Reacting to Soviet propaganda that shined a light on US racism toward Black and other racial minority citizens, the United States rushed to demonstrate and practice the equality and rights promised to all individuals regardless of skin color. The Cold War also looms over federal and state reforms prior to the 1960s. Alien land laws and anti-miscegenation laws were struck down by the US Supreme Court in 1948 (*Oyama v. State of California*) and 1967 (*Loving v. State of Virginia*), respectively. The California Supreme Court had overturned the states' anti-miscegenation laws in 1948 (*Perez v. Sharp*). Race-based immigration exclusions and ineligibility to naturalize were ceased with the passage of the McCarran-Walter Act in 1952. (Chan 1991; Gotanda 1996; Takaki 1998; Spickard 2009).[4] A true reopening of America's gates for Japanese and other Asian immigrants, however, would not come until 1965 and the passage of the Immigration and Naturalization Act. Through the lens of the Cold War, the much lauded postwar reforms that publicly represented a tipping point in the expansion of domestic rights and granting of racial equality under the law are reenvisioned as a performative benevolence serving the imperialist and capitalist interests of US empire on the world stage. Such reforms did not reflect a meaningful shift in the pervasiveness of US racism or a rise in anti-racist goodwill at home. The civil rights period, then, while certainly impactful, did not suddenly change the broad local and national perceptions of belonging and citizenship for Black, Indigenous, and other people of color, Japanese Americans included. Without a doubt, race continues to be a limiting factor in the recognition of belonging into the present day.

Postwar Non-migration and the Shape of the Japanese American Community

While 1965 is generally seen as a watershed moment in Asian American immigration, Japanese immigration to the US did not resume in significant numbers at this historical juncture (Chan 1991; King-O'Riain 2006; Spickard 2009; Takaki 1998). Following its World War II reconstruction, the Japanese economy saw significant growth buttressed by the Cold War military-industrial complex and needed to maintain its labor supply. Immigrants from Japan averaged less than five thousand per year through 1989. Beginning in 1990, immigration from Japan slowly began to rise but remained low, with only 7,100 immigrants in 2010 (Nakano 2014).[5] In practical terms, Japanese immigration had minimal impact on the demographics of the existing Japanese American population.

The time gap in immigration and the relatively short time period of immigrant entry from Japan (1880s–1924) allows for a seemingly uniform generational cohort structure within the Japanese American community. Within this structure, generation from point of immigration maps fairly neatly on historical generation based on birth year: issei (immigrant, first generation), nisei (second generation), sansei (third generation), yonsei (fourth generation) (Glenn 1988; Omi et al. 2019; Spickard 2009; Tsuda 2016; Yanagisako 1992). On the US mainland, the first generation, issei, arrived prior to 1924 due to restrictions on immigration of Japanese laborers beginning in 1908 with the signing of the Gentlemen's Agreement and full exclusion of all Japanese immigrants with the Immigration Act of 1924.[6] The majority of their nisei children were born between the years 1918 and 1940 (Glenn 1988; Yanagisako 1992). Sansei were born from the 1940s through the 1960s. The vast majority of yonsei were born from the early years of the 1970s through the end of the century. This generational structure is ubiquitous in the everyday vernacular of the ethnic community but is also federally institutionalized. Japanese Americans are the only ethnic group to have generational labels—issei, nisei, sansei, yonsei, gosei—enumerated in the ancestry code list of the US Census Bureau (Omi, Nakano, and Yamashita 2019). While newer waves of Japanese immigration post-WWII certainly complicate this tight generational structuring, the majority of Japanese Americans trace their ancestral roots to immigrants arriving prior to 1924 and identify themselves by these distinct generational categories (Fugita and O'Brien 1994; Glenn 1988; King-O'Riain 2006; Nakano 2014; Tsuda 2016; Yanagisako 1992).

Demographic Shifts in Postwar Southern California

Postwar mobility driven by the Cold War military-industrial complex and post-1965 immigration fundamentally changed the demographic landscape of Southern California and the communities that the sansei and yonsei in this study called home (McGirr 2001; Zhou et al. 2008). The suburbs of Los Angeles and Orange Counties flourished in the postwar period. Beginning in 1950, the Orange County population grew an astounding fourteen-fold, from 216,224 to over three million, in 2010. Over the same period, Los Angeles County more than doubled in size, from 4.1 million to nearly 10 million residents (Forstall 1995; United States Census 2010). While delayed by racist housing and lending restrictions, the general population growth was followed by a racial demographic shift that would turn both Los Angeles and Orange into majority-minority counties by the turn of the twenty-first century.

Within this growing racial diversity of the Southland, the ethnic diversity of the Asian American segment of the population increased tremendously. In 1960, Asian Americans represented 1.8 percent and 0.8 percent of Los Angeles and Orange Counties, respectively. By 2010, Asian American populations accounted for 13.5 percent of Los Angeles County and 17.7 percent of Orange County. Given the changes to immigration laws beginning in 1965, Asian American diversity in terms of ethnicity and national origin saw meteoric growth, but with a diminishing Japanese American presence. In 1960, the US census enumerated only three Asian categories: Chinese, Filipino, and Japanese.[7] In that year, Japanese Americans made up 71.1 percent of all Asian Americans in Los Angeles County and 75.6 percent of Orange County. By 2010, the US census would list twenty-two distinct Asian American ethnicities (Nakano 2013), and Japanese Americans would account for only 6.8 percent and 5.4 percent of all Asian Americans in Los Angeles and Orange counties, respectively. As will be shown, this postwar demographic shift is especially significant for Japanese Americans' understanding of their own ethnicity, race, and social position within local and national communities.[8]

Because the growth in ethnic diversity relied on the immigration of new Asian American groups, it was also accompanied by a shift in the generational and nativity breakdowns of the Asian American population. While the Japanese American population had been predominantly US born since the 1930s, Asian Americans entering after 1965 began to shift the nativity balance back toward the foreign born. Until 1970, the majority of the aggregated Asian American population in Los Angeles and Orange Counties and throughout the state were native born. However, in 1970, Asian America returned to a predominantly foreign-born population. From 1980 forward, the total population of Asian

Americans was predominantly foreign born (Nakano 2013). Throughout this period, the vast majority of Japanese Americans have been US born (Nakano 2013).

Japanese Americans in Los Angeles and Orange Counties: A Partial Demographic Profile

Despite minimal immigration, the Japanese American population in Los Angeles and Orange Counties continued to expand through the baby boomer generational phenomenon and domestic migration patterns in the closing half of the twentieth century. The Japanese American population in Los Angeles County grew from 36,761 in 1950 to 141,028 in 2019. Over the same time period, Orange County's Japanese American population expanded from just 1,186 to 54,977. Federal statistics from the US Census Bureau and other agencies along with some privately funded surveys allow some insight into the historical and contemporary status of the Japanese American population along a number of often assimilationist-oriented metrics. However, none of these data sources alone collect all the necessary variables or sample broadly enough to capture significant numbers of smaller ethnic populations like Japanese Americans. Instead, even a partial story of contemporary Japanese Americans must be pieced together from existing federal statistics collected by multiple agencies. This is particularly true in terms of generation and multiraciality, two characteristics that are central to the changing face of the Japanese American community. Data on these two characteristics do not appear simultaneously in any federal database. The US census collected data on mother's and father's birthplace until 1970. From this data, it is possible to tabulate the third plus generation of Japanese Americans by coupling parental birthplace with respondent nativity. Disaggregating between sansei and yonsei, however, becomes less precise and can only be based on assumed birth year ranges shared by the third and fourth generations, respectively.[9] The multiraciality and multiethnicity across different generations of Japanese Americans, however, is unknown, as the census did not begin to track multiracial identification until 2000.

The 1970 US census—the last federal data source that allows for a tabulation of Japanese Americans up to the third generation—shows that over 76 percent of Japanese Americans were native born in the US. Similar percentages existed in Los Angeles and Orange Counties with 77 percent and 79 percent, respectively. By combining this information with information of parental birthplace, I estimate that among the native born in Los Angeles and Orange Counties, 62 percent and 56 percent, respectively, were nisei. In 1970, the sansei had already become 36 percent of Los Angeles County's and 43 percent of Orange County's total Japanese American populations stemming from pre-1924 immigration. If yonsei are estimated to have been born beginning in 1965, they made up a small, but certainly growing, portion of the Southland Japanese American population. After 1970, and without the collection of parental birthplace data, it becomes impossible to disaggregate the native-born population among nisei, sansei, yonsei, and increasingly the native-born children of postwar immigrants. However, these demographics gleaned from the 1970 census, coupled with knowledge of fairly minimal postwar immigration from Japan and a continuing native-born majority, provide a strong indication that the later generations of the Japanese American population make up a large, if not majority, share of the contemporary Japanese American population in Los Angeles and Orange Counties.

It was not until the 2000 US census that individuals were allowed to identify with more than one racial category. In every census before the year 2000, individuals, regardless of their actual racial background, were forced to be counted as only one race. For this reason, we have no federal data on multiracial and multiethnic Japanese Americans before this date. Despite the dearth of federal data, the broader historical record and social science academic studies demonstrate that multiracial and multiethnic Japanese Americans have long been part of the community. Literary scholar Andrew Leong notes that Japanese America, extending back to the 1880s, has always included community members who were mixed race (Leong 2019). Social science scholarship also provides insight into mixed-race Japanese Americans and general intermarriage rates prior to their availability in federal data. In 1973, Kikumura and Kitano found that outmarriage among Japanese Americans was an increasing trend and reached 49 percent in Los Angeles County by 1972 (Kikumura and Kitano 1973). It is only logical to assume that such unions produced multiracial and multiethnic offspring. Given such early evidence of a sizeable mixed-race segment of the Japanese American population and institutional limitations of the US census up until 2000 that forced multiracial and multiethnic individuals into singular racial identifications, the Japanese American population was likely undercounted in the second half of the twentieth century. To demonstrate this fact, between the 1990 and 2000 US censuses, the number of individuals who identified only as Japanese fell from approximately 847,500 to 796,700. However, because the 2000 US census allowed individuals to identify with more than one racial category, the complete Japanese American population totaled more than 1,152,000. Nearly one-third of the Japanese American population in the year 2000 identified with more than one race. Certainly, these multiracial and multiethnic Japanese Americans were not all newly arrived immigrants or born in the intervening decade. They always existed but were only now being counted properly. It may also be possible that the mixed-race Japanese Americans who had been forced to choose one race prior to 2000 had normalized a non-Japanese single racial identification and opted to not identify with multiple races when given the opportunity. Some people may not have been aware of their mixed-race heritage due to this longstanding institutional erasure. It is also likely that this undercount would be more prevalent in the native-born and later-generation segments of the population that are more multiracial and multiethnic than the Japanese American population as a whole (King-O'Riain 2019). However, because of the thirty-year gap between when generational breakdowns could be tabulated in 1970 and when multiracial statistics began being captured in 2000, we cannot know this fact with any certainty.

The 2000 and 2010 censuses capture the multiracial and multiethnic makeup of Japanese Americans in Los Angeles and Orange Counties. In 2000, multiethnic and multiracial individuals accounted for 19.3 percent of Los Angeles County's Japanese American population and 25.1 percent of Orange County Japanese Americans. By 2010, these figures grew to 26.4 percent and 33 percent, respectively. The multiethnic and multiracial population is particularly prevalent in the native-born segment of the Japanese American population.[10] In Los Angeles County, 87.7 percent of multiracial and multiethnic Japanese Americans were native-born in 2010 compared to 89.1 percent of Orange County's population. There is no further insight into generational status beyond nativity.[11]

Federal Data and Assimilation's Incomplete Truths

Without a doubt, federal data provided by the United States Census Bureau, the Bureau of Labor Statistics, and other agencies and offices are invaluable sources of robust longitudinal information enabling and shaping our understanding of inequalities and trends across any number of segments of the US population. The federal government is unmatched in its resources and ability to reach out to all US residents for the purposes of data collection. While the information provided by the US census and other federal data sources is vast, it cannot be comprehensive. It is limited by the quantity and quality of questions it can ask and who decides to provide responses. Of course, the US census is not meant to be comprehensive, and we cannot forget this fact in our sociological analyses. We must be cognizant of the shortcomings and omissions and consider them in our conclusions and subsequent theory building.

The Japanese American case lays bare the shortcomings of the US census across its recent history in terms of immigrant generation and multiracial identification. Because the Japanese American population is relatively small, federal data is among the few locations of large-scale data collection on this group. It is census data that has been used consistently to verify the assimilationist success of Japanese Americans (Alba and Nee 2003). However, as multiraciality and generation play such a large role in shaping the Japanese American experience, the census's inconsistent capturing of this information paints an incomplete picture. While the availability of such data may not change the sociological conclusions on Japanese American assimilation, the data would certainly illuminate more about the shape and trajectory of the Japanese American community.

Other issues also arise in the usage of US census data to understand Japanese Americans and integration processes and inequality more broadly. The US census and other federal sources provide data on outcomes at the time of the survey (e.g., household income, years of schooling completed, marital status). Even as longitudinal surveys, census outcomes tracked over time provide insight into trajectories but not the lived experiences that produce such trends. How groups and individuals arrived at particular outcomes and continue to live their daily lives in those outcomes is just as important—arguably more important—than the outcomes themselves in understanding integration. The "how" can tell how race and other statuses and conditions help or hinder such outcomes and shape everyday lives. This is certainly true for Japanese Americans.

In this chapter, I have leveraged permutations of federal data to provide a rough outline of the demographic shape of the contemporary Japanese American community. Such context, while incomplete, remains important. However, the outcomes offered by federal data are incomplete truths. To provide a more complete picture and a fuller understanding of Japanese American experiences and outcomes, the chapters that follow focus on the everyday negotiations and practices created and completed by Japanese Americans in response to their complex social positions. Essentially, Japanese Americans navigate their identities and interactions, form communities, and claim recognition of their belonging as racialized subjects and with maintained ethnic salience despite positive assimilationist outcomes evidenced in existing federal data.

3

The False Promise of Assimilation

Tricia had all the trappings of an all-American teenager growing up in the suburbs of Southern California in the 1960s. She was a top student in her high school class and was named the head cheerleader. Shortly before Tricia, a third-generation Japanese American, raised her pom-poms, sociologist Milton Gordon published his foundational work *Assimilation in American Life* (1964). In this text, Gordon outlines seven types of assimilation but focuses on structural assimilation as "the keystone in the arch of assimilation" (Gordon 1964, 81). For Gordon, structural assimilation includes "large-scale entrance into cliques, clubs, and institutions . . . on the primary group level" (71). Once structural assimilation is achieved, all other forms of assimilation should fall into place. This includes what Gordon references as forms of receptional assimilation, which include an absence of prejudice and discrimination. Contemporary studies of immigrant incorporation have come to focus on socioeconomic and residential integration as proxy measures of structural assimilation (Alba and Nee 2003; Charles 2007; Massey and Denton 1993).

A superficial comparison of Tricia's life story and the definition of structural assimilation seems to forebode the fulfillment of assimilation's promise—the American Dream—for Japanese Americans. Tricia's suburban residence and educational achievement serve as evidence of socioeconomic upward mobility and residential integration. With the mantle of head cheerleader, Tricia exemplifies the endpoints of both acculturation and structural assimilation as an active participant and leader in a quintessential American pastime. Despite these truths, Tricia's own recollections of her high school days are not filled with simple fond nostalgia but also hold a sense of melancholy:

> Where I grew up and went to high school, there were only like maybe, less than a handful of [Japanese Americans]. And I kind of always felt

alienated even though I was a cheerleader and stuff, I didn't really feel a part. So, you know, people think, "Oh head yell leader. She's probably really rowdy and did all this bad stuff with all the other cheerleaders." I never did that. I just kind of stayed by myself.

Tricia would continue to describe her sense of alienation as resulting from, at least in part, racial and cultural differences. For Japanese Americans, this is assimilation's false promise. While nominally members or leaders of mainstream organizations and institutions, a persistent racial positioning as outsider and other remains. Participation in a mainstream institution like cheerleading did not automatically grant Tricia acceptance and camaraderie, hallmarks of Gordon's receptional forms of assimilation.

Tricia's experiences—common among sansei and yonsei—mark the incomplete perspective and racial blind spot of contemporary assimilation theory. They demonstrate that acculturation and structural assimilation are insufficient to provide the recognition of belonging by other community members and that such recognition is often withheld along racial lines. While sociology, its allied social sciences, and broader public discourse continue to rely on versions of the assimilation framework to understand hopeful immigrant trajectories toward integration and belonging, Japanese American history seen through an ethnic studies lens has long displayed the false promise of assimilation. From the complicated impacts of the World War II mass incarceration to the origins of the model minority myth, Japanese Americans have been entangled in assimilation's melancholic false promise again and again. Across history and into present-day later-generation experiences, the Japanese American racial uniform has always placed a limit upon Japanese American assimilation.

Assimilation Success and the Pretense of the Model Minority Myth

The story of Japanese American assimilation is the postwar mythology of the model minority. The suburban setting of this story underscores the achievement of residential integration, a facet of assimilation theory that assumes success with diminishing physical and social distance from whites (Alba and Nee 2003; Charles 2007; Gordan 1964; Massey and Denton 1993). Residential integration is, of course, only one of many benchmarks successfully met by Japanese Americans in their postwar mobility story. Nearly all later-generation Japanese Americans are exclusive English speakers. Japanese Americans have education attainment levels and occupational statuses above that of native-born whites. Japanese Americans have among the highest median household incomes for any ethnic or racial group. Japanese American outmarriage rates are also high, at 53 percent among native-born Japanese Americans. As a result of high rates of outmarriage, native-born Japanese Americans are an increasingly multiracial and multiethnic population, with 40 percent of the population identifying with more than one race or ethnicity. Point by point, Japanese Americans seem to empirically meet the assimilation criteria deemed most important in contemporary sociology and give life to the model minority myth.[1]

However, we must recognize the gap that remains between the alleged ideals of assimilation—full integration and lack of differentiation—and the lived experience of later-generation Americans of color. Model minority status is the end result of a theoretical framework that focuses more on change over time—"it gets better"—and dubious cultural explanations than on the structural limitations—a sociological hallmark—of race on the assimilation process. While assimilation theory portends race neutrality, the model minority myth functions on more explicit racial logics. The very term *model minority* invokes the position of national abjection—referencing the marginal foreigner within—and the state of racial melancholy—the sought after, but racially unattainable status of full belonging (Cheng 2000; Shimakawa 2002). To label a group a model but leave it a distinct minority is to protect the overlayed boundaries of whiteness and Americanness and present a dishonest critique—if not outright attack—on other "less successful" and therefore less deserving minority groups (Ramírez 2020). The model minority myth awards a superficially higher status to one minority group to make them more palatable to, but still defined outside of, the white racial group, and it pits minority groups against each other. The model minority myth, then, is not a reward for any exceptional hard work on the part of Asian Americans. Rather, it is a cover for the maintenance of white supremacy.

Cold War Logics and the Model Minority Paradox

Beyond the racial divide-and-conquer tactics of white supremacy, the origins of the model minority myth further reveal racial logics that coincide with the Cold War and an era of seeming racial progress. As noted in the previous chapter, the postwar period is often marked by reforms at the state and federal levels with an arc toward justice. From the removal of anti-miscegenation, alien land laws, and racist immigration and naturalization restrictions to civil rights, voting, and fair housing, the US made great strides to remedy the racist sins of its past. However, as noted previously, the postwar tidal wave of civil rights and immigration reforms broadly benefiting racial minority communities was not a result of ideological shifts in the racial criteria of who belongs and is deserving of equality in the minds of the US public or policy makers; it was instead tied to geopolitical military and economic interests and to efforts to contain Cold War communist threats (Dudziak 2000). While this incomplete expansion of rights and protections were important regardless of motivations, it was foreign—not domestic—interests that ultimately tipped the scales in favor of justice. As the Cold War heated up in Asia, the social and political positioning of Asian Americans began to shift. Confrontations with communist China over Taiwan, the Korean Peninsula, and Southeast Asia drove a shift in the racial positioning of Japanese Americans during this era. The same perceived foreignness and association with a foreign power that led to Japanese American mass incarceration during World War II became an asset during the Cold War and afforded an expansion of domestic rights and opportunities.

This symbiotic relationship between forever-foreigner perceptions and the expansion of civil rights is clearly demonstrated in the movement of Japanese Americans into the Southern California suburbs. Suburbanization has always been a racialized and deeply racist process (Kruse 2005; Zarsadiaz 2022). As the Southern California suburbs developed and sprawled, they were a safe haven for white flight, as urban neighborhoods became more racially and ethnically diverse. White suburbanites further safeguarded their new homes and neighborhoods against racial minority intrusion through de jure and de facto practices of redlining (Kurashige 2007). In some ways, the Orange and south Los Angeles County suburbs developed around Japanese Americans, given the ethnic group's deep roots in the region's prewar agricultural industries. But Japanese Americans also moved to these developing suburbs from other parts of California and the country. Here, Cold War interests to maintain the US alliance with Japan collided with the exclusionary racism of local homeowners' associations, banks, and city councils. Similar to the shift in rhetoric around federal civil rights and the treatment of racial and ethnic minorities for the sake of Cold War global interests, Japan's new role as the central Cold War ally in the Pacific led to a change in discourse surrounding the treatment of Japanese Americans and their place in local Southern California communities (Brooks 2009; Kurashige 2007). The shifting position of Japan in Cold War geopolitics enabled Japanese Americans to gain residence in predominantly white neighborhoods; neighborhoods that continued to deny residence to other racial minorities (Brooks 2009).[2] Japanese Americans were accepted into suburban neighborhoods not because they were recognized as equal Americans by their white neighbors. Rather, they were seen as local representatives of Japan who needed to be treated with dignity for the sake of diplomatic relations (Brooks 2009; Kurashige 2007). This residential integration and supposed reduction in social distance highlighted rather than diminished the perceived racial difference of Japanese Americans vis-à-vis their white neighbors, because Japanese American acceptance into the neighborhood was based on their assumed foreignness.

Japanese American movement into the predominantly white suburbs of Southern California and its basis in Japanese American foreignness reflects a larger discourse on Japanese Americans as the model minority. Again, from an assimilation standpoint, residential integration serves as a key metric for reduced physical and social distance and general acceptance. As a validating step toward assimilation, Japanese American suburbanites embody the model minority mythology. As noted, reforming the discourse around Japanese American assimilation success away from one of wartime military and economic threat and toward the rhetoric of the docile model minority was meant to demonstrate to the world the virtues of the US brand of liberal democracy, where anyone can make it regardless of race (Lee 1999; Wu 2014). If Japanese Americans, as visible racial minorities, were able to achieve the American Dream, systemic racism clearly could not be the cause of more general racial inequalities seen among other racial minority groups, African Americans, in particular. Japanese and other Asian Americans were used as pawns and a racial wedge by the US government to promote a virtuous image of the US abroad (Brooks 2009; Cheng 2013; Lee 1999; Wu 2014).

The anti-Black and racism-denialist underpinnings of the model minority mythology demonstrate that Japanese American upward mobility and movement into the white suburbs should not be taken at face value—good faith progress toward greater racial equality and assimilation. Beyond anti-Blackness, other foundational assumptions undergirding the model minority mythology further demonstrate its oppressive intentions. The model minority label is not applied in recognition of Japanese American Americanness and belonging. Just as Brooks (2009) and Kurashige (2007) demonstrate how the positioning of Japanese Americans as foreigners enabled their entry into white suburban neighborhoods, model minority status itself is predicated on a persistent foreign imagining of Japanese Americans and is tied to Cold War politics (Lee 1999; Wu 2014). Wu (2014) connects the origins of the model minority myth to the parallel rise of racial liberalism in the US and the importance of Asia in the postwar global order. The mantle of the model minority was placed on Japanese and Chinese Americans as "persons acknowledged as capable of acting like white Americans while remaining racially distinct" (Wu 2014, 5). Sociologist William Petersen, in one of the earliest applications of the model minority label to Japanese Americans in his 1966 *New York Times Magazine* essay, "Success Story, Japanese-American Style," explained Japanese American assimilative success as a result of cultural vestiges from Japan, which emphasized family and hard work. Across multiple generations, Japanese Americans persevered against "the highest barriers our racists were able to fashion in part because of their meaningful attachment with an alien culture" (43; also see Wu 2014 for discussion of the foreign cultural roots of Japanese American success). Despite cultural parallels and their attempts to conform to white middle class norms and socioeconomic successes, Japanese Americans persist as racially distinct subjects, inextricably tied to a perception of foreignness.

This is the assimilationist paradox of the model minority myth—to be a model of assimilation success but remain a visible foreign minority outside the bounds of full community membership and the white racial category it requires. As Brooks (2009) states regarding Japanese American movement into the California suburbs, they were "neighbors" but "alien;" "friends" but "foreign." For all their empirically measured successes in terms of residential integration, socioeconomic status, educational attainment, and intermarriage, Japanese Americans acceptance is recognized only through their perceived foreignness, which is to say that they are not recognized members of the national, or local, community. If Japanese Americans, and Asian Americans more broadly, are held up as the model minority, it is imperative not to lose sight of the racial and racist underpinnings of the mythology. The model minority myth is a sleight of hand that provides particular types of access and success while simultaneously denying the oppressions faced by other racial minorities as well the recognition of full citizenship of Asian Americans. The model minority myth underscores that assimilation success in socioeconomic terms is an insufficient measure of full citizenship and belonging.

Selective Narratives of Assimilation and the Multigenerational Impact of Mass Incarceration

Beyond its perpetuation of the foreigner racialization, the model minority assimilation story of Japanese Americans has been curated to follow a particular narrative that omits important historical and contemporary realities. Elsewhere, I have argued that Japanese Americans as an ethnic community define their boundaries not just through notions of common culture and ancestry but also through a particular historical and racialized narrative (Nakano 2018). This narrative provides the historical details and plot points of the model minority myth. This narrative centralizes WWII, through mass incarceration and military service, as a pivotal moment for Japanese Americans to demonstrate their belonging and jumpstart their postwar assimilation achievements (Nakano 2018; Omi, Nakano, and Yamashita 2019). The devastating racist experiences during incarceration and in military service in segregated combat units are an impetus for rapid postwar assimilation within the collective narrative of Japanese American ethnicity (Nakano 2018; Omi, Nakano, and Yamashita 2019). The narrative, actively constructed by ethnic organizations such as the Japanese American Citizens League and by large-scale social scientific studies like the Japanese Evacuation and Resettlement

Study, Issei Story Project, and Japanese American Research Project, highlights the causal link between postwar assimilation and mass incarceration (Wu 2014). Through this narrative linkage, the WWII mass incarceration of Japanese Americans casts a long shadow over multiple generations of Japanese Americans and far beyond the closing of the last camp in 1946 (Nakagawa 1995; Simpson 2002). The indelible mark of the incarceration and of WWII experiences impacts how Japanese Americans conceptualized and practiced ethnic identity and community throughout the postwar period and into the present day.

Within the Japanese American ethnic narrative, postwar social acceptance and upward mobility are the result of the demonstrated valor of Japanese American WWII veterans of the all-nisei 442nd Regiment/100th Battalion and the dutiful and peaceful cooperation of Japanese American incarcerees (Kurashige 2002; Nakano 2018; Wilson and Hosokawa 1980). The narrative explains that in reaction to their wartime treatment, Japanese Americans—nisei in particular—practiced a quiet patriotism and 110 percent Americanism, which downplayed their Japanese heritage (Spickard 2009; Wilson and Hosokawa 1980). Nisei parents made a conscious choice not to teach their baby-boomer sansei children the Japanese language and kept other Japanese cultural practices as private affairs if they kept them at all (Fugita and O'Brien 1994; Kurashige 2002; Spickard 2009; Wilson and Hosokawa 1980). Sansei and yonsei in this study were also quick to connect Japanese American acculturation—or Japanese cultural loss—with the incarceration experience, demonstrating the embeddedness of this logic within the community. Japanese American upward mobility, educational success and admittance to top universities, movement into white neighborhoods, and even marriage into white families is all tied to WWII incarceration and military service within the Japanese American narrative (Glenn 1988; Kurashige 2002; Nakano 2018; Wilson and Hosokawa 1980).

The provided evidence connecting Japanese American assimilation to WWII incarceration is dubious at best. For example, it is true that sansei and yonsei overwhelmingly do not speak Japanese (Alba and Nee 2003; Spickard 2009), but this may be attributable more to anticipated paths of acculturation in response to time, contact, and environment rather than to the mass incarceration experience. Rumbaut (2009) demonstrates that in the United States, historically and across ethnic groups, language abilities are lost over time and generations. By the third generation, a very small minority of any ethnic population speaks their mother tongue with any amount of fluency (Alba et al. 2002; Lopez 1978; Rumbaut 2009; Rumbaut, Massey, and Bean 2006). Other aggregated outcomes of structural forms of assimilation—residential integration, intermarriage, and institutional participation—are also empirically verified and support the model minority myth. On deeper inspection and contextualization, however, such achievements often occur in racialized and ethnic-specific ways. What should be obvious through even the most casual of observations is that in the postwar period and into the present day, the Japanese American community continues to exist. Wartime racism simultaneously taught Japanese Americans the necessity of assimilating and the importance of community—ethnic community in particular—as a safeguard against enduring white racism and anti-Asian nationalism. Mass incarceration can then be understood as changing the Japanese American community, but it certainly did not lead to its demise. In many ways, mass incarceration strengthened Japanese American community bonds in new forms. While former incarcerees sought to distance themselves from all things Japanese, this clearly did not include other Japanese American people. Rather, Japanese Americans in the postwar period joined other Japanese Americans in activities and institutions modeled after those within the white mainstream. As Kurashige (2002) notes, in the prewar period, these postwar institutions and activities paralleled mainstream counterparts but rarely intersected. Scholars have shown the continuing postwar importance of Japanese American churches (both Buddhist and Christian), festivals, sports leagues, and social and political organizations (Chin 2016a, 2016b; Fugita and O'Brien 1994; King 2002; Kurashige 2002; Lim 2005; King-O'Riain 2006; Levine and Rhodes 1981; Matsumoto 2014; Omi, Nakano, and Yamashita 2019; Takahashi 1997; Tsuda 2016).

The postwar persistence of the Japanese American ethnic community and institutions despite the coercive assimilationist tactics embedded within the strategy of WWII mass incarceration is not the only convenient oversight within the Japanese American assimilationist narrative. In the midst of incarceration, resettlement in eastward regions of the United States with lower concentrations of Japanese Americans was also part of the larger federal project of removal. However, despite being re-settled in eastern and midwestern locations like Chicago, "loyal" nisei, thought by federal authorities to be the most likely to assimilate, sought out other nisei for companionship and formed community where none had previously existed (Wu 2014). After the war, the vast majority of incarcerees returned to the West Coast (Weglyn 1996). While not all prewar residents decided to return to Southern California after the closure of the camps and the evacuation orders were rescinded, Los Angeles remained a postwar beacon for the ethnic community. Regardless of where they lived prior to the war and incarceration, Japanese Americans were drawn to Los Angeles and Orange Counties, and the ethnic population recuperated its prewar size of around thirty-eight thousand within five years of the camps' closures (Kurashige 2008; Nishi 1958). Despite a narrative of US patriotism, integration, and distancing from Japanese culture and heritage, physical Japanese American communities built and rebuilt themselves across the West Coast during the postwar period. On their return to Los Angeles, many Japanese Americans formed ethnically concentrated neighborhoods in places such as Gardena, the San Gabriel Valley, the Crenshaw district, and the Westside (Kurashige 2002). As previously noted, Japanese Americans remain among the most regionally concentrated ethnic groups in the US (Portes and Rumbaut 2014), concentrated on the West Coast, in Southern California in particular.

While WWII mass incarceration certainly shaped the postwar trajectory of Japanese Americans, its relationship to Japanese American assimilation is not linear, nor has it produced the "twilight" of Japanese American ethnicity (Alba 1985). As historian Lon Kurashige (2002) argues, Japanese Americans are examples neither of assimilation nor its assumed opposite, ethnic retentionism. Rather, he calls for an analysis and understanding of integration that does not simplify the persistence of ethnic identity as the antithesis of assimilation processes (Kurashige 2002). Japanese American collective reflection on WWII mass incarceration highlights this false dichotomy. Furthermore, the incarceration may have galvanized certain assimilationist trajectories, but it also holds a central place in how Japanese Americans define their ethnic history and the boundaries of their ethnic community through narrative (Nakano 2018). The ethnic narrative with incarceration as a pivotal plot point forms the basis for ethnic connection among later-generation

Japanese Americans who did not directly experience incarceration and should otherwise be fully assimilated nonethnics. Yet again, this demonstrates a persistence of ethnicity unanticipated by assimilation theories.

Racialization and Marginalization Despite Acculturation

While the previous sections demonstrate the uncertain footing of the model minority myth and a complicated, nonlinear historical trajectory of mobility, the false promise of Japanese American assimilation is also evident in the contemporary experiences of sansei and yonsei. Here, I turn to the experiences shared in my interviews with Southern California sansei and yonsei. As third- and fourth-generation Japanese Americans, sansei and yonsei are without question acculturated and accustomed to US mainstream institutions. Sansei and yonsei saw their culture as basically American and felt comfortable and integrated within the broader community. Brenda, a sansei, joked, "I'd forget I was Japanese. I'd forget I was not white until I looked in the mirror. Oh! I am not blonde!" Humor aside, Brenda's words demonstrate the depth of cultural similarity felt by Japanese Americans with their non-Japanese American, particularly white, peers. Nonetheless, Brenda's racial uniform is a constant reminder of her inescapable otherness. A generation later, Megan, a multiracial yonsei, experienced a similar feeling of racial othering: "I mean, I didn't feel not American. I just felt like there was obviously something that stood out about me that people would ask me about." As Japanese Americans continue to wear this racial uniform in their movement into the middle class, they continue to face limitations on their membership in their local and national communities. Regardless of the cultural compatibility that sansei and yonsei felt among non-Japanese Americans, racial difference remained palpable and continued to create social distance from their mostly white peers in the Southern California suburbs.

Beyond acculturation, sansei and yonsei also shared their extensive participation in local mainstream organizations and institutions in their communities and schools, again pointing towards structural assimilation (Gordon 1964). This high-level participation frequently included long-term memberships and leadership positions (recall Tricia, the head cheerleader, who opened this chapter). The sansei and yonsei I interviewed were often former student government representatives, class presidents, honor society members, and high school and college varsity athletes. Despite such evidence of structural assimilation, respondents often report a simultaneous sense of marginalization while actively participating in their respective organizations.

The finding of persistent marginalization despite acculturation and structural assimilation mirrors previous studies of immigrant-origin communities of color and the minority middle class, including Tuan's (1999) seminal study on later-generation Asian Americans (also see Tsuda 2016 on Japanese American racial marginalization). Similar to these previous studies, later-generation Japanese American marginalization from the white-dominant mainstream is most frequently felt through experiences with prejudice, overt racism, and microaggressions. Sansei and older yonsei were most likely to report experiences with overt racism and even violence. Outside of WWII mass incarceration, Linda shared the most extreme case:

> I remember getting called "Jap" and "Nip" and I didn't even know what that meant. And I came home and asked my mom and dad. . . . But otherwise, the only other huge thing is, one time they did burn it into our grass, the word *Nip.*

Common across the lifetimes of all sansei and yonsei were reports of racial microaggressions. Sue and colleagues (2007) define racial microaggressions as "brief and commonplace daily verbal, behavioral, or environmental indignities, whether intentional or unintentional, that communicate hostile, derogatory, or negative racial slights and insults toward people of color" (271). For Asian Americans, microaggressions most frequently imply foreignness, lack of acculturation, and racial lumping. Later-generation Japanese Americans were no exception, as Jennifer, a multiethnic yonsei, and Franklin, a multiracial gosei, so cogently revealed:

> They see someone who looks like a certain race. They don't see your ethnicity, your generation, your background, your family. All they see is your race. So they'll say things like, "We love the way she looks when you guys are ice-skating." Or "We love Panda Express." Or "Oh, have you ever had

dim sum before?" And it's so funny, because they're not—I'll tell them that's not actually the right culture, but it's just, I think that that's the first thing people see.

—Jennifer

The first thing is everyone will ask you what you are. You tell them, "I'm half German, half Japanese." The first thing they always ask you is, "Were you born here?" Obviously, I was born here, I think. Then they say, "Do you speak any Japanese?" "No." Then they go, "Were your parents born in Japan?" "No." "Do they speak any Japanese?" "No." "Do you know how to cook Japanese food?" "Kind of." It feels like the line of questioning, it happens from everyone, it's always the same questions. It's checklists trying to see exactly how Japanese you are. . . . They expect you to have the same thing, that your parents were either first- or second-generation, and then they're just always almost disappointed to hear you're not more of a functioning Japanese person.

—Franklin

Both Jennifer and Franklin demonstrated frequently occurring assumptions faced by later-generation Japanese Americans based solely on their race. As Jennifer stated, race is all people can see. This often leads to racial lumping—confusion with other Asian ethnic backgrounds. Franklin, a multiracial fifth-generation Japanese American, relayed the racialization of Japanese Americans as forever foreigners through the consistent expectations of Japanese origin and knowledge. Such expectations continue even when people are aware of his generation and his American upbringing. Highlighting the particular foreign mantle placed on Japanese ethnicity, Franklin further explained that he is never asked if he speaks German or if he was born in Germany, despite his equal heritage in Japan and Germany. German ethnicity is an acceptable variation within American citizenship; Japanese ethnicity is not.

Participants in my study continued to claim an ethnic identity and community, in part due to such microaggressive comments and the failure of others to recognize them as American and legitimate members of their local communities because of their non-white racial uniform. These findings are similar to those of Zhou and Lee (2007), who find that second-generation Asian Americans who have birthright citizenship and would be deemed "successful" according to traditional assimilation measures continue to feel marginalized due to frequent social interactions that demonstrate how others do not view them as "American." Sansei and yonsei, despite their strong claims on American identity, are well aware of their continued racialization as a non-white racial other. As Andrew, a yonsei, put it:

> I guess I've always felt that no matter what, no matter how I act, the job that I have, the clothes that I wear, I still always look Asian, you know, and I feel like that because you will always be treated like that. I feel for me, even if I became a successful multimillionaire, right? I would be seen as, "Oh that one Asian guy, you know, who is a successful multimillionaire."

Andrew's words echo Robert Park's conception of the persistent Japanese American racial uniform. Just as Park observed the racial uniform worn by Japanese Americans in 1914, Andrew observes that the same uniform inescapably marks and stigmatizes Japanese Americans over a century later.

Instances where the impact of the racial uniform was made clear for Japanese Americans were common throughout the experiences and memories among sansei and yonsei. Recalling uncannily similar situations in two different generations some twenty-five years apart, Darren, a sansei who grew up in the 1960s, and Crystal, a multiracial yonsei who grew up in the 1990s, described how they were romantically paired with other Japanese Americans solely on the basis of race:

> One of my friends was throwing a party. They were going to invite all the guys that hung out together, and they were trying to come up with a list of girls to invite to the party, too. And then one of the kids said, "Well, you know, we'll invite this girl and that girl, but gee, there's no girl for Darren." Well, the difference was because they were all Caucasian. There wasn't a Japanese girl in my class, and I wouldn't be included.
> —Darren

> There were mostly Latino and white students. I think sometimes there was just, like, myself and my brother who were the Asian students. Actually, no, there was one other Japanese American. We weren't friends;

we were enemies. [laughs] I think we hated each other because people always were like, "Oh, you two should get married," and we were like, "Why, because we're Japanese?" and they were like, "Yes." I think that made us hate each other, which is really weird.

—Crystal

In these two contrasting time periods, Darren and Crystal could be paired only with other Japanese Americans at the margins of their social circles where interracial relationships seemed inconceivable. Regardless of whether such comments and the preceding microaggressions are read and interpreted as innocent small-talk proddings or playful jokes between friends, they continue to reinforce the forever-foreigner status and racial othering of Japanese Americans. This message is clear: Japanese Americans aren't really American. White people are American. Darren's, Crystal's, and other Japanese Americans' experiences demonstrate that diverse friendship networks do not always equal postracial acceptance. Rather, they may also highlight how an individual can remain marginal and differentiated in racial terms even within spaces that should mark belonging. This is the false promise of assimilation. Acceptance and fully recognized membership are not guaranteed to accompany acculturation and socioeconomic mobility. Race—the racial uniform—continues to matter.

4

How to Be Cool at Deer Park

Japanese Village and Deer Park offered only seasonal, part-time work, a typical middle-class teenage rite of passage. For many of the sansei (third-generation) Japanese Americans, who came of age in the suburban communities south of the city of Los Angeles in the late 1960s and early 1970s, Deer Park was summer employment or an after-school and weekend job. However, Deer Park had a seemingly disproportionate importance in the lives of former sansei employees and to the broader local Japanese American community. The ethnic impact of Deer Park is even more surprising when considering the orientalist and commercial underpinnings of the park, far from an intentional site of ethnic community building. Deer Park's ownership and management shared that they saw no explicit connection with the global Cold War amelioration of the World War II image of Japan as military and ideological enemy. However, they undoubtedly profited from the cultural shift and emerging popular interest of the US public in karate, Zen Buddhism, bonsai trees, and all things Japanese (Kim 2010; Klein 2003; Mettler 2018; Simpson 2002; Tan 2004). Emerging Japanese cultural interest in Southern California in the late postwar period was underscored by the opening of the Descanso Japanese Garden in 1966 and the Long Beach Yokkaichi Japanese Friendship Garden in 1964.

The need to project a façade of authenticity logically led Deer Park management to actively seek out Japanese-looking employees to interact with park patrons. But what brought otherwise assimilated sansei to Deer Park? Perhaps sansei felt a nostalgic and symbolic connection with the amusement park's cultural theme. However, the paradoxical position of US-born-and-raised sansei employees "playing Japanese" deserves critical examination. As this chapter will show, cultural representation was only a small draw for potential sansei employees. What, then, did sansei find, or what was created, at Deer Park that kept them coming back year after year for low-wage—and for some, inconvenient—part-time work? In short, the answer is community and belonging. Sansei came to Deer Park in search of ethnic community that might provide them with a previously unattainable sense of belonging. Such a search is at sociological odds with scholars who contend that by the third generation, immigrant-origin communities should have minimal cohesion and only symbolic and optional ethnic attachment (Alba 1985; Alba and Nee 2003; Gans 1979, 2005). Ethnicity should not impact life chances or shape everyday lives, relationships, and community formations. Nonetheless, ethnicity played a strong role in bringing sansei to Deer Park.

The maintained importance of ethnicity and community-seeking efforts of sansei resulted from their feelings of marginalization within their local, predominantly white communities, an affect of non-belonging. Deer Park is a case study in local, mundane negotiations of belonging and ethnic-community-seeking practices—non-belonging's performative effect—stemming from a persistent racialization as forever foreign. Deer Park illuminates the formation, persistence, and meaning of ethnic community for sansei coming of age in the late 1960s and early 1970s and throughout their lives. The performative effect is not just a search for ethnic community but can also be read as a search for a mutually recognized citizenship.

The presence of local Japanese American youth playing the role of Japanese villagers at Deer Park creates a critical opportunity to understand the racialized foreignness of Japanese faces and bodies and how Japanese Americans understood and navigated this perceived racial uniform. Despite being generations-deep residents of Southern California, Japanese Americans were largely invisible in political and social terms within their predominantly white communities. Furthermore, at the local and national level, Japanese Americans—along with other Asian Americans—continue to be viewed as forever foreigners regardless of their generation and upbringing. Deer Park highlights the ways in which Japanese Americans become visible within their local suburban Orange County communities as "authentic" foreign residents of a Japanese village but simultaneously resist the erasure of their local American identities. Suburban sansei youth, lacking a sense of belonging and recognized membership within their local communities, actively sought out such communities of belonging and found themselves at Deer Park.

Employees constructed their own local belonging among other Japanese Americans and established more confident claims on local community membership and US citizenship through their specifically co-ethnic interactions with coworkers at Deer Park.

One key way sansei employees asserted their local citizenship was through visual cultures that demonstrated their claim on local membership and the US. As a visual spectacle and an amusement park, Deer Park both sustained its own well-manicured visual culture and allowed for the creation of a visual culture of citizenship among sansei employees. These visual cultures survive in the promotional and personal photographs and images from Deer Park, as well as in the memories of former employees. The photographs and images display how sansei employees visually negotiated the fulfillment of foreign fantasy by "playing" Japanese while simultaneously asserting their local belonging. I explore how sansei utilized fashion cues and other visual practices (e.g., hairstyles, makeup, color choices) rooted in local American popular culture to assert a visual dimension to their incidental claims of citizenship and create their own communities of belonging. While such cultural and visual cues went largely unnoticed by park guests, such cues were centrally important in communicating local identity and "coolness" to fellow sansei employees. Through local mainstream visual and cultural practices, sansei became visible and legible to each other, opened the possibility of building a community of belonging, and formed the foundations of local citizenship.

Deer Park as Amusement?

Deer Park did not feature rides or roller coasters. Its attractions drew on cultural themes to produce "the enchantment of Old Japan." Beginning with little more than a small deer pen, the park expanded over its short lifespan to include a koi pond, teahouses, giftshops, a dove pavilion, a Hokkaido bear pit, a pearl-diver lagoon, and amphitheaters and stadiums for cultural performances (figures 4.1, 4.2, and 4.3). The commercial appeal of Deer Park rested on the creation of a foreign and exotic atmosphere that transported park guests to another place and time. In addition to the Japanese ambiance, the park added animal stage shows featuring sea lions, dolphins, bears, and tigers. The authenticity of

Figure 4.1. Illustrated map of Japanese Village and Deer Park at its height, circa 1971. Courtesy of Vicki Ohira Yoshikawa.

Figure 4.2. Postcards displayed the built environment of Deer Park that attempted to mimic an ancient Japanese village. Courtesy of Karen Yoshikawa.

Figure 4.3. To augment the realism of Japanese architecture and landscaping, Deer Park postcards also utilized Akitas, a Japanese dog breed, and Japanese American employees. Courtesy of the author.

the cultural performances and the built environment executed by Japan-trained professionals stood in stark contrast to the animal shows, which held strong entertainment value but little basis in "old Japan." Bears, sea lions, and dolphins were not the traditional jesters of the Imperial Japanese court. While some of the human performers, as well as the landscapers and chefs, were immigrants trained in their respective crafts in Japan, the vast majority of Deer Park staff, particularly those regularly interacting with park guests, were born and raised in the local suburban communities of Los Angeles and Orange Counties. In terms of staffing, Deer Park explicitly recruited ethnic Japanese youth, relying on word of mouth and publicity in local Japanese American newspapers. The faces and bodies of local sansei employees, especially women dressed in Japanese costume, were used to add to the illusion of an ancient Japanese village. Deer Park proprietors leveraged the racial uniform of sansei employees to augment the park's orientalist façade.[1]

Popular culture historian Russell Nye (1981) describes amusement parks as created and understood by patrons as a fantasy, a produced spectacle simultaneously dazzling every sense. Deer Park, with its mimicry of an authentic ancient Japanese village mixed with fanciful animal shows, aptly fits Nye's definition. However, to say Deer Park can be understood as purely fantasy and entirely separate from the world outside its gates privileges the perspective of park patrons, broadly racialized and classed as white middle-class families. This perspective denies the fact that Japan, Japanese people, and Japanese Americans are real entities contemporaneous with the park itself. To disconnect the park from the outside world would be to deny the preexisting geopolitical and domestic racial ideologies circulating in and around the park shaping patrons' and employees' understandings of their park experience. In addition, separation of theme park and "real" worlds denies the presence of park employees for whom the park constituted a part of their daily lives. While sansei and other employees could certainly get wrapped up in the fantasy and faux nostalgia of Deer Park, they did not lose sight of the space as a workplace that was not intended to cultivate Japanese American ethnic or racial identities. Deer Park, with its Japan-focused theme and employment of local Japanese American youth, highlights the shortcomings of understanding the amusement park as simple fantasy and the ability of park patrons to fully separate their park experience with the real world. Deer Park is what sociologists Michael Omi and Howard Winant call a racial project, "an interpretation, representation, or explanation of racial identities and meanings" and organize such identities and meanings in economic, political, and social hierarchies (2014, 125). As a fantastic journey to a foreign land, Deer Park served to reinforce the perceptions of foreignness of Japanese American employees, despite their being locally born and raised. Rather than view the amusement park as mere fantasy and entertainment, I understand Deer Park as a setting where the real lives of sansei were played out through cross-racial interaction, a site of racial formation (Omi and Winant 2014). In this space, Japanese American racialization, community building, and citizenship claims can be given in-depth examination in light of the local context and a broader structural and ideological racial milieu. Bringing together the façade of ancient Japan, local sansei employees, and predominantly white middle-class family visitors, Japanese Village and Deer Park provides an ideal—perhaps fantastic—site to illuminate the relationship among foreignness, belonging, and visibility.

Revisiting Method: Interview and Visual Sources

Taking full advantage of the visual spectacle of Deer Park, this chapter differs from the other empirical chapters in this book by drawing on two separate data sources: a subset of the full sample of in-depth interviews and an original visual archive. I draw from interviews conducted with former Deer Park employees (forty-one of ninety-three total interviews). The recollections of former employees, however, can tell only part of the story. For this reason, I also collected visual artifacts from Deer Park. This visual archive was accrued from the personal collections of former Deer Park employees and consists of 404 unique Deer Park–related images. In utilizing visual images as a source of data and object of knowledge, I draw on two traditions often overlooked in sociological studies: visual sociology and visual cultures. Both fields take seriously the role of the visual in expressing meaning and providing insight into the social world. Deer Park, as an amusement park, was filled with visual stimuli and relied heavily on the visual to establish its authentic experience. At Deer Park, much of this visual imagery was captured on film in the form of promotional photographs appearing on postcards and other memorabilia, as well as in press releases and brochures (209 of 404 total images). The visual aspects of society and culture present in and around Deer Park are also apparent in the personal photography taken and shared by former employees (195 of 404 total images). Coupling a visual analysis with in-depth interviews, this chapter recreates the visual context of Deer Park to understand how Japanese Americans were racially viewed within their local communities and daily lived experiences. Taking visual culture seriously, I explore how Japanese American employees negotiated their belonging and leveraged visual imagery in navigating their claims on local community and citizenship.

Beyond the utility of visual methodologies for this project, I also root this study in visual representations to highlight the common elision of the visual basis on which racial and ethnic judgments are often made (also see Knowles 2006; Obasogie 2013; Omi and Winant 2014). Too often, studies on race, particularly those dealing with Asian American integration, continue to rely on ideological measures such as stereotypes and prejudice or material measures such as socioeconomic outcomes. Given Asian Americans' upward mobility, many scholars conceive of

Asian Americans as undergoing a process of racial whitening (Lee and Bean 2010; Twine 1997; Warren and Yancey 2003). Such arguments seem plausible if we understand race to be a vaguely cognitive social construction with little basis in the visual. This is not the case. We must also consider that in our interpersonal interactions, racial and ethnic cues are often visually stimulated. In this way, visual sociology and cultures and the reviewing of photographs of Japanese American employees at Deer Park can provide additional insight into the continuing importance of displays and visions of race even in light of seeming assimilation.

Drawing from visual sociological methods, this study examines photography as the product of social actors and understands the practice of looking as a social process (Harper 1988; Sturken and Cartwright 2009). Photographs are social objects that "reflect the lifeworlds and social relations of their makers and users" and "hold documentary information about their subjects" (Caulfield 1996, 57). Photographs are "arrested moments" within a particular historical and political narrative (Knowles 2006, 512). In examining photographic data, I am mindful simultaneously of the "myth of photographic truth" and the need to investigate more fully the encoded and decoded meanings embedded within the image (Sturken and Cartwright 2009, 16; also see Hall 1993; Slater 1995). Caulfield (1996) understands the construction, viewing, and interpreting of the photograph as discursive practices. The photograph is constructed, viewed, and understood from different vantage points: the photographer, multiple audiences, and the photographic subject. Each of these actors attempt to use the photograph to convey a particular message in relationship to one another. In this way, Caulfield builds on the earlier insights of Roland Barthes on the embedded meanings within an image: denoted and connoted messages (Barthes 1977; also see Chavez 2001). Denoted messages relay the image as reality. What you see is what you get. Connoted messages, however, consider the signs and symbols embedded within the image and read them within particular historical, social, and institutional contexts. Taking Caulfield and Barthes together, I focus on the discursive practices of viewing and creating photography, taking into consideration relevant historical time frames, social structures, ideologies, and institutional constraints.

In analyzing the photographs, I first divided them by photographer positionality and intended audience: professional/promotional and amateur/personal. Personal photographs were further disaggregated by location of the photograph: workplace and non-workplace. I treat each image similar to a textual document and open-coded them for common themes as they pertain to the various levels and attributes of analysis. I examine each group of photographs as a set and do not provide an in-depth analysis of any singular photograph. The images included in this chapter were chosen as representative of the full sets in a way similar to selections of quotations from textual documents or interview transcripts. In describing the visual culture portrayed in Deer Park photographs, I focus on the foreign and local representations of self by Deer Park employees. I argue that the foreign and the local are perceived realities that are negotiated by Japanese Americans and are often simultaneously displayed in attempts to negotiate communities of belonging and claims of citizenship. Such negotiations become evident through both promotional and personal photographic images, and such visual evidence is further corroborated by the words and recollections of former Deer Park employees themselves.

"Part of the Landscape": Racial Uniform as Gendered Work Uniform

BRENDA: They [park guests] probably thought we were from Japan, even though we spoke perfect English.

JACK: We were probably just as Americanized as they were. I think sometimes they did approach me and go, "Do you speak English?" Yes, I do.

BRENDA: I don't think they saw us as Americans. They saw us as . . .

JACK: Part of the landscape.

BRENDA: People from Japan, imported to work.

JACK: Kind of role-playing a little bit, you know, it's like, when you put on the Japanese costume, you put on the Japanese façade and, you know, you become Japanese.

BRENDA: We put our hair up, and we had little, you know, ornaments in our hair, so you kind of put on your costume so to speak. . . . You really didn't have to do too much, because you look the part. You were Japanese, and I think maybe that's why they wanted it to be authentic Japanese people to work there because you didn't have to play a part, you just . . .

JACK: You just have to look the part.

BRENDA: Yeah, which we already did. I mean, that's part of our heritage.

There is no avoiding the performative Japaneseness required of sansei employees at Deer Park, given the amusement park's central theme. This was not an active performance, however. While not using the explicit language of race, Brenda and Jack, a married sansei couple who met while working at Deer Park, discussed how convincing their racial uniform was for park guests. Sansei such as Brenda and Jack "didn't have to play a part," because from the vantage point of park guests and management, their racial uniform did the acting for them. They became naturalized into the built environment mimicking ancient Japan. They became "part of the landscape," inhabitants of an exotic fantasyland, part of the ambiance and façade of Deer Park. Sansei employees were invisible to park guests as Americans, seen as foreign to and separate from the "real America" that stood just outside the park gates. The cross-racial interactions at Deer Park served to reinforce the forever-foreigner perception of Japanese Americans.

Park management expected employees to portray the role of authentic Japanese villagers. However, sansei workers provided a dubious sense of authenticity. In keeping with assimilationist trajectories that predict a predominant pattern of English-only households by the third generation (Portes and Rumbaut 2014), the upbringing of these local sansei youth provided minimal exposure to Japanese language and culture. Few sansei employees had even visited Japan as tourists, and fewer still had any notable command of the Japanese language or strong familiarity with Japanese culture of any time period. While park guests readily accepted sansei employees' performed Japaneseness, the ability of sansei to provide an authentic portrayal of "old Japan" remains questionable. Recognizing, perhaps subconsciously, popular assumptions of foreignness associated with the sansei racial uniform, Deer Park proprietors cared little about the cultural knowledge-base of their Japanese American employees. Many former employees remember being hired on the spot, often attributing their quick hire to their Japanese surnames and appearances. Cynthia, who remembered a great amount of detail about her first and only interview to work at Deer Park, noted a lack of concern on the part of management about her personal knowledge and authentic representation of Japanese culture. Steve recalled that when he was hired at the park, "they [management] said, 'Here, you can dress like your ancestors.' So, you got to play the part of being the Japanese of Asian background. Because you looked the part, so you could play the part." None of the former employees I spoke with recalled being asked about Japanese language skills or familiarity with Japanese culture. Some even recalled being told to hide or downplay their Americanness. Another sansei employee, Denise, worked as a pearl diver bringing oysters to park guests waiting by the side of the lagoon. She was instructed by management, "'Don't speak, don't speak, because we want the illusion that you're from Japan.' So, you couldn't talk." Denise was being asked to maintain the illusion of foreignness displayed by her Japanese face. An illusion that might have been shattered if allowed to converse with park guests with her unaccented English. This was the racial uniform at work.

The leveraging of the racial uniform was not only apparent in the explicit dictates from management in hiring and training processes but was also inscribed in dress code policies. Policies relating to proper work clothing were stricter for women. Female employees working as hostesses in the deer field, working in the gift shops, and even those working behind high counters at the teahouse eateries or working administrative jobs in managerial offices out of view of park guests were required to wear *yukatas*, lightweight cotton kimonos, along with all the traditional embellishments (figure 4.4). Angela recalled her experiences working with the strict—and impractical—uniform policies in one of the teahouse eateries:

> All the girls had to wear kimonos. So you have to wear the undergarment and the kimono and then you had the ties that bound you and then the obi. Then, because I worked in food service, I have to wear a white apron, the Japanese kind, over all of that. Oh, and then you had to wear tabis [Japanese socks with a split between big toe and other toes] and then some, like, slippers, and that got really, really hot in the summertime, especially in the kitchen where there's all this heat being created, you know, from all the food production. So it was pretty uncomfortable, and I often

wondered why we in the teahouse had to wear the kimonos, because there wasn't much that they could see—from the chest up maybe—from over the counter.

Once hired at Deer Park, employment was gendered beyond the different standards in work uniforms. From the recollections of former

Figure 4.4. With few exceptions, Sansei women employees were required to wear *yukatas*, here shown in a gift shop. Courtesy of Gary and Sheri Nakano.

Figure 4.5. Sansei men employees in their varied work attire—*happi* coats and work shirts. Courtesy of Vicki Ohira Yoshikawa, Gary, and Sheri Nakano.

employees, the gender balance among Deer Park employees was skewed toward women. As such, Deer Park is revealed as simultaneously a racial and a gender project, leveraging a particularly feminine image of Japan. The differing visual representations of male and female employees parallel the gendered processes of racialization and assimilation experienced by Asian American men and women across history (Espiritu 2008; Glenn 1988, 2002; Kim 2010; Lim 2005; Matsumoto 2014). Women in particular have often played a central role in the amelioration of Asia and Asian people in American popular culture, scholarly, and political discourses (Kim 2010; Shibusawa 2006; Simpson 2001). As Asia became transformed in the US public and political imagination into a prime target for communist expansion, Cold War logics reconfigured Japan's image into friendly ally in a highly gendered way (Kim 2010; Shibusawa 2006). Jodi Kim (2010) describes the shift of Japan's image from one of dangerous militaristic aggression, generally read as masculine, to a re-gendering of Japan as a docile and peaceful ally, portrayed through feminine imagery.

As previously mentioned, women throughout the park, save those working as pearl divers or as part of the sea-life shows, were required to wear yukatas. Male employees had more variation in their uniform based on where in the park they worked. Maintenance staff, who were mostly a mix of Japanese American and Mexican American men, were an exception to traditional Japanese costume and were provided with standard work shirts. Most other male employees wore *happi* coats (a wide, straight-sleeved, hip-length cotton overcoat) of varying colors depending on their department (figure 4.5).

The gendered dress code and provision of work attire were constructed to maintain a professional uniformity all while keeping up the passable façade of an ancient Japanese village. The authenticity of the work garb mandated by Deer Park, however, was a façade in more ways than one. Generally speaking, yukatas and happi coats were not the daily attire of contemporary or ancient Japan. Nor are yukatas and happi coats gendered in the way Deer Park categorized them. Yukatas are, in fact, worn only occasionally during the hot summer months and have both male and female variations. Happi coats were traditionally worn by house servants or during festivals and used to demarcate familial or village affiliations, not gender differences. Nonetheless, yukatas and happi coats were recognizably foreign and plausibly authentic to the predominantly white middle-class patrons of Deer Park. Deer Park took costume an additional step by intentionally recruiting and hiring ethnic Japanese employees, who matched the foreign scenery and theme of the park (corroborated in an interview with the park's former general manager). Female employees, particularly in the early days of the park, were almost exclusively Japanese American. Male employees, on the other hand, included individuals of other racial backgrounds, although they remained predominantly Japanese American. Non-Japanese American male employees were generally relegated to positions that were not as visible to park guests, such a maintenance or kitchen staff.

Descriptions by employees and promotional images of park staff demonstrate how the Japanese faces of sansei employees were part of their work uniform as much as any piece of clothing. While dress codes were fairly stringent in terms of clothing, other policies related to employee appearance were markedly more lax. Former employees and the former general manager recalled employees being required only to maintain a tidy appearance and keep hair off the shoulders. There were no other explicit policies regarding hair and makeup during work hours; there was no expectation of female or male employees to don authentic hairstyles and makeup of ancient Japan to match their garb. The fact that hair and makeup policies were more lenient than clothing policies speaks directly to the intention of Deer Park management to leverage the physical racial attributes of sansei employees as part of the authentic appearance of the park. From the standpoint of park management, the sansei's innate Japanese look made policies regarding hair and makeup unnecessary.

Beyond the recollection of former employees, the gendered racial project and gendered racial uniform are on full display in the promotional photographs and materials generated by Deer Park. These materials, with their heavy representation of young, racially Japanese women, confirm the ways that the employees' racial uniform played a central role in selling the authenticity of the park alongside the architecture and other aspects of the park's built environment. In many of these photographs, they are literally positioned as "part of the landscape." While their presence is certainly visible, they are not autonomous subjects in any of these photographs. Women in these photographs hold demure poses, complete with parasols and traditional Japanese kimonos in keeping with the Western-held image of the feminine East (Kang 2002).

Figure 4.6. In promotional and souvenir images, young Japanese American women were often positioned as decorative objects within the landscape. Courtesy of Gary and Sheri Nakano.

Rather than being the subjects of these promotional photographs, these women appear as thematic lagoon-side decoration, as part of rock gardens, or as dispensaries for deer or dove feed. In this way, Japanese American women literally became inseparably embedded in the built foreign façade of Deer Park (figures 4.6, 4.7, and 4.8).

Racially Japanese men appear far less frequently in promotional photography compared to women (figures 4.9 and 4.10). The images containing male subjects do not have them fading into the background but continue to dehumanize them as show performers. A handful of images show both white and Japanese American male animal trainers. In these

Figure 4.7. Rather than be featured in the foreground of professional photographs of Deer Park, women were often positioned in the background. Courtesy of Gary and Sheri Nakano.

Figure 4.8. A young sansei woman is posed as lagoon-side decoration among the black swans. Courtesy of Gary and Sheri Nakano.

Figure 4.9. The infrequent appearance of men in promotional images often centered around martial arts performance. Courtesy of Karen Yoshikawa.

Figure 4.10. Cultural shows featuring karate were simultaneously masculine and a demonstration in self-defense and artistic control. Courtesy of Gary and Sheri Nakano.

images, people are not the main focus; however, the high proportion of white men in these pictures suggests a racial and gender hierarchy in occupational status within the park. Skilled positions, such as animal trainers, were reserved for white male employees, with a few Japanese American men mixed in. Racially Japanese male imagery dominates in the promotional photographs of the cultural shows featuring martial arts. Such male depictions may seem to work against the reimagining of Japan as a demilitarized and docile ally, but such performances were couched within an array of shows demonstrating the art and beauty of ancient Japanese culture rather than aggression (Krug 2001; Skidmore 1991). The samurai sword fight show was ornately costumed and categorized with performances such as the tea ceremony, traditional dance, and kabuki (Skidmore 1991). The karate show was introduced into the park in recognition of the growing popularity of Japanese martial arts in the United States following World War II (Tan 2004). The popular discourse around karate focusing on the peaceful and self-defense orientation of Japanese martial arts also held true in the Deer Park performances. In this way, these masculine and militaristic aspects of Japanese culture and people also underwent a process of gendered racial rehabilitation whereby even seemingly aggressive representations were reclassified as performative, artistic, and non-threatening.

Through these photographs and the recollections of former employees regarding their everyday interactions with park guests, Japanese Americans are rendered visible yet invisible. Their presence is surely visible and recognized as part of the park and its landscape. However, the audience's gaze on these images or during a park visit would be wholly unaware that the employees pictured were US-born sansei from the local community. Sansei employees reside and are visible as Japanese villagers only within the confines of the foreign fantasy space of Deer Park. They are neither revealed nor understood as part of the local community, despite their physical presence in suburban Orange County, the location of Deer Park. Sansei remained invisible in terms of presence and belonging within their local community and the US nation. Despite being part of the largest Asian American ethnic group in the entire state of California during this time period, their third-generation status, and their being physically part of local Orange County communities, these Japanese American youth only became visible to park guests in their representation of a foreign culture.

The particular purpose of promotional photographs requires an intentional invisibility of any possible local representations. However, such invisibility of local American identity and culture in the behavior and bodies of sansei employees was not limited to the still images. This invisibility played itself out within the interactions between park employees and guests through the assumptions of sansei foreignness. It is beyond question that park guests willingly immersed themselves in the fantasy of Deer Park and also—perhaps unconsciously—disconnected the employees who populated this fantasy world as Japanese villagers from their real lives as American teenagers outside of the park gates. The easy acceptance of sansei employees as foreigners and the genuine surprise on the faces of park patrons when they discovered that sansei employees spoke unaccented English or had grown up in the surrounding cities underscores the invisibility of sansei Americanness to park guests. Certainly, the context of Deer Park augmented the expectation of employee foreignness on the part of white park patrons, and Deer Park's employment of Japanese American youth strategically cued off a preexisting social assumption of Asian American foreignness—a lack of recognition of Asian American belonging within the US. However, park guests in their immersion into the fantasy of Deer Park consistently looked past numerous visual, cultural, and interactional cues that pointed to the American upbringing and identification of sansei employees. Employees within Deer Park promotional photographic images were not as docile and compliant as the pictures may show on first glance. The visible foreignness seen through the gaze of the general public audience did not negate the inherent Americanness of sansei youth who grew up in the local communities and neighborhoods in Los Angeles and Orange Counties. As Lisa reminded us, "In our real lives, we [sansei] grew up with all those people [in LA and Orange counties] anyways."

Resisting Invisibility and the Visual Construction of Americanness

Sansei employees were not oblivious to their racial uniform whether at work or in their local communities. They were well aware of how it played into their employment at Deer Park and their invisibility as local subjects. Such interactional microaggressions with park guests were ubiquitous in the memories of former employees. As Jack mentioned earlier, sansei racial uniform and "looking the part" was accompanied by assumptive questions like "Do you speak English?" Michelle, another sansei employee, similarly recalled, "There were a lot of people that, because we were wearing kimonos, they thought we didn't know English. So they made hand gestures about, 'Where do I find the bathroom?' or 'A place to eat?'" Not only were park patrons shocked by English language abilities or the lack of foreign accents, but they also imagined accents that did not exist. In an informal conversation about Deer Park, a white woman who grew up in the Los Angeles suburbs—likely alongside some sansei—and visited Deer Park in her youth, casually and erroneously shared that she remembered all the employees speaking with Japanese accents. Of course, sansei, born and raised in the US to parents born and raised in the US, did not speak with foreign accents. Further underscoring management's successful leveraging the sansei's racial uniform in constructing the visage of Deer Park for park guests, Jill stated, "I guess they [park guests] thought we were authentic because we looked the part. I looked the part." Or as Brenda noted earlier, park guests assumed that sansei employees where straight from Japan, "imported for work."

As the racially charged, erroneous assumptions of park guests were readily apparent to sansei employees, they responded to such, at times ridiculous, microaggressions with their own micro-assertions of local, American identities and belonging ranging from the matter of fact to the downright snarky. In one interaction, Tricia shared:

> What's funny is the tourists that came, you know, they were pretty ignorant [laughs]. They would look at us and they'd go, "You speak English?" And we're going, "Yeah." And they look at our tabis [split-toed socks] and go, "Do you only have two toes?" "No, that's just a Japanese sock."

Echoing Tricia's experience with patrons assuming sansei foreignness, other employees shared their common retorts:

> Every once in a while, you would get a Caucasian guy who spoke Japanese and we [sansei employees] would go, "Hey! We don't know what you're saying!"
> —Robert

We talked to people. They kind of expect you to speak Japanese, and I
didn't speak any Japanese. So I learned how to say "I don't know how to
speak Japanese" [in Japanese].
—Patricia

Witty comebacks, reminiscent of what Tsuda notes as examples of
the "everyday struggles for racial citizenship" among later-generation
Japanese Americans (2016, 40), were not the only way sansei employees
pushed back against their invisibility and the assumptions of their foreign upbringings. They also demonstrated their Americanness through
visual cues. Outside the park and out of the traditional Japanese garb,
sansei employees were voracious consumers of popular youth culture
and would have been indistinguishable from any other American teen—
save for their racial uniform. The high school and college-aged sansei
were exposed to the same television programs and movies and read
the same popular culture and fashion magazines as their white peers.
Former employees recounted flipping through the pages of *Tiger Beat*
and *Seventeen Magazine* and sharing fashion and makeup tips during
break times and after hours socializing. Such behaviors echoed those
found a generation prior among young nisei (second-generation)
women prior to WWII who perused *Look* magazine, wore poodle skirts,
Max Factor red lipstick, and permanent waves in their hair (Lim 2005;
Matsumoto 2014). In their own era, sansei drew on the same popular
1960s and 1970s trends and styles as their white American peers, imple-
menting them on Japanese American bodies. These sansei youth did not
leave this American style at the park gate. Taking a deeper look at the
promotional photographs of Deer Park, the vibrant colors of the kimonos, hairstyles, and face makeup of the young women pictured reveals
their American heritage. Within the confines of Deer Park's work dress
code, which attempted to portray them as foreign, the young sansei
women, as well as the men, constructed a visual culture through color
choices, hair, and makeup that demonstrated their local identities and
worked toward a recognized belonging. Even in the highly manicured
and staged contexts of promotional photographs seen in gift shop postcards (figures 4.11 and 4.12), the personal, contemporary, and American
style of sansei young women is visible. Even the yukatas themselves
drew from the vibrant color schemes popular during the late 1960s and

Figure 4.11. Contemporary styles drawn from American youth popular culture can be seen in hair, makeup, and color choices of young women in promotional images. Courtesy of Karen Yoshikawa.

Figure 4.12. Even in the traditional tea ceremony performance, styles familiar to American youth culture were evident. Courtesy of Karen Yoshikawa.

Figure 4.13. Contemporary popular culture style of sansei employees evident in personal photographs taken during work hours. Courtesy of Vicki Ohira Yoshikawa, Gary and Sheri Nakano.

early 1970s rather than the more muted natural-dye tones used in traditional silk kimonos. Teresa recounted, "The females could wear any colors that they wanted to. . . . So some of the females had really more ornate kimonos." Such hairstyles, makeup, and yukata are anachronistic to "ancient Japan."

In addition to promotional images, personal photographs from in and around the workplace are informative in demonstrating how hairstyles and makeup all maintained a distinctly contemporary American flavor while accompanying work attire of "traditional" Japanese dress. The fashion accents of young men and women who were employed at Deer Park very much mirrored the fashions depicted in the fashion, popular culture, and lifestyle magazines from the same period. Young men sported shaggy longer hairstyles in their happi coats, and young women wore elaborate fashionable up-dos, simple makeup, and long eyelashes in addition to their yukatas (figure 4.13). As mentioned previously, the only dress code policies relevant to grooming and makeup required women to keep their hair off their shoulders with a short haircut or up-do and men to be clean shaven. For men, hair also could not extend beyond the shoulder. While the relatively lax policies regarding hair and makeup demonstrate a reliance on the sansei racial uniform as part of their work uniform, the policies also provided space for creative expression among employees, and employees drew creative inspiration from the youth culture that surrounded them as they grew up.

Within the space of Deer Park and despite their portrayal as foreign Japanese villagers, the fashion choices made by sansei employees were a means through which they resisted their invisibility and assumed foreignness and laid claim to belonging and citizenship within the local Orange County community and broader national imaginary. In stating that sansei youth at Deer Park established citizenship through American fashion, I do not mean to project any intentionality on the part of Deer Park employees. In fact, interviews with former employees revealed that they utilized contemporary American youth fashion because it was all they knew. Having grown up in Los Angeles and Orange Counties, American popular culture and fashion were as ubiquitous for these local sansei as they would be for any American teen. They had little reference for any other trends and were certainly unfamiliar with traditional Japanese hairstyles and makeup. Regardless of intention, the practice of local visual culture in the fashion choices of sansei were not consistently recognized by broader society, as represented through interactions with park patrons. All the while, these sansei had hairstyles and makeup that were no different than any other American teenager, perhaps no different than the shocked patron. Suffice to say, the American fashion and aesthetic markers of belonging of the Japanese American youth were largely invisible to park patrons. Under the hair and behind the makeup was a Japanese, and ultimately foreign, face. Despite their resistance and their visual construction of Americanness, the experiences of sansei at Deer Park demonstrate how the visibility of racialized foreignness—the racial uniform—supersedes the visibility of the domestic aesthetic and visual culture on the Japanese American body within the racial landscape of Southern California and the broader nation.

Although the visual culture constructed by sansei, which asserted their local membership and belonging, was not readily recognized by Deer Park patrons or within the frames of promotional photography, such displays remain important artifacts as simultaneously intrinsic aspects of sansei identity and culture as American teens and personal assertions of local identities and citizenship. Beyond the individual benefits stemming from fashion choices, visual culture is also always socially communicative. Sansei fashion and visual culture signaled to others and aided in the formation of communities of belonging at Deer Park. Despite the invisibility to park guests, American fashion cues were readily visible and legible to other sansei employees. The primping and cultural cues seen particularly in the personal photographs from both inside and outside the workplace can be read as an attempt to present an aesthetic that would be appealing, recognized, and legible as contemporary cool to other sansei employees and find acceptance within the Deer Park social scene. Sansei signaled their cool to one another as a means to assert their local identities and familiarity with American popular culture, a claim on belonging and citizenship. While there are certainly many avenues to social acceptance at Deer Park, part of legible coolness meant displaying visual markers of contemporary American fashion within the confines of the work dress code through kimono color choice, hairstyle, makeup, and dress in non-work attire. These similarities in fashion were not just individual claims but also aided in the construction of an extensive social life at Deer Park. The legibly cool enabled the formation of relationships, a social network, and ultimately a community based in ethnicity and common interests. The photographic images, promotional as well as personal, from Deer Park demonstrate that clothing, hair, and makeup were important ways in which sansei were able to express this legible coolness to each other.

The Social Life of Deer Park

Considering the relatively short-lived existence of the Orange County tourist attraction—only eight years—and its relatively small size compared to neighboring amusement parks (e.g., Disneyland and Knott's Berry Farm), Deer Park had an unusually large impact on the lives of its employees and the Japanese American community in Southern California. Many employees worked only during the busy summer season but returned to Deer Park again and again, citing the fun and friendship with other Japanese Americans that characterized the experience. As Angela shared, "It was just so much fun and I—we had become a very close-knit group that worked among, you know, good friends." Deer Park was much more than just a workplace and a paycheck. Christine and her sister Julia both worked at the park:

JULIA: Definitely weren't working there for the money.

CHRISTINE: No, and it was funny because by the time I stopped working there, sometimes I forgot to pick up my paycheck.

JULIA: Oh, we all did that.

CHRISTINE: I forgot to pick it up because . . . I don't know, it was like I'm over . . . making a lot of money, you know. It was just so much fun.

To say that Deer Park had a vibrant social scene is an understatement. Personal photographs taken during work hours (figures 4.14–4.17) show that employees would socialize during break times and within their respective work areas and departments at the park. Cynthia and Christine captured the social atmosphere during work hours:

It seemed like a break the whole day because it was pretty—it was so much fun. Break time, we would try to—like our friends, all of us, when we were some of the older ones that had been there for a while, we would try to work it, so that even if we were in different areas, we would get our breaks at the same time. So we would meet in the break area. We knew the guys in the kitchen. They would make special stuff for us. I mean it was really just social hour. I think at break time, you know, we just go in there and have fun talking to everybody and then you know probably took a little bit of advantage of the park because they were so lax about a lot of things, so breaks, lunch times might have been a little longer than they were supposed to. —Cynthia

We were all young then, but it was probably the coolest job I have ever had, not because it was like partying all the time . . . but we would be rolling on the floor in our kimonos and laughing, you know, playing around with guys. . . . It was just a ball! —Christine

Most former employees remember being recruited by family and friends who lured them in with stories of getting paid to have fun and socialize.

Figure 4.14. The break room at Deer Park was noted for its fun and social atmosphere. Courtesy of Gary and Sheri Nakano.

Figure 4.15. Employee socializing would happen even on the clock; it was "like a break the whole day." Courtesy of Gary and Sheri Nakano.

Figure 4.16. Many romantic relationships grew out of Deer Park on-the-job socializing, including among the author's parents, pictured here. Courtesy of Gary and Sheri Nakano.

Figure 4.17. Many employees would return to Deer Park after their shifts to hang out with their friends who were still on the clock. Courtesy of Gary and Sheri Nakano.

The active social life surrounding the park was a deciding factor for joining the staff and maintain employment year after year.

The socializing among Deer Park friends also extended outside of work hours into personal time. Many former employees recalled ending their work shifts and then reentering the park to continue hanging out with their friends who were still on the clock. Even beyond the ticket gates, Deer Park was an all-encompassing social scene. Lisa recollected how employees would spend nearly all their time with Deer Park friends—even going on vacation together:

> A lot of us got together after work. . . . I remember my friend's house, and we would all go out there to . . . maybe Cypress (a neighboring city). Tons of us, we would just go there and play cards. They had a pool table. Tons of us would drive there at night or after work and play pool till twelve or one o'clock then come home and go to work the next day. So you were with these people all the time.

For many employees, Deer Park and the friends and community they made there were central features in their lives and the main hub of their social networks. The Deer Park social network came to encompass a wider set of Japanese American youth from the local area who did not work at Deer Park. These individuals were drawn by the same promise of a vibrant ethnic community that offered a broad array of social activities. Former employee Lisa further expanded on some of the broader social activities that sprang up in and around Deer Park.

> We actually, on Friday or Saturday nights, would bring bands [to the park] and would have dances in the evenings. So the kids would come back [afterhours] and we would have dances. There was a lot of activity geared towards families during the day and then at night, I think it was mainly the Asian [Japanese American] kids that would come and dance to the bands of the era. It was neat. You go and meet people from different cities.

In addition to dances hosted at Deer Park after hours with live cover bands, employees organized a bowling league, sports nights at local gyms, car rallies, and numerous other events and activities (figures 4.18 and 4.19). During at least part of Deer Park's lifespan, employees

Figure 4.18. Personal photographs show the diverse social life of Deer Park that included sports nights at local gymnasiums for volleyball and basketball games. Courtesy of Gary and Sheri Nakano.

organized a social club, Bushido, that collected membership dues to help fund and organize these social gatherings. Within the Deer Park social scene, there was seemingly something for everyone.

Building Ethnic Community

As described by former employees and depicted in personal photographs, the robust social life offered through the Deer Park network would be enviable and attractive to any teen or young adult. For sansei, however, this social life took on an amplified importance not only for a sense of belonging so often missing in their neighborhoods and

Figure 4.19. Deer Park employees also organized dances with live band music often hosted at the park afterhours. Courtesy of Gary and Sheri Nakano.

schools but also for the ethnic connections it provided. As Lisa alluded to in her previous quote, the social life at Deer Park was predominantly enjoyed by the Japanese American employees. The park became a particularly ethnic meeting place and destination for sansei, a locus of ethnic community building. As discussed in the introductory chapter of this book, Deer Park brought together a critical mass of Japanese American youth who largely grew up in predominantly white neighborhoods and schools in the Southern California suburbs. Darren noted, "[Before Deer Park,] I had never been around as many Japanese people in my life that I didn't personally know from family. And so yeah, that was—it was great." The draw to Deer Park was not race neutral. Perhaps the great irony of Deer Park was that in their attempts to build the illusion of a foreign fantasy world by leveraging the Japanese American racial uniform, they brought together American teens and created a space for American community building. Without Deer Park, many of the sansei employees may not have found a strong ethnic community in their lives. Angela, who was recruited by her friend Valerie, reflected on what drew her to Deer Park:

> I think the way my friend Valerie, who already worked there, described it to me was there were just a lot of Japanese kids that worked there, and it was an amusement park and it's just a lot of fun. And I thought, well, I could use a summer job. So that's why I went.

Returning to the words of Lisa:

> It seemed like a nice place to work. And there were people like me! Young people, we had common interests. My friend worked there and her sister, so you kinda already knew people who worked there. And then the [Japanese American] people who were working with me at Disneyland, they left that job and came over to Deer Park. It was the camaraderie and friendships. That's kind of the core of it all, really . . . It was an experience that I don't think anyone would have given up.

Fun was clearly a draw for Angela and Lisa, but so too was the critical mass of Japanese American youth who would be found at Deer Park—and not at other potential workplaces. Deer Park's promise of a robust social life actually drew workers away from other, often higher paying, jobs. Among other Japanese American youth, sansei like Angela, Lisa, and Valerie found a sense of similarity, comfort, and belonging that had been missing from their "assimilated" suburban lives. This critical mass allowed for exposure to a broad and diverse range of Japanese Americans and enabled them to find commonality and community. Recall Donna, who lamented that she felt she had little in common with the few other Japanese Americans at her high school. But at Deer Park, "it was a good experience to see all different kinds of Japanese with different backgrounds and everything and a big group of them." From Donna's words, common ethnicity was an insufficient characteristic for building friendships, but it was not a superfluous factor, either. In fact, Donna and other sansei often yearned for ethnic spaces and friends that would provide a sense of comfort and belonging they felt lacking in their daily lives.

To be sure, most of these sansei were active participants in their home communities and schools and reported friendships and social lives with non-Japanese classmates and kids from their neighborhood based on similar interests, hallmarks of structural assimilation. However, these same individuals often recalled a lingering and unshakable sense of being different from their white peers despite friendships and similar interests. Deer Park friendship provided something different. Laura reflected on this ethnic bond:

> I think, of course, I became much closer to those, you know, with the same background with me and same family background; and the cultural, you know, sort of the American and Japanese culture combined.

At Deer Park and among other Japanese Americans of their same age and generation, they didn't feel different anymore. They found a sense of belonging. Again, recall from the introductory chapter Jack and Brenda, a married couple who met at Deer Park and shared about the commonality and community found there. Brenda verbalized an affect of marginalization and non-belonging growing up in white suburbia and "just feeling a little bit the odd ball out . . . They were little instances that would happen. I don't know what it was, an odd feeling." But at Deer Park, Jack found it "amazing how similar everybody was" and that he never really confronted how different he felt from the white peers he grew up with "until you meet a lot of Japanese people and then think, 'Oh my gosh! They're like me!'" Brenda previously echoed these sentiments as she realized that at Deer Park and among other Japanese Americans, "oh you weren't odd at all. It's just, it's because you're Japanese."

Feeling American Citizenship through Common Racial Experiences

While focusing on ethnic similarities, Brenda's sentiments also allude to the fact that the ethnic friendships and community built at Deer Park were more than common cultural idiosyncrasies. Deer Park relationships provided an additional level of comfort and understanding based not just on common ethnic experiences but on racialized ones as well. Bonds were formed not just over commonalities based on cultural practice and shared history but also in commonalities in social interactions driven by their externally perceived racial body—their racial uniform. Prior to Deer Park and in relative ethnic and racial isolation, Deer Park employees were surprised to find that they shared common experiences of growing up visibly and culturally Japanese American in a still white-dominated society. In this way, the Deer Park story is not just about Japanese ethnics finding each other; it is a particularly American story driven by the particular racialized experiences of third-generation Japanese Americans as they attempted to navigate assimilation's empty racial promise. Through Deer Park, many sansei were able to find their community—a space of local belonging—and a basis from which to build a broader sense of citizenship—common ethnic and racialized experiences based in the unique US racial landscape. Of the eye-opening experience and the discovery of comfort and belonging, sanseis Darren and Tricia shared:

> When I worked at Deer Park, it was just an eye-opening experience. . . . I think that at that point, I really didn't have a sense of who I was. I had just begun to realize, like I said, at the beginning of high school that I was different. I don't think I was ever consciously aware that I was different. Physically I looked different, but I never thought of myself as being different.
> —Darren

> I don't know, for me it [Deer Park] was comfortable. It was really different. I mean, I came from mostly white people, and then all of a sudden here's all these Japanese that were like me. . . . But it was just . . . it just was different. You just felt more like you were a part of them.
> —Tricia

Within this new community of belonging, sansei felt they had to explain less about themselves and their experiences because it seemed that fellow sansei had an innate and intimate knowledge that had previously been restricted to familial spaces. Such knowledge was, of course, not innate but rather the result of common cultural backgrounds and racialized experiences growing up with a Japanese face in lily-white suburbia. Sansei strengthened their sense of belonging through the discovery of others who shared similar racial and ethnic encounters. Realizing that their lives were not aberrational but part of a broader and uniquely American set of experiences also enabled them to be more active participants within their community beyond ethnic networks. Cynthia, a yonsei who was a contemporary of most of the sansei in my sample, spoke about this very impact from the connections and community she built as an employee at Deer Park:

> Up until that moment [of working at Deer Park], I don't think I really identified with being Japanese or anything. The thing is, once I started working at the park and became probably more aware of being Japanese and being so comfortable with all the people that I was meeting and the friends that I was making, I was much more comfortable talking to, the customers and didn't feel self-conscious, didn't feel. . . . I mean, because I felt like they were coming to visit some place where I belonged, where I felt a sense of belonging. If anything I'd say Deer Park probably brought out more of my own personality. I didn't feel as introverted and feel as awkward and feel, you know, I felt a lot more comfortable about expressing my opinion. I don't know how my life would have gone if I hadn't worked at the park.

Cynthia found a sense of self and pride, as well a sense of belonging, among the sansei at Deer Park who shared similar experiences of marginalization and racial difference. Within this community, she was better able to assert herself and claim the space of Deer Park as her own. Denise similarly connected comfort and belonging with self-esteem. Denise pointed to the importance of Deer Park in combating the racial marginalization and melancholy she experienced in her daily life:

> Deer Park, that was my self-esteem. I felt like I was okay. It was okay to be Japanese, and I was glad. I think I would've grown up wishing I was *hakujin* [white] if I did that differently. Everyone was everyone's friend. It was just like a utopia for sanseis.

Deer Park provided a place to belong. Even though the sense of belonging expressed by both Cynthia and Denise was limited to the ethnic community found at Deer Park—"a utopia for sanseis"—sansei were exposed to the unquestioned recognition of their membership and were able to actualize and embody their citizenship. Such exposure and actualization made them increasingly aware of what had been missing in their lives beyond Deer Park and prepared them to lay claim to a broader citizenship. Donna spoke about the foundation of belonging found at Deer Park:

> Growing up in a period where there were not very many Japanese and Japanese Americans, there was prejudice in the way you got treated where they kind of make fun of you for being Japanese in school. But at Deer Park, I think the self-esteem is different because you weren't made fun of for being Asian. You're the majority. When I was growing up, being Asian or Japanese American, you're the minority and you're treated somewhat like that. So Deer Park gave me an opportunity where a lot of Asians that are Japanese Americans that I'm now one of them and so, it's sort of like you're not the minority anymore. I think you get to carry that as you go along too. There's a little bit of Japanese American pride because you're around all these people where it's a good thing being Japanese American. I think it helps you going forward.

The Broad Reach and Enduring Impact of Deer Park

The sense of local belonging Donna, Cynthia, Denise, and others found at Deer Park was not confined to that particular place and time—"You get to carry that as you go along." It would have a profound impact on their general self-esteem and sense of themselves as full members and citizens of their local communities and society at large. As Cynthia built her self-confidence within the ethnic community, she took that sense of self and community with her into her life outside of Deer Park:

> I mean, I was somewhat active in high school. . . . I was in the—I started in the drill team and everything. I did that and that was actually because of a friend of mine from my neighborhood in La Mirada who said, "You

need to join the drill team! It's a lot of fun! You'll have a good time!" So I did that, but I didn't really feel all that much a part of it. And then I started working at Deer Park and gained a lot of confidence from that and from there I just, then I ran for office and became a little bit more involved in high school. . . . So yeah, Deer Park gave me an identity. I mean I realized how important it was to be Japanese American and to be proud of that. I think it just, it made me aware of that, but it also made me feel—well, I don't know. . . . Well, other than I guess just a sense of belonging and a place to bond, you know, somewhere where I belong and felt totally comfortable. I could be myself. People understood me.

Growing up in the predominantly white suburbs, Cynthia had ample opportunity to be involved in school and neighborhood activities. She just never felt fully integrated into these groups. But Cynthia's Deer Park experience and the sense of belonging she found within the ethnic community changed her perspective and enabled her to become a more active civic participant in her high school and her community. That is to say, sansei claims on local and national citizenship and membership have an ethnic basis rather than a basis grounded in an ethnic attenuation.

Glen shared a sentiment similar to Cynthia's of finding a community of belonging at Deer Park and noted the immediate and long-term impacts such community had on his recognition of his racial minority status and on the strengthening of his sense of security and confidence. Following his time at Deer Park, Glen enrolled at a prestigious local university and related how the sense of confidence he built at Deer Park made him feel that his experiences were not anomalous but valid and worthy of sharing in his university courses. He felt increasingly comfortable speaking up in class to share his opinions on both racial and nonracial topics. Glen would later go on to attend law school and explained that finding people who had lived lives similar to his provided a foundation for a sense of belonging within a broader American community, within which he had the right to participate. Local ethnic community was a strong factor in Glen's decision and confidence to become an active member in his college courses and a civic actor as a lawyer.

In addition to the sense of citizenship found at Deer Park, the relationships and social connections also extended beyond the space and time of Deer Park. Deer Park employees shared that many of their friendships have lasted into the present day and remain some of their strongest relationships. Sharing a sense of connection with fellow former employees even despite long gaps in seeing each other, Michael said:

> Deer Park to me, it was always the lifelong friendships. In fact, that's one thing my daughter would always tell me when we go shopping or go anywhere. I have to stop and talk to somebody, say hi to an old friend. It's kind of a joke. "How many times is Dad going to stop and talk to somebody?" Wherever we go, I'll talk with somebody. I told them, "I'm rich with friends." I'm proud that I can go someplace and say, "Hey, there's someone I can go talk to and get caught up."

Cynthia summed up a similar point, sharing that her closest group of friends continue to be those she made at Deer Park. "The best friends I have are the friends I made at Deer Park. Even though we may not see each other very often. . . . I still feel a really strong connection to everybody." These sustained relationships demonstrate the long-lasting impact of Deer Park and the special place the experience holds in their lives. As a further testament to the lasting nature of Deer Park relationships, a reunion was held in 1986, over ten years after the park closed, with over two hundred attendees, including former employees and their family and friends.

Beyond friendships, Deer Park was also the site for blossoming romances, many of which became marriages and families. Lisa commented, "That's where I met my husband. That's where Jack met Brenda. Where Diane met Nick. A lot of people met [future spouses] there at Japanese Village." Within the diverse social gatherings in and around Deer Park, there was ample opportunity to meet potential dates and romantic partners. Robert, Lisa's husband, joked that potential romance was *the* reason he and his brothers decided to work at Deer Park. He exclaimed:

> Check out all the girls! That's the only reason we worked there! It was a social gathering. You have to take into account how many people met and got married there. . . . Before you went to Deer Park, most

people probably didn't know a lot of Japanese people. Before I went there, I don't think I ever dated someone Japanese.

From a sociological standpoint, the building of relationships, romantic or not, is unsurprising and perhaps inevitable in circumstance of frequent contact brought about by reduced social and physical distance, another result of structural assimilation (Gordon 1964). However, structural assimilation, and the interracial relationships it portends, assumes a diminishing of ethnic connection, a movement away from ethnic community. The sansei at Deer Park did just the opposite. They sought out contact with co-ethnics and built relationships, even marriages. Combined with earlier sentiments shared by sansei employees of racial marginalization in their schools and neighborhoods and the ethnic and racial belonging sought and found at Deer Park, the formation of meaningful and long-lasting platonic and romantic relationships with other Japanese Americans exposes an unquestionable need to understand processes of integration as being fundamentally shaped and limited by race.

While the formation of such intraethnic unions is noteworthy on its own, these unions also had longer-term structural impacts on the Orange County Japanese American community and population. Returning to the words of Lisa, who expanded on this point, "Truly, the fourth generation [yonsei] would look totally different if not for [Deer Park]." As Robert noted, many had never dated another Japanese American before Deer Park and probably would not have without Deer Park. The marriages formed at Deer Park led to the formation of families and to a fourth generation, yonsei, who were born into a robust ethnic social network. Deer Park not only created a space for belonging for residentially dispersed suburban sansei but enabled the creation of a significant yonsei population in the region—myself included—and laid a structural foundation for the maintenance of community among those yonsei. While times change and the yonsei grew up in a Southern California much different from the one of their parents, the following chapters reveal the similar racialized experiences of yonsei and sansei in their respective adolescence as well as contemporaneously. For both, such experiences demonstrate and shape their citizenship practices and racialized path of integration.

Conclusion

Deer Park had an outsized impact on the Japanese American community of Southern California sansei and provides deep insight into the workings of affect in the processes of integration and lived experiences of citizenship. The seeking of ethnic community by sansei at Deer Park and the belonging through culture and common racialized experiences found there contests assimilationist assumptions regarding the dampened importance and impact of ethnic and racial identities for the third generation of an immigrant-origin population. Race and ethnicity shaped the affect registered by sansei outside and inside the park. The lack of belonging and unrecognized citizenship felt outside the park was in large part what made Deer Park an appealing workplace. Inside Deer Park, sansei formed community that provided them with an affect of recognition explicitly based in ethnicity and shared racialized experiences. This is the persistent impact of race and ethnicity on the lives of these third-generation Japanese Americans. The distinct practices developed by sansei in the process of seeking out and forming community are performative effects. This includes the particular visual culture that displayed local identity and belonging. Recognition of local identity through visual culture did not come from the "mainstream" or the white park guests but from other sansei. Such ethnic community-seeking and formation among sansei highlight alternative origins of belonging that do not centralize whiteness. The particular visual culture developed and demonstrated at Deer Park, a suburban middle-class workplace, constitutes a minority culture of mobility. Japanese Americans leveraged visual culture and circumvented the racialized terms of belonging denied to them in their daily lives before and outside of Deer Park. At Deer Park, among sansei, they found a new feeling of citizenship.

5

The Racial Replenishment of Ethnicity

Janet grew up in Orange County and worked at Deer Park during her high school years. Like other sansei, she transitioned into adulthood during the late 1960s and early 1970s. She met her husband, Doug, another sansei who grew up in Los Angeles, in college. During our collective conversation, the three of us spoke of their early adulthoods. Janet described her experiences in this way:

> That was just a gathering place where all the Asian kids go—at the Deer Park. Even though a lot of them, like Susan and Cathy, they never worked at Deer Park, but they went too. They're all involved with all the Deer Park, you know, dancing and activities . . .
>
> . . . I always stood around with the Asian crowd—when I think about it, the Japanese crowd—because I lived at Deer Park. . . . You know, it was all Asian out there for me growing up. . . . Doug, I don't know what he did. He had—I think he had Asians, too.

Further in our conversation, we turned to their later adulthood and the raising of their yonsei children in the Orange County suburbs in the 1980s and 1990s.

> JANET: You know, when we first moved here, it was all white, okay. So I mean, all those schools—they went to Diamond Bar High, and it was still pretty much white, but by the time Stacey [their youngest daughter] got there, it turned Asian.
>
> DOUG: It was like sixty, fifty-five percent Asian and when Matthew [their oldest son] was there maybe twenty-five percent. . . . I mean, where we are right now, it's a little too Asian maybe from a demographic perspective, but I surely much rather have our kids growing up here.

As a yonsei who grew up in the Orange County suburbs, I was reminded during the flow of interviews of the casual conversations I myself had—and continue to have—at family gatherings or community events. The banter was easy and familiar. There was little need to dissect the meanings of words in our shared vocabulary. While this level of acquaintance was invaluable in uncovering the nuanced racialized experiences of sansei and yonsei in Southern California, I have to admit that at times, peculiar word usages would not always strike me as particularly significant in the moment. However, patterned behaviors reemerged as an empirical finding after data collection of the project ended and I pored over the transcripts of my interviews. I suppose this is why we hold our research to such rigorous procedures and standards. In the case of my conversation with Doug and Janet, they made an unnoticed linguistic and cognitive pivot in their usage of the term *Asian* as they discussed their friends and neighborhood across two different time frames. When using the term *Asian* to describe people during their youth in the 1960s and 1970s, Janet and Doug had a common understanding that this referenced other Japanese Americans. This is evident in the usage of "Asian kids" and "the Asian crowd" to describe the community formed at Deer Park, which was almost exclusively Japanese American. Flash forward to their adulthood, when the term *Asian* takes on a different meaning. During this time of their lives, over twenty years later, *Asian* referred to anyone who was of an Asian ethnicity, particularly those assumed to be immigrants who were not Japanese. *Asian* was no longer synonymous with Japanese Americans. In fact, it explicitly excluded them.

This linguistic and temporal idiosyncrasy noted in my conversation with Janet and Doug was remarkably consistent and common in the casual language used by sansei, who similarly grew up in the Los Angeles and Orange County suburbs in the 1960s and 1970s. In other interviews, the linguistic pivot became more accentuated when sansei interviewees caught their own linguistic imprecision of the usage of the term *Asian* in describing different temporal contexts. Donna, another sansei Deer Park employee, corrected her usage of *Asian* to equal *Japanese American* when speaking of her youth in the 1960s:

In high school . . . there were like maybe three Asian boys and that wasn't really a good experience of three Asian boys because they were not . . .

very good examples of what even Asian Americans could be like, *or should I say, Japanese Americans because they're Japanese American* [emphasis added].

Similarly, Teresa demonstrated the linguistic pivot in the usage of the term *Asian* as it applied in the context of her later adulthood and her children in the 1990s and 2000s. Now, *Asian* no longer referenced Japanese Americans, and Teresa explicitly made this clarification:

I think [my kids] made friendships with a lot of Asians, *probably Chinese might be more so* [emphasis added]. They seemed to have found an interest in Asians, but as far as the Japanese part—growing up, them getting together with our family—they also were introduced to Japanese American culture.

This pivot is an example of how macro-level structural forces can impact mundane behaviors at the individual level. In particular, this pivot is a manifestation of the Immigration and Naturalization Act of 1965 and its demographic impact in the everyday lives of sansei at Deer Park and across suburban Southern California. It is the immigration-driven demographic shift that shaped and reshaped Japanese American local practices of citizenship produced through a racial replenishment of ethnicity, ethnic identity and community replenished and shaped by the arrival of and interaction with similarly racialized, but ethnically distinct, immigrants. This replenishment of ethnicity is another example of the affect of citizenship's performative effect. Here, non-belonging, manifested as a forever-foreigner perception of later-generation Japanese Americans, leads to identity negotiations by sansei and yonsei that simultaneously aligned them with and distinguished them from other Asian Americans, immigrants in particular.

In the historiography of Asian America, the year 1965 looms large. It is the year President Lyndon B. Johnson signed the Immigration and Naturalization Act. This law would fundamentally alter the trajectory of the Asian American population in terms of size, diversity, and community formation (Chan 1991; Lee 2016; Nakano 2013; Takaki 1998). After over half a century of severe restriction and exclusion, depending on national origin, from immigrating to the US, the golden gates were re-opened to Asia (Chan 1991; Lee 2016; Takaki 1998). While the law was passed and signed in 1965, it did not go into effect until 1968, one year after Deer Park opened its gates. As such, the Deer Park experience of sansei coincided with this watershed moment in Asian American history but was largely unaffected by the law's long-term impacts of growth and diversification of the Asian American population. That would unfold in the subsequent decades. However, the Deer Park sansei, who largely came of age in the late 1960s, experienced firsthand the demographic transition sparked by the Immigration and Naturalization Act of 1965. It is within the historical context and demographic reverberations of the Immigration Act of 1965 that sansei learned and relearned the racial and ethnic definitions of *Asian*.

The interchangeable usage of *Asian* and *Japanese* by sansei when discussing their youth is an artifact of the pre-1965 demographic reality during their childhoods—and at least until the 1980 US census—where Japanese Americans were the largest Asian American ethnic group in Southern California. This linguistic slippage among sansei is, then, less surprising. During sansei childhoods, to be Asian in Southern California was to be Japanese. This was not true in sansei adulthoods or in the lives of their yonsei children, who largely came of age in the 1990s and 2000s. During this time frame and with the full impact of post-1965 immigration waves from Asia, sansei changed their usage of *Asian* to describe a broader set of ethnic backgrounds and to reflect the growing diversity of the Asian American population. The exclusion of Japanese Americans from such references to "Asians" in adulthood also alludes to the ways in which Japanese Americans attempt to distinguish—and at times distance—themselves from other Asian Americans within a growing and increasingly diverse milieu. The strange double usage of this single word is emblematic of the shifting constructions of community boundaries for sansei and yonsei and the broader impact of the post-1965 demographic shift on the everyday negotiations of Japanese American racial and ethnic identity.

This chapter explores how Japanese Americans come to define their communities of belonging in light of the demographic shifts driven by post-1965 immigration. The making and remaking of such community boundaries are banal, affective practices of citizenship. The communities they delineate are performative effects. Sansei and yonsei demonstrate that the communities of belonging being sought are not singular or static in their boundaries. Conceptualizations of community and identity are multiple and dynamic. They shift in response to structural and demographic changes both within and outside the Japanese American population. Conceptualizations of community and identity are more complicated than a persistence of ethnicity. For sansei and yonsei, communities form at the intersections of race, ethnicity, class, and generation in ways deeply impacted by the patterns of immigration that have shaped and reshaped the US demographic context. In particular, this chapter reveals the impact of broader Asian immigration—with a notable absence of any sizable immigration from Japan—on the identity and community formation practices among sansei and yonsei. In turn, such community formation practices shape how sansei and yonsei see their own position within the racial and ethnic landscape of the US and how they define their sense of belonging and their claims on local and broader citizenship.

Expanding Immigrant Replenishment

The notion of racial replenishment of ethnicity is not without its antecedents. Tomás Jimenez (2009) provides an informative baseline for understanding the impact of immigration on a long-standing US ethnic community. He demonstrates the impact of the continuous flow of Mexican immigrants and persistent racist nativism on the ethnic identification and culture of later-generation Mexican Americans, positing an "immigrant replenishment" of ethnicity. The continual flows of immigrants from Mexico in response to labor needs and proximity bring with them a direct replenishment of culture and identity for all Mexican Americans regardless of generation. The highly visible nature of large-scale Mexican migration also impacts and emboldens nativist and racist sentiments against Mexican Americans, again, regardless of generation. Such sentiments contribute to later-generation Mexican Americans' maintenance and awareness of their persistent racialized difference and the continued importance placed on ethnic identification and culture.

Jimenez's study provides important insights into the role of immigration in shaping the identity and culture of ethnic communities already in the US. However, his focus on the relationship between later-generation Mexican Americans and Mexican immigrants limits the application of his framework to within an singular ethnic community. The particularities of the Japanese American case offers a broader framework. Japanese immigration was slowly cut off beginning in 1907 with the Gentlemen's Agreement and culminated with full exclusion in 1924. Japanese immigration did not have the opportunity to be continuous as with the Mexican-origin case, and it also did not see a resurgence in the postwar period as with other Asian immigrants. Nonetheless, immigration still has a significant impact on Japanese American identity and community-building practices. Japanese Americans are impacted not by a steady flow of Japanese immigrants but by a large influx of immigrants from other Asian nations, with whom there is a shared US-based racialization. The large-scale entry of similarly racialized immigrants from other parts of Asia, particularly after the Immigration Act of 1965, has helped shape contemporary Japanese American racial and ethnic formations.

This common racialization results in the racial lumping of Japanese Americans with other Asian American groups regardless of ethnic and generational differences. Class context is also key to understanding the impact of racial lumping; driven by immigration hyper-selectivity and systemic racism, Japanese Americans, more recently arrived Asian American communities, and whites all inhabit the same physical middle-class spaces and therefore have frequent interaction (Lacy 2007; Lee and Zhou 2015). Racial lumping is magnified in such settings and impacts Japanese American negotiations of identity and community in two seemingly contradictory ways. First, interaction and racial lumping with more recently arrived Asian Americans leads later-generation Japanese Americans to recognize, maintain, and assert their ethnic difference from other Asian American groups. In this way, the persistence of Japanese American community and identity is a form of "reactive ethnicity" (Portes and Rumbaut 2001). Ethnic identity maintains and gains importance for later-generation Japanese Americans in reaction to the racial lumping with other Asian Americans and the racial discrimination and marginalization that accompanies it. Of course, such reactive ethnic distinction does not wash away the Japanese American racial uniform, which they continue to share with other Asian Americans. This relates to the simultaneous second impact of racial lumping:

Japanese Americans recognize that their common racialization with other Asian Americans produces similar lived experiences. Such shared experiences form the basis for relationships along racial lines as well as explicit racial solidarities and identities as Asian Americans. The negotiation of racial and ethnic identity by sansei and yonsei is a fundamentally intersectional one. The response to the immigration of readily middle-class and similarly racialized Asian immigrants is the *racial replenishment of ethnicity*.

Conceptual Foundations of a Racial Replenishment of Ethnicity

To make sense of a racial replenishment of ethnicity, it is important to reiterate the conceptual boundary between race and ethnicity as they apply to the Japanese American case. Race and ethnicity are distinct yet mutually interacting constructs. Omi and Winant define race as "a concept, a representation, or signification of identity that refers to different types of human bodies, to the perceived corporeal and phenotypic markers of difference and the meanings and social practices that are ascribed to those differences" (2014, 111). I focus on "the perceived corporeal and phenotypic markers" that sansei and yonsei share with many post-1965 Asian immigrants. Perceived phenotypic markers support a common Asian racialization, which in turn produce "the meanings and social practices" taken up in Japanese American community formation and affects of citizenship. In contrast to race, Cornell and Hartmann define ethnicity as "a collectivity within a larger society having real or putative common ancestry, memories of a shared historical past, and a cultural focus on one or more symbolic elements defined as the epitome of their peoplehood" (2006, 19). Here, the reliance on shared history and symbolic elements in defining ethnic peoplehood is particularly useful. For later-generation Japanese Americans, ethnic persistence focuses on symbolic attachment to generational status and long family histories in the US, particularly WWII mass incarceration, as well as shared cultural practices (Nakano 2018). Such attachments and practices distinguish later-generation Japanese Americans as an ethnic group separate from other Asian Americans despite shared racialization.

Clarified definitions of race and ethnicity are important for understanding the mechanisms and processes of a racial replenishment of ethnicity. These processes and their outcomes, however, also demonstrate that race and ethnicity are simultaneous and interlocking, each affecting the other. While this study does not operate on a panethnic definition of Asian American, the panethnicity literature does offer important insight into the relationship between race and ethnicity in the identity and community formations of individuals.[1] Okamoto (2014) and Nakano (2013) argue that panethnic identification does not spell the end of ethnicity identity. Rather, panethnic and ethnic identities are conceptualized as layered, flexible, and interlocking structures. The racial replenishment of ethnicity exemplifies these same types of overlaps and intersections between racial and ethnic identities and communities where sansei and yonsei find their sense of belonging and citizenship, particularly at the local level.

Structural Underpinnings: Demographic Shift and Class Status

While a racial replenishment of ethnicity is animated at the local, interactional level, it is predicated on two structural underpinnings: the shift in immigrant demographics ushered in by the passage of the Immigration Act of 1965 and subsequent reforms and the upward mobility and middle-class status of Japanese Americans in the postwar period.

Incremental changes to US immigration law beginning during WWII and the rise of a global communist threat in the postwar period culminated with the Immigration and Naturalization Act of 1965. This reform ushered in a new era of Asian immigration from China, Korea, India, and the Philippines, and subsequent reforms in immigration and refugee laws led to new flows of Southeast Asian newcomers (Chan 1991; Lee 2016; Takaki 1998). Notably absent from these new Asian immigration waves was a substantial representation of Japanese immigrants. Figure 5.1 shows the Japanese immigration in relation to immigration from all of Asia to the US from 1965 to 2010. While annual Asian immigration grew from just over 20,000 in 1965 and approximately 75,000 in 1969— the year after the implementation of the Immigration and Naturalization Act—to nearly 420,000 annually by 2010, Japanese immigration remained low and fairly constant across the same time span, averaging near 5,600 annually and only breaking 10,000 immigrants once, in 1993. From 1969 to 2010, Japanese immigrants accounted for a decreasing

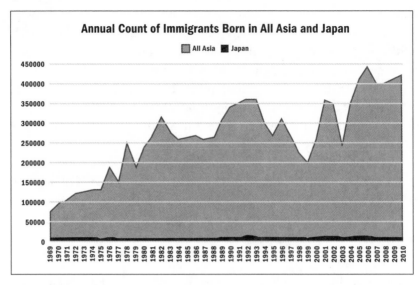

Figure 5.1. "Annual Count of Immigrants from Japan and Asia by Country/Region of Birth, 1969–2010," US Department of Homeland Security, *Yearbook of Immigration Statistics 1969–2009.*

proportion of Asian immigrants and only about 2 percent of all Asian immigrants to the US across the forty-year time period (figure 5.1).

The overall growth of the Asian American population and proportional decline of Japanese Americans was mirrored at the local level in Los Angeles and Orange Counties. From 1960 to 2010, the Asian American percentage of the population grew from 1.8 percent to 13.5 percent in Los Angeles County and from 0.8 percent to 17.7 percent in Orange County. In 1960, Japanese Americans made up 71.1 percent of all Asian Americans in Los Angeles County and 75.6 percent in Orange County and continued to hold a majority through 1970. Such statistics provide context for sansei's interchangeable usage of the terms *Asian* and *Japanese* when speaking of their adolescences in the 1960s and 1970s. Japanese Americans made up the strong majority of all Asian Americans. To be Asian was to be Japanese during this time period in Southern California. However, by the 1990s, the percentage of Japanese Americans within the Asian American population dwindled and, in 2010, Japanese Americans would account for only 6.8 percent and 5.4 percent of all Asian Americans in Los Angeles and Orange counties, respectively. In this new ethnic demography, to be "Asian" no longer meant to be "Japanese." It followed that for sansei in their adulthood—and yonsei in their adolescence, the usage of the term *Asian* changed as well to reference something other than Japanese American.[2]

The strong majority held by Japanese Americans in Southern California was not displaced by the growth of a singular Asian ethnic group. Rather, the decline was driven by the tremendous growth of multiple ethnic groups within the Southland's Asian American population. Between 1960 and 2010, the US census–enumerated Asian ethnic categories grew from three to twenty-two (Nakano 2013). Increased diversity shifted the Asian American population into a more variegated group based on ethnicity and also shifted the population from predominantly US born to predominantly foreign born (Nakano 2013). Because of the minimal influx of new Japanese immigrants in the postwar period, Japanese Americans have been a predominantly native-born population since the 1930s. From the postwar period until the 1970 US census, all other Asian American ethnic groups were also majority native born. After 1970, however, the influx of new Asian immigrants shifted the nativity breakdown of Asian Americans toward a predominantly foreign-born population. It is in this context of diminished representation and an increased sense of difference along lines of ethnicity, nativity, and generation that sansei and yonsei define their communities of belonging in dynamic ways.

Beyond the idiosyncratic use of the term *Asian* observed among sansei respondents, both sansei and yonsei demonstrated a strong awareness of the growing size and diversity of the Asian American population in the Southland. Again, sansei, who grew up in the 1960s and 1970s, when Japanese Americans dominated the relatively small Asian American population, experienced this demographic shift firsthand. Doug and Janet, the sansei couple, noted this shift when describing the changes they witnessed in their neighborhood on the border of Los Angeles and Orange Counties.

DOUG: Out of our whole [housing] tract of two hundred some odd, we
    were like one or two Asian families when we moved in here in '83 but
    now it's like 65 and 80 percent mostly Chinese and Korean, but—
JANET: All the whites moved out.

Doug and Janet remarked on the increasing and notable presence of other Asian American ethnicities within their neighborhood and local community, an unnoted manifestation of white flight. For their part, yonsei, having grown up in the 1980s and 1990s within a more diverse suburban setting, still experienced some of the increased diversification. While 1965 marked a watershed moment for the Asian American population, its growth and diversification continue well into the twenty-first century. Doug and Janet's son Matthew, who entered high school in the mid-1990s, corroborated his parents' observations on the changing makeup of his neighbors and classmates during his youth.

> My parents moved here after I was in preschool, I think. The [white] population was a lot larger when we first moved here, and I just felt like as I got older there were more Asians coming into this area. And even today, I know that the area, like the high school, is even more Asian . . . I would say more Korean and Chinese.

The local neighborhood and school changed from predominantly white to increasingly Asian, although not Japanese. The growing presence of a diverse array of Asian American ethnicities was evident across the Southern California suburbs. Kristina, a mixed-race yonsei, remarked on a similarly ethnically diverse, but minimally Japanese American, Asian American population in her high school and hometown of Garden Grove:

> I think I had maybe one or two other friends that were Japanese American. The majority of the Asian or Asian American people that were at my school were Vietnamese. Vietnamese would be the majority; probably next would be Korean and Chinese, then Japanese, Cambodian, Laotian, and like all that other stuff. . . . So of my graduating class, which is maybe about just under four hundred people, there were two [Japanese American] people that I knew personally.

Nicole, another multiracial yonsei, observed a similar shift as she grew up in Arcadia, a Los Angeles County community. She noted the rapid change in the percentage of Chinese American students at her high school taking place in under a decade:

I guess at Arcadia, yeah, I hung out with my white kids, but it was really mixed at the time. Now, you go to Arcadia High School and it's probably 75 percent, 80 percent Chinese. It's so saturated, the area. So it's a lot different than when my brother grew up. He went to Arcadia—he's seven years younger than me—and a lot of his friends were Chinese kids. So it's just kind of very different.

Further south in Lake Forest, yonsei Jonathan pointed out the same trend in his Orange County hometown:

Lake Forest is a small suburb . . . predominantly white. When I was growing up, more Asians started coming in my teenage years, probably overspill from Irvine [a neighboring city]. It was an upper middle-class community.

Jonathan's comment directly references not only the shifting ethnic and racial makeup of his hometown but also its class status. While such explicit references to class were rare across my interviews, residence in the Southern California suburbs marks a particularly middle-class status that formed the foundations for experiences of all sansei and yonsei participating in this study. Whether examining the sansei experience growing up in predominantly white neighborhoods or the yonsei experience in increasingly Asian American neighborhoods, middle-class status dictates the location of Japanese American upbringing and the racial demographics of their interpersonal interactions. The similar class status among Japanese Americans, whites, and post-1965 Asian American immigrant families directly contributed to their physical proximity and increased interaction (Lacy 2007; Neckerman, Carter, and Lee 1999). The middle-class status of Asian Americans arriving post-1965 directly resulted from the preference categories of the Immigration and Naturalization Act, which prioritized the entry of immigrants with professional degrees and high occupational skills, allowing these newcomers to quickly enter into the US residential middle class (Lee and Zhou 2015). The ethnic and class demographic shifts resulting from the 1965 immigration reforms produced a high level of contact between later-generation Japanese Americans and other Asian Americans, making similarities and differences highly observable. Such comparisons and contrasts were evident not only to Japanese Americans but also to the broader community, which often lumped Japanese Americans into the same racialized category as other, more recently arrived, Asian Americans.

Racial Lumping with Asian Immigrants

Within the context of the growing Asian American middle-class and decreasing proportion of the Japanese American segment of that population, sansei and yonsei recognize the ways Asian American ethnicities are lumped into a singular racial category. Regardless of generation and assimilation successes, Japanese Americans face the same stereotypes and discrimination as all Asian Americans, what Mia Tuan (1999) and others have described as the forever-foreigner syndrome. Tracy, a yonsei, and Donna, a sansei, stated this succinctly:

> I think that to people who were not Asian, they felt like we [Japanese Americans] were kind of just clumped in with all the other Asian groups, which is not necessarily true, like, we didn't have a lot of similarities with each Asian group, Chinese, Korean, Vietnamese. It was all a little bit different. But we were always just kind of clumped in with those groups.
> —Tracy

> I think people confuse Japanese Americans with—they lump you together with all the different Asians. And they lump *American* Japanese in with *non-American* Asians [emphasis added]. So with the coming of non-American Asians, like immigrants, that's what people are saying.
> —Donna

Tracy and Donna both demonstrated a strong awareness of the racial lumping of Asian Americans of diverse ethnic backgrounds into a single group by non-Asian observers (Espiritu 1992). Donna took lumping a step further by observing that not only are Japanese Americans lumped with other Asian Americans, but they are lumped with Asians of different generational statuses, particularly "non-American" immigrants. There is a direct causal relationship. Japanese Americans are seen as forever foreigners because they are lumped with more recently arrived immigrants, immigrants who would not be present if not for post-1965 immigrant and refugee waves.

The predominance of the forever-foreigner racialization of Asian Americans runs counter to Japanese Americans' understandings of themselves, their community, and their multigenerational history within the US. While later-generation Japanese Americans were the predominant Asian American ethnic group nationally and locally in Southern California until at least the mid-1970s, the maintenance—and perhaps amplification—of forever-foreigner stereotypes highlights the increasingly marginal position of later-generation Japanese Americans within the Asian racial umbrella. This invisibility is further underscored by the assumptions often encountered by sansei and yonsei regarding their immigrant generational status when interacting with other non-Japanese Asian Americans. Carrie, another yonsei, recalled one such interaction:

> People ask you all the time, "What nationality are you? Where are you from?" You know where they say it a lot? The nail salon. They [Vietnamese American salon employees] always ask me. "Oh, where are you from? What nationality are you? What country do you come from?" Sometimes people will think that I'm not born here, because most of them probably weren't born here. So they assume that I wasn't born here also.

While the Vietnamese American salon workers' words can be read as a seeking of common experience and perhaps racial solidarity, they make an incorrect racial assumption of foreignness, which highlighted for Carrie a feeling of difference and distance from other Asian Americans. This racial lumping and forever-foreigner assumptions by other Asian Americans is not necessarily a simple internalization of widely circulated racist tropes concerning Asian Americans. It may also reflect the decreasing population and visibility of later-generation Asian Americans within the local communities of Southern California and in the nation overall. The general lack of exposure to later-generation Asian Americans is evident in the comments by many sansei and yonsei where they recalled shock expressed by other Asian Americans regarding their later-generation status or the unaccented English of an older adult of Asian descent. For sansei and yonsei, later-generation status and parents and grandparents who were native English speakers is part and parcel of their Asian American experience. Regardless of the reasons behind assumptions of forever-foreigner status, Carrie's interaction with the Vietnamese American salon workers served to highlight the differences between herself and Vietnamese Americans, regardless of any racial similarities. The interaction illuminates the pervasive practice of racial lumping and the erroneous assumption of forever-foreigner status, even among other Asians Americans. Such assumptions implicate a complex misunderstanding and invisibility of Japanese American history, the Japanese American present, and the broader racial impact of post-1965 immigration.

While sansei and yonsei feel their history, culture, language, and circumstance should mark them as distinct from the postwar waves of immigrants and refugees from Asia, later-generation Japanese Americans are lumped with other Asian Americans without consideration of their generational status, for which there are no bodily markers.[3] They remain similarly perceived as forever foreigners and immigrants. The revived and highly visible influx of Asian immigration eclipses the realities of later-generation Japanese Americans in the eyes of mainstream culture and society. As the words of Tracy, Donna, and Carrie demonstrate, Japanese Americans are keenly aware of their racial lumping with other Asian Americans imposed by mainstream society. While such perceptions have existed throughout the history of Asians in the US, their persistence is certainly augmented by the large-scale migration from Asia beginning in the 1970s and continuing into the present day.

Unsurprisingly, sansei and yonsei do not simply accept this common racialization. Their awareness of racial lumping is equaled by their understanding of Japanese American experience as unique in terms of history, culture, and generational status. Such lumping forces Japanese Americans to think about themselves in relationship to these new immigrants and the forever-foreigner racialization they share. As Japanese Americans are racialized as Asian, the Asian American milieu surrounding them impacts how they view themselves and how they understand how others view them. The renewed flow of other Asian immigrants and the inability of mainstream America to distinguish among different Asian American ethnic groups leads to a persistent salience and replenishment of ethnic *and* racial identification and community for sansei and yonsei in Southern California.

Persistent Ethnic Distinction and the Importance of Generation

In recognizing their position within the growing ethnic diversity of the Asian American population, sansei and yonsei do not lose sight of the distinctiveness of Japanese American ethnicity and experience. In fact, as already demonstrated in Carrie's experience, intra-Asian American interactions often serve to reinforce the differences and to augment their individual ethnic identity. Comparisons between Japanese Americans and other Asian Americans is magnified by their shared class status and colocation in middle-class spaces. This location also places them under the white gaze given the generally strong representation of whites in middle-class spaces. As the proportion of later-generation Japanese Americans diminishes, Asian American racialization is shaped by the perceived characteristics and experiences of other, more recently arrived, Asian American immigrants that make up the vast majority of Asian America. The subsequent racial lumping leads to a reactive and replenished importance placed on a uniquely Japanese American identity within the Asian American racial umbrella. Jill, a sansei, discussed this distinction through her relationship with her Chinese American in-laws:

> My son is married to a Chinese American girl, and I just see their culture as so different. Because the parents and the grandparents, I can't relate to that so much. We're miles apart in that way, but we still love each other and like each other. It's very interesting. There's such a difference that I see and feel that I really hold on more to my Japanese Americanness and appreciate it and want to perpetuate that.

For Jill, the differences between Japanese Americans and Chinese Americans became much more apparent through her extended contact with her daughter-in-law's family. Jill explicitly states that such observable differences led her to want to maintain her distinct Japanese American identity and culture. Doug, the sansei who earlier discussed with his wife, Janet, the increasingly Asian—but not Japanese American—neighborhood, also did not readily feel a sense of commonality with his racially similar neighbors, and he expressed an increasing sense of being a minority in his own community.

> Yeah, you just feel like a minority. It's so weird how our kids grew up, one generation removed. I was actually talking to some of my friends. When we were going to school it's like, oh they're Chinese. . . . I mean, you had friends that were Chinese or Korean whatever, but you always knew the differentiation between Asian groups. Whereas nowadays, man, the kids. I mean, my son's friends are Chinese, Korean. I mean, we've been invited to like eight or nine weddings and it's like Chinese, Koreans, whatever. It's like the kids don't think about ethnicity anymore.

Doug's assertion that he feels like a minority now that there are more Asian Americans in his area is peculiar. Afterall, he had been a minority when his city was predominantly white. However, being an overshadowed minority within the Asian American population feels different to Doug from when he was a visible racial minority among a white majority. This reaction references how minoritization occurs under the white gaze. To be sure, Doug does not see himself as white. He is very much aware—and made aware—of his racial difference. When Doug and his family were one of few Asian Americans, he felt there was a more accurate understanding and visibility of his Japanese American identity and history. However, the unique Japanese American experience became less visible with the increasing presence of other Asian Americans of varied generational and ethnic backgrounds. From Doug's standpoint, as the Asian American population became predominantly non-Japanese and foreign born, racial lumping led to increased assumptions that all Asian Americans hold the same immigration history, a history that he and his family did not share. Doug's description of his racial position demonstrates an awareness of how the social perception of Japanese Americans, particularly through the white gaze, is impacted by the increasing presence of other Asian Americans of varied generational and ethnic backgrounds. In the face of racial lumping and confusion with other Asian Americans, Doug feels an increased sense of minoritization and marginalization. Doug's response to this negative affect was to reminisce and reassert the ethnic distinctiveness of Japanese Americans.

Doug also projected his concerns about the loss of ethnic distinctiveness onto his children. Doug's struggle to reconcile his personal sense of ethnic distinctiveness and his perception of his children's lack of ethnicity—"It's like the kids don't think about ethnicity anymore"— mirror the particular sansei shift in the usage of the term *Asian*. Formative sansei experiences that defined *Asian* as synonymous with *Japanese* were no longer true in the formative experiences with yonsei. As such, the linguistic idiosyncrasy is not present among yonsei who largely did not experience the demographic shift following the 1965 Immigration and Naturalization Act but grew up in its resulting ethnic and racial milieu. There is lament in Doug's comments on the diverse Asian background of his son's friend group. He worries that the perceived lack of ethnic distinction stemming from the white gaze is being internalized by his children. Doug's yonsei children, however, told a very different story about themselves and their experiences. While they certainly found commonality and friendships across ethnic lines, each of Doug's children reported a strong awareness of the differences in history, generation, and acculturation between Japanese Americans and other Asian Americans. Doug and Janet's daughter Stacey recalled interactions with her Korean American friends that highlighted, rather than erased, ethnic boundaries:

I remember some of my Korean friends would say, "Oh, my grandmother wouldn't like you." Because I would date Korean guys, but I wouldn't meet their families. It was kind of weird that way because of the history [of Japanese war crimes against Koreans before and during WWII].

Such interactions were not unique to Stacey. Elizabeth, another yonsei, reflected on a similar situation:

I did have a boyfriend in high school who is Korean, and his grandma didn't want to meet me because I was Japanese, and there was a lot of—I think it was just a misunderstanding of, you know—our family was not even in Japan at that time.

To be clear, both Elizabeth's and Stacey's families were already present in the US for at least two generations prior to WWII and had been incarcerated by the US government while the Imperial Japanese army committed atrocities against the Korean people. Regardless of these historical facts, Elizabeth's and Stacey's interactions with Korean American friends and their families, particularly immigrant parents and grandparents, accentuated two intertwined forms of lumping. Similar to Carrie's interaction with Vietnamese American workers at the nail salon, Elizabeth's and Stacey's experiences demonstrate a racial lumping through the assumption of the immigrant generation by these Korean Americans. Because Elizabeth and Stacey are Asian, they must be first or second generation and therefore have a close connection with Japan. Because Elizabeth and Stacey are ethnically Japanese, they are inextricably tied to the war crimes of Imperial Japan, regardless of their current generation and location or the location of their families during World War II. Again, these forms of lumping produce experiences that serve to highlight the social distance and differences between these two ethnic groups. Furthermore, Elizabeth's statement regarding her family having not been in Japan during WWII makes implicit reference to the centrality of multiple generations and a deep history in the US in the Japanese American conception of ethnicity. This conception of ethnicity clearly diverges from Stacey's and Elizabeth's understandings of Korean American ethnicity, which seem to be tied to homeland histories and the immigrant experience.

Beyond such historically based antipathies and divergences, sansei and yonsei draw on differences in generational status and the accompanying family history in other ways. Jennifer, a yonsei, described the difficulty of building connections across generational difference: "It was hard to relate to most Korean, Chinese, or Southeast Asians, because they were first generation or second generation. So that's a cultural divide, and it's really hard to associate." The importance of generation in the Japanese American sense of ethnicity is further underscored by the usage of generationally based identifiers, such as sansei and yonsei. Such terms are a common feature in Japanese American vernacular and within interview responses in this study to describe self-identity and community. Recall that Japanese Americans are the only ethnic group to have generational groupings enumerated in the ancestry code list of the US Census Bureau

(Omi, Nakano, and Yamashita 2019). More than a naming convention, generational identifications allow Japanese Americans to position themselves and demarcate community boundaries with co-ethnics through an assumption of a shared ethnic history (Levine and Rhodes 1980; Montero 1980; Tsuda 2016). It is not uncommon for Japanese Americans to ask each other their generation in introductory conversations.

Crystal, a mixed-race yonsei, expanded on the generational differences she observed between herself and her Asian American peers of other ethnic backgrounds:

> A lot of the other folks in the room [of an Asian American college organization event] were second generation, so when they were going around talking about issues, they were talking about being the children of immigrants, that experience, and assimilation and all these things. And as a fourth-generation Japanese American, you're just like, "I don't know. My dad grew up in LA. His dad grew up in Fresno and then LA. We are just like Californians." So it was really hard to have conversations with people. They were expecting me to contribute, and I'd be like, "I have nothing. I have nothing to talk about on these conversation points."

Generation is deeply embedded within sansei and yonsei sense of ethnic identity and community and creates social distance with Asian American peers who are often immigrants or the children of immigrants. Here, Crystal drew on her family's history and multiple generations in the US as boundary markers between herself and the mostly second-generation Asian American event attendees. As a fourth-generation Japanese American, Crystal felt a great deal of social distance from and "nothing to talk about" with her second-generation classmates despite the shared racialization that ostensibly made Crystal interested in attending the event in the first place.

While discussions of generational differences often evoked history and place-based distinctions, assertions of generation also dovetailed with assertions of cultural differences with other Asian Americans. Such assertions of cultural differences are intertwined with generational identity as sansei and yonsei connected their longer generational history in the US with a higher level of acculturation and "Americanization." Yonsei Carrie pointed out this simple causality: "Japanese Americans are more Americanized because we've been here longer." Stacey expanded on the connection between generation and acculturative differences when comparing herself, as a yonsei, to her other Asian American friends: "Among my friends, they are mostly first or second generation. So they are more with their culture than with American culture. Like a lot of their parents only speak Korean or Chinese."

In general, sansei and yonsei feel considerable distance from Japanese culture, following the logics of assimilation. Sansei and yonsei respondents in this study referenced acculturation into mainstream American culture as part of their cultural ethnic identity. Beyond the multigenerational history of Japanese Americans in the US, acculturation was seen as a direct result of the particularities of that history. Yonsei Tracy illustrated:

> If the conversation gets to that level, definitely I'll say something about it. They'll ask me why I don't speak Japanese, and I'll let them know. All these things happened. We were interned. The Japanese Americans were trying to assimilate towards American culture, so they didn't want to be perceived as being different by speaking this other language. So there's a lot of history behind why a lot of people don't speak Japanese anymore.

Tracy framed the acculturation of Japanese Americans, through the example of language loss, as a reaction to racism and the WWII mass incarceration experience. While the true causality of Japanese American acculturation may be more complicated than Tracy described, she points to the way in which sansei and yonsei draw strong connections between cultural practices and the long and tumultuous history of Japanese Americans in the US.

In highlighting the acculturation of Japanese Americans, I do not mean to diminish the unique ethnic culture that was equally discussed and practiced by the respondents in this study—a Japanese American culture, distinct from Japanese culture. While Tracy readily outlined a history that has led to a diminished Japanese cultural connection and heightened level of acculturation into US mainstream society, she also shared the myriad ways in which a distinct Japanese American culture remained salient in her life:

Obviously, the internment camps, things like that, just that part of history. We went to Manzanar [an internment camp] and saw all of that history, so that's really what I think about when I'm thinking about Japanese American culture. Being a part of SEYO, it was a huge [Japanese American youth sports] organization. The Buddhist churches have the *hanamatsuris* and all the *obons* [Japanese festivals].[4]

Mirroring her earlier emphasis on history in shaping the acculturation trajectory of Japanese Americans, Tracy also named that same unique history as an important part of what defines Japanese American ethnicity. She expanded on her conception of Japanese American culture by centering various institutions that continue to shape and connect the ethnic community. Andrew, another yonsei, similarly noted the significance of such institutions for the community and culture using the language of hybridity. Such hybridity of institutions is a microcosm of Japanese American ethnicity:

It is this weird hybrid culture that's not Japanese at all, but it's not American, it's right in between. It includes American sports like basketball in huge Japanese American leagues. It includes Buddhist churches and Methodist churches, but that are all Japanese American. It includes . . . yeah, like Boy Scouts that are all Japanese American. And that's the specific hybrid culture . . . that's how I define it because that's what I grew up in.

While any of these institutions, such as basketball and Boy Scouts, may seem like typical Americana, they take on a distinctly Japanese American flavor. In Southern California, Japanese Americans have acculturated and adopted American institutional types but do not necessarily join mainstream institutions themselves. Rather, they have historically created parallel institutional structures that are membered predominantly by Japanese Americans (Kurashige 2002). For sansei and yonsei in suburban Southern California, participation in one or more of these institutions is seen as integral to identifying as Japanese American. As Henry, a yonsei, flatly stated, "If you're a yonsei, you play basketball. If you grew up in Orange County, that's pretty much it." Institutional participation and the community connections it fosters are important sites of cultural transmission and maintenance. As Crystal stated, "I think our Japanese American culture has become less about the actual culture of Japan or Japanese things and more about how we interact as a community."

Intra-Ethnic Divisions: Japanese Americans and Japanese Immigrants

The importance of generational status and level of acculturation in the construction of Japanese American ethnic identity and community is also evident in the way sansei and yonsei compared themselves with Japanese immigrants who came to the US after 1965 and their children.[5] Most respondents stated that they had little interaction with or knowledge of contemporary Japanese immigrants and their children, so-called shin-issei and shin-nisei, respectively. This was true even among individuals with heavy involvement in Japanese American community institutions. Carrie admitted, "I don't actually think I've ever really had a lot of interaction with someone who was Japanese Japanese and not Japanese American. I only interact with Japanese Americans, so I don't really know." Given this perceived absence, it may be assumed that post-1965 Japanese immigrants maintain their own separate institutions and could even be considered a distinct ethnic group from later-generation Japanese Americans (see Gutiérrez [1995], Jimenez [2009], and Ochoa [2004] for similar internal ethnic boundaries based on generation among Mexican Americans). Even in instances where Japanese immigrants and later-generation Japanese Americans are physically present in the same spaces, there is a sense of distance and difference between them. Kimi, a yonsei who grew up in a neighborhood with a sizeable Japanese American population, commented on such differences:

> In my neighborhood, at school growing up there were a lot of Japanese American kids. And I guess it's a little misleading to say Japanese American, because some of them weren't really—some of them were, like, Japanese citizens who were here for a couple years because their dad worked for Toyota, and they got relocated here for five years. I had a few friends like that in elementary school. . . . They spoke Japanese, and I didn't. Actually,

now that I think about it, I do remember feeling that when I was little, feeling alienated from the kids who were fluent because I didn't speak.

Growing up in the Gardena/Torrance area of Los Angeles County, a region known for its high concentration of Japanese Americans and Japanese immigrants, Kimi noted the distinction between Japanese immigrant and Japanese American residents. It would be "misleading" to name these two distinct groups living in the same middle-class neighborhoods as a single ethnicity. For Kimi, such differences are very real and accentuated by the language difference between the two communities. Jason, a younger sansei, observed a similar separation on the college campus where he works:

> There's a club, I forgot what it's called, it's pretty much about Japan. They held their meetings in *nihongo* [Japanese language]. They talk about Japan, about manga and other stuff going on in the motherland. They don't talk about Japanese American stuff. Matter of fact, I don't think there's any Japanese Americans in that club. Then there's the Japanese American club. It's a bunch of Japanese Americans. The meetings are in English. We talk about cultural programs, internment, the JACL [Japanese American Citizens League], and other things more Japanese American-related. I see that as the great distinction between Japanese and Japanese American.

The two clubs are distinct social spaces on the same campus with little or no overlap. While the main language spoken at each club meeting—a marker of acculturation—is a significant difference between them, Jason also notes the differences in the interests and activities of each club. In this way, the differences between Japanese immigrant students and later-generation Japanese American students goes beyond language. Differences are also cultural, generational, and historical. The history of Japanese American World War II mass incarceration and the JACL—so central to the construction of Japanese Americanness (Nakano 2018)—have less relevance for Japanese immigrants who arrived after 1965. Despite the similar class status between Japanese immigrants and Japanese Americans, as demonstrated by similar residential and higher education locations, generation and history remain salient boundary markers between these two groups that would largely be assumed to share the same ethnicity. Similar to their sense of difference and distance from other Asian Americans based on generation and sense of acculturation, later-generation Japanese Americans feel distinct from these other Japanese ethnics on the same basis.

The replenishment and maintenance of ethnicity for Japanese Americans, then, is primarily driven by race and racialization, not co-ethnics and Japanese culture. To distance themselves from the forever-foreigner racialization they are ascribed, sansei and yonsei assert their personal, family, and community experiences alongside generation and history as fundamental to an ethnic identity that is distinct and worthy of maintenance and notice. Overall, the words of sansei and yonsei consistently demonstrate an awareness of the racial lumping of Japanese Americans with other Asian American ethnic groups—including more recently arrived Japanese immigrants and their children—which serves to heighten their sense of ethnic distinctness and the need to assert it. Hence, a racial demographic shift brought on by the arrival of similarly racialized Asian immigrants is responsible, at least in part, for the replenished ethnicity of later-generation Japanese Americans. Japanese Americans do not receive a cultural replenishment from any of these newly arrived immigrants, including those from Japan.

Racial Community Formation with Asians like Me

Racial replenishment impacts Japanese American community and identity formation not only in ethnic terms, but racial terms as well. As the growing diversity of the Asian American population and racial lumping led to a strengthening of ethnic identification, it also opens the possibility of racial community and relationship formations. Such formations do not happen independently from each other, rather race and ethnicity coexist, interlock, and shift simultaneously in mutually affecting—and seemingly contradictory—ways (see Nakano [2013] for similar interlocking relationship between ethnic and panethnic identities among Asian Americans; also see Okamoto [2014]). Japanese Americans are well aware of how their common racialization creates similar lived experiences for all Asian American regardless of ethnicity and generation. Such awareness has led Japanese Americans in post-1965 Southern California to look toward other Asian Americans to build communities of belonging at the same time that they have sought out and maintained ethnic community. The seeking of racial community by Japanese Americans highlights how such communities are not constructed based off race as a static identity but rather as an affective lived experience. Sansei and yonsei in this study spoke of racially oriented communities based on common racialized experience as well as a similar level of acculturation and upbringing within the distinct racial landscape of Southern California and the US. Community is built with individuals whom sansei and yonsei perceive as "Asian like me."

Many of my respondents recognized their linked fate with other Asian Americans due to their common racialization in political terms (Espiritu 1992).[6] In particular, the more politically active respondents in this study often made reference to the murder of Vincent Chin (see chapter 1). Crystal, a multiracial yonsei, related this watershed moment in Asian American history:

> I think the reason we [Asian American activists] always bring that incident up is because it was a very high-profile incident of a Chinese American man being killed because people thought that he was Japanese, because people just can't tell Asians apart. They don't know the difference. They don't care to know the difference.

While Vincent Chin's murder has long served as a historical touchstone, Asian Americans, as a racial community, were once again reminded of such dangers during the COVID-19 pandemic. Given media attention on the Chinese origins of the virus, anyone racialized as Chinese—regardless of ethnicity—were scapegoated and blamed for the pandemic, leading to a dramatic rise in racist violence against these individuals and communities. While the anti-Asian sentiment and violence as shown in the parallel cases of Vincent Chin and the COVID-19 pandemic are deplorable on the basest level, they exemplify the lack of differentiation and the racial lumping that Asian Americans experience on a daily basis. Sansei and yonsei readily recognize that regardless of their generation and asserted ethnic distinction, mainstream society continues to view Asian Americans as interchangeable. The murder of Vincent Chin and now COVID-19-related hate crimes serve as beacons and rallying points for the need of Asian American community building across ethnic lines, particularly within the political realm.

The recognition of common racialized experiences, particular to the US context, is not limited to political solidarities. Yonsei Andrew shared how racial similarity factors in his relationships and community building: ’

> It's interesting because the relationships that I built in college . . . my circle of friends is predominantly Asian American. Yeah, it was almost 100 percent Asian, and I just became okay with it at a certain point, because it's just easier to connect with them. And yeah, I'm not going to give some political bullshit, "Oh you know, it's about building community" because it is, but I think more important for me, it is just more comfortable. You knew where I was coming from. We had the same jokes, similar cultures, right? I just connected with them. . . . And sometimes they are unspoken reasons. Sometimes, being Asian American I think just connects you to other Asian Americans naturally. For me, I just feel sometimes it's such a natural connection and this is just so easy, you know. And maybe it has everything to do with, "Oh my god, I'm in a room full of white people, but phew, there's another Asian American here."

Andrew highlighted the common racialized experiences shared among his Asian American peers that provides an "unspoken" and "natural connection." Growing up and living as a minority in the US is a particular, albeit unfortunate, claim on an American identification and creates empathy between Asian Americans. This is the sense of relief Andrew felt in finding another Asian American in a room full of white people. There is an assumption that another Asian American has experienced the same racialized life as Andrew. Respondents in my study not only identified similar racial stereotypes faced by Asian Americans but also reflected on how growing up racialized as Asian and forever foreign in the US produced a particular shared experience for Asian Americans regardless of ethnic background. Shared racialized experiences in the US context helps to identify other Asian Americans as "Asian like me."

In addition to growing up within the US racial context, another main factor in constructing racial Asian American relationships and communities is perceived similarities in levels of acculturation. This aspect of "Asians like me" highlights the ways in which other Asian Americans who are more acculturated and "Americanized" are perceived in ways deemed similar to later-generation Japanese Americans. Multiethnic yonsei Jennifer shared this sentiment within her relationships in two ways—her organizational participation in high school and her group of close friends:

> There wasn't a lot of non-international Asian guys in high school, because of the makeup of the school. Anyone who was second generation or above was part of the Chinese student organization. Also, there were just a lot more Chinese people. It's a bigger and more developed club than the Japanese club is on campus. They tend to be louder and more gregarious, and I think that appeals to me more to be among loud and gregarious people.

Jennifer looked beyond ethnicity toward a racial community but drew a distinction between international students and second- and later-generation Asian American students. She found greater affinity with US-born Asian Americans. Her preference was, of course, not really about nativity or generational status but about a more "American" set of behaviors—"louder and more gregarious"—she perceived as more similar to herself. These loud and gregarious second-generation Chinese Americans were "Asians like me." The foreign-born, Asian international students were not. Speaking about her friends more generally, Jennifer added:

> My group of friends would be, like, 70 percent Asian. I don't know; that's a made-up number. . . . It was just people who I thought were just like me, and I don't really consider myself Asian or not Asian. I'm just an American citizen.

Again, for Jennifer, commonality was found with her friends across ethnic lines but within the racialized boundary of being Asian. She clearly asserted a deracialized American identity for herself and her friends, similar to what Tsuda (2016) discusses as racialized citizenship. But contemporary racial realities continued to impact Jennifer's friendship choices as she seemed nonetheless drawn to friends of a similar racial background.

The process of seeing similarities between later-generation Japanese American experiences and those of other Asian American ethnics continues to be intimately tied to the shifting demographic diversity of the Asian American population in Southern California. As discussed at this chapter's outset, the sansei in my study, who entered adulthood in the 1970s, experienced the demographic shift firsthand. In contrast to their childhood conceptions that had a distinctly ethnic focus due to the high percentage majority of Japanese Americans within the broader Asian American community—to be Asian was to be Japanese—sansei in their adulthood increasingly saw community in racial terms, reacting to the common racialization with a more diverse set of Asian ethnicities arriving after 1965. In their appreciation of this common racialization, sansei do not seek out relationships with other Asian Americans based on similar phenotype alone. In relating the experiences of building relationships and individuals with whom they felt the greatest commonality, sansei respondents would also make frequent references to "Asians like me." As Angela, a sansei, said in describing her ability to find commonality with other Asian Americans, "I think as far as the other Asians, it kind of depends on how long they've been here and how they have assimilated into the main culture." We also see a similar reference in the words of Mary:

> The American-born ones probably have similar experiences to what I have. Like my good friend is Chinese . . . I mean American Chinese, Chinese American, and she's had the same experience I had when we were younger about being made fun of because you're Asian. But we don't talk about it a lot . . . but we probably have mentioned it once because I think that I remember her saying something like that.

Levels of acculturation, which beget higher levels of comfort for Mary and Angela, also come with assumptions about birthplace and generation. Actual generational status is of limited importance. Such assumptions make these other, non-Japanese Asian Americans seem more similar to sansei and yonsei, particularly due to parallel experiences with racism. It is not just race or ethnicity that construct the "Asian like me" category but how race is similarly experienced within an explicitly US sociohistorical context.

The boundaries around "Asians like me" are also constructed within a particular class context. Barbara and Jason, also sansei, echoed Angela and Mary's remarks in describing "Asians like me" and highlighted how this impacts their relationship and community building within their workplaces.

It is easier for me to communicate with an Asian person—not necessarily Japanese person, but an Asian person. I tend to gravitate that way at work, two of my good friends at work, one is Chinese and one is like Filipino . . . it seems I can talk to them more, you know, understand and it's always been that way from me, at least at work. I gravitate more towards Asians. I feel more comfortable with them.
—Barbara

For example, being in a fraternity-sorority as an Asian American, there's a similar empathetic situation going on where a minority in this group would feel comfortable overall, but we'd feel most comfortable with each other [other Asian Americans]. And there's some things that people just get. We don't have to explain stuff when we're hanging out, while my Jewish friends or Latino friends or African American friends, sometimes I have to explain stuff. They didn't grow up with it. It's just easier not to have to explain stuff, not to have to teach, just to be, you know.
—Jason

The setting of Barbara's and Jason's workplace observations, a corporate office and a college campus, respectively, mark particularly middle-class experiences. These middle-class locations place later-generation Japanese Americans in close proximity and high contact with similarly class-situated Asian Americans of other ethnic backgrounds. Shared class settings certainly bolster the sense of similarity of Japanese Americans with other Asian ethnic groups. The increased levels of interaction among these groups within middle-class spaces also leads to shared racialized experiences with discrimination and the ability to see commonality across ethnic lines. In this way, class status and class-specific settings heavily shape the ethnic community and identity formations of later-generation Japanese Americans. Such community and identity formations with "Asians like me" reflect particular behaviors and practices that shape the cultural practices and behaviors of this minority middle-class community (Neckerman, Carter, and Lee 1999).

While respondents recognized their shared racial status with all Asians, they found a deeper commonality and community among Asian Americans most fluent in a broader American culture. "Asians like me" refers to the recognition of common racialized experience of Asian Americans who grew up or have substantial socialization in the US and are perceived as more "Americanized" or acculturated. To be sure, the definition of "Americanized" was fuzzy at best and generational status is often inferred, not known. For example, Doug and Janet's yonsei son, Matthew, described his Asian American group of friends as "Korean and Chinese, but we all just kind of grew up third or fourth generation. So we are Asian but grew up more Americanized." Given the immigration histories and demographics of the Korean American and Chinese American communities around Matthew's Southern California home, it is likely that his friends are actually first or second generation. However, because he sees them as similar to himself, he assumes they share a similar generational status. Regardless of the veracity of such generational perceptions, what is clear are sansei and yonsei feelings that both experiential and racial similarity remain important in building community within the contemporary ethnic and racial diversity of suburban Southern California. "Asians like me" are Asian Americans who grew up in the same racial milieu of the US and experienced what it meant to be racialized as Asian in the US. Importantly, the racial milieu of the US in the post-1965 era, particularly the diversity of the Asian American segment of the population, is created as a direct result of immigration reform and the large influx of immigrants from various regions and nations of Asia. It is the population growth of similarly racialized immigrants (and their children) from parts of Asia other than Japan that sets the structural foundation for the logics of "Asian like me." Thus, the construction of racial commonality and community is another result of racial replenishment.

The Mutual Effect of Race and Ethnicity

Beyond demonstrating the broader impact of immigration on the ethnicity and community formations of existing resident populations, the racial replenishment of ethnicity also provides insight into the intersectional and interlocking relationship between race and ethnicity. Here, it is important to acknowledge not only the multiple identities held by individuals and communities in terms of race and ethnicity but also the mutual effect these identities have on each other. As demonstrated among ethnic and panethnic identities (Nakano 2013; Okamoto 2014), the meaning and assertion of ethnic and racial identities in everyday interactions are impacted and shaped by one another.

Sansei and yonsei assert their particular ethnicity as a direct result of their racial lumping with other Asian Americans and the racialization as forever foreign. Reacting against the mantle of forever foreigner, Japanese Americans define their ethnic identity through symbols and historic events (e.g., generation, WWII mass incarceration) that demonstrate their long history in the US. Japanese American culture focuses on institutions and practices that bring the community together in ways that significantly diverge from Japanese culture and underscore their fluency in US cultural institutions (e.g., basketball leagues, Christian and Buddhist churches). As the words of sansei and yonsei in the Southern California suburbs make apparent, ascribed racial identifications and racializations affect the persistence and shape of ethnic identity.

Moving in the opposite direction, ethnicity also affects the ways race is operationalized and bounded by later-generation Japanese Americans. While sansei and yonsei readily recognize that they are racialized as similar to other Asian Americans regardless of nativity or generation based on a perceived common phenotype, their own ethnic boundary formations that highlight acculturation and racialized experiences in the US context impact how they perceive their racial community. Sansei and yonsei perceive the Asian Americans they feel closest with to have similar upbringings and experiences of growing up racially Asian in the US. This bounded racial subset of Asian Americans is defined this way because of how Japanese Americans conceptualize their ethnic identity. In effect, perceptions of racial similarities—that is to say perceived common physical characteristics—are limited by the perceptions of ethnic similarities, perceived common history and culture.

While I continue to assert the need to maintain conceptual distinction between race and ethnicity, they are not without their overlap and impact on each other. As seen in the case of later-generation Japanese

Americans, the interlocking relationship between race and ethnicity produces a complex array of affiliations and belonging. For instance, commonality is felt with other racially similar Asian Americans who are perceived to have similar cultural socializations and experiences in a racialized US society, but less social proximity is felt with recently arrived Japanese immigrants—despite their explicit ethnic similarity—because they do not share in the same Japanese American history and lifelong racialized experiences in the US. As distinct social structures and systems of oppression, race and ethnicity must be conceptualized as relational, simultaneous, and linked. The effects of race and ethnicity are mutual. Race shapes ethnicity; ethnicity shapes race—"They are positioned and therefore gain meaning in relation to each other" (Glenn 2002, 13).

Conclusion

The influx of Asian immigration, particularly resulting from the class bias embedded within the immigration reforms beginning in 1965, resulted in two interwoven and seemingly contradictory outcomes for sansei's and yonsei's sense of ethnic and racial identity and community. First, post-1965 waves of immigrants and refugees from Asia—but not Japan—led Japanese Americans, who are racially lumped with Asian newcomers, to feel a heightened need to assert their ethnic distinctiveness, particularly by drawing on their deep US history and levels of acculturation. In this way, the arrival of similarly racially Asian immigrants replenished and reinforced the distinctness of Japanese American ethnic identity and community. Second, the racial lumping with Asian immigrants of other ethnic backgrounds highlights for sansei and yonsei the persistence of a shared racial marginalization as forever foreign regardless of their generation, replenishing and reinforcing an affect of non-belonging. Recognizing shared experiences with the distinct brand of US racism but also maintaining their own sense of acculturation and Americanness, sansei and yonsei construct shared identity and community across Asian ethnic lines with "Asians like me," those perceived to have similar US upbringings and experiences of racial marginalization as Asian Americans.

The recognition of commonality with other Asian Americans is also predicated upon the shared class location of Japanese Americans and other Asian Americans. Taken together, the ethnic identity and community maintenance and construction of community with "Asians like me" are examples of minority middle class cultural practice and the performative effect of the affect of non-belonging—the lack of recognized citizenship. Racial replenishment of Japanese American ethnicity is enabled by the shared middle-class status among many later-generation Japanese Americans and Asian American immigrants, which places them into high levels of interaction with white mainstream society. Importantly, the class mobility of many newly arrived Asian American immigrants is largely the result of the system of preferences put in place by the Immigration and Naturalization Act of 1965, which privileged the entry of high-skilled and highly educated immigrants more likely to readily enter the US middle class (Lee and Zhou 2015). The racial replenishment of ethnicity, then, exemplifies a minority culture of mobility whereby ethnic and cultural practices by middle-class minorities clearly impact and structure their daily lives in meaningful ways (Neckerman, Carter, and Lee 1999).

As I argue throughout this book, the Japanese American case is ideal for tackling some of the open questions on the functions of race, ethnicity, and class in the long processes of integration as an upwardly mobile, later-generation, immigrant-origin community of color. While studies of immigrant integration focus on the dampening of ethnic identity and affiliation, the racial replenishment of ethnicity among sansei and yonsei demonstrates the opposite: the persistence—perhaps, strengthening—of ethnic identity and community. Because the impetus of this ethnic persistence is racially based, the racial replenishment of ethnicity exemplifies the lasting impacts of race in the integration experiences into the later generations. Mainstream perceptions of Japanese American racial difference, manifested in the racialization and lumping with other Asian Americans as forever foreigners, gives rise to feelings of marginalization and a lack of belonging. In this way, the racial replenishment of ethnicity and its structuring of identity and community are a performative effect of the Japanese American racial uniform and citizenship's affect.

6

Have Ethnicity, Will Travel

Over the course of my interviews, several former Deer Park employees shared a story of a sansei coworker who lived in Barstow, California, some 120 miles from Deer Park, best known to most Los Angeles and Orange County residents as a place to stop for gas and the site of the original Del Taco near the halfway point on a Las Vegas road trip. While the story was referenced across a broad range of interviews about Deer Park, it was never told with exactly the same facts. Some said that he worked only on weekends. Some said that he stayed with family or friends while he worked. Others said he made the commute daily. Most had vaguely heard about this guy but didn't know much else about him. I never found out who this man was, nor did I put too much effort into the search. The facts of the story were not what intrigued me. Rather, the repetition and circulation of this story—not its veracity—demonstrate a common recognition among sansei employees of the importance of a place like Deer Park. Whether true or not, this story lived on to be shared in multiple interviews because it was believable and relatable to sansei employees. While not quite as extreme, most of the sansei employees I spoke with had verifiable one-way commutes that averaged between fifteen and twenty miles to Deer Park despite similar work opportunities closer to home. While such distances may not seem terribly far for a Southern California commute, they are considerable when taking into account that Deer Park provided only a minimum-wage, part-time job. But distance was a small obstacle to overcome for the sake of the community and belonging found among fellow sansei at the park. Because of their own experiences and attachments at Deer Park, it was understandable to former employees, even years after the park's closure, that a sansei kid living out in Barstow would travel over two hours to work at such a special place.

The story of the employee traveling from Barstow serves as an allegory for the concerted efforts made to find belonging and the persistent importance of ethnic community in obtaining such belonging. Such observable efforts and importance—performative effects of citizenship's affect—were not unique to sansei who found their way to Deer Park. The importance of ethnic community and its connection to a sense of belonging was also evident among sansei who did not work at Deer Park and yonsei who came of age in the 1990s and 2000s. Sansei and yonsei, who largely lived dispersed in predominantly white neighborhoods in Southern California, continue to wear a racial uniform, a visible marker of difference racialized as not belonging. Unrecognized membership in their local communities would lead sansei and yonsei to seek belonging among co-ethnics at places like Deer Park and anywhere they could be found, with minimal regard to time traveled. This chapter explores the creative community-seeking strategies and practices employed by later-generation Japanese Americans. Along with a willingness to travel significant distances for ethnic community, Japanese Americans across the Southern California suburbs formed ethnic relationships by happenstance in some unexpected places. This search for community is an active and demonstrable process that simultaneously exemplifies a performative effect of the affect of non-belonging and a localized practice of citizenship. As a performative effect shaped by race, class, and geography, the search for community and belonging among suburban sansei and yonsei also reveals a distinctly middle-class form of affective citizenship practice. How sansei and yonsei search for and find ethnic community and achieve a sense of belonging is part of a middle-class minority culture of mobility.

Minority Cultures of Mobility and the Limits of Structural Assimilation

While the allegory of the Barstow employee makes plain the continued importance of ethnic community and concerted effort made by Japanese Americans to find such community, the reason for such importance and effort are an unspoken subtext in the story. This subtext was seamlessly understood by the sansei employees who heard and shared the story: Japanese Americans growing up in predominantly white neighborhoods faced stigmatization and lack of recognized belonging associated with their racial uniform. They had to find the affective dimension of their citizenship elsewhere.

As previously noted, the vast majority of Japanese Americans in the Los Angeles and Orange County suburbs did not live in ethnic neighborhood clusters as they had prior to their World War II incarceration. Following the 1950s white flight migration to the suburbs, upwardly mobile Japanese Americans took advantage of the new residential developments on the urban periphery. Between 1950 and 1960, the Japanese American population in Orange County more than tripled, from 1,186 to 3,890. The population continued to grow rapidly to 10,645 in 1970 and 21,841 in 1980 (*Orange County Almanac*). As immigration from Japan did not significantly increase following the end of the US ban on Japanese immigration in 1952, the vast majority of this growth was a result of domestic migration into the county's new suburban developments.

Despite the growing size of the Japanese American population in Orange County and south Los Angeles County throughout the postwar period, residential clusters of Japanese Americans did not develop. Movement into the suburbs of south Los Angeles and Orange Counties resulted in the dispersal of the Japanese American community. Sansei and yonsei respondents consistently described their neighborhoods as predominantly middle class and white, occasionally with substantial portions of Latine and Asian American neighbors. Save the few who grew up in communities with somewhat larger Japanese American populations, such as Gardena and Torrance, none reported a notable number of Japanese Americans living in their vicinity. In this way, the Japanese American experience seems to follow assimilation theory's prediction of movement to the suburbs and whiter neighborhoods as an outgrowth of their upward socioeconomic mobility (Charles 2007; Massey and Denton 1993).

Beyond residential integration, sansei and yonsei also reported active participation in neighborhood and school activities and clubs fulfilling the criteria of structural assimilation through participation within "cliques, clubs, and institutions of the host society" (Gordon 1964, 71). Structural assimilation, along with its corollary, spatial assimilation, is theorized as "the keystone in the arch of assimilation," the piece that secures everything into place (81). Having seemingly achieved structural assimilation, the sansei and yonsei in this study should reap the full

promise of assimilation: the disappearance of ethnic difference and recognition as indistinguishable members of a society. The full promise of
assimilation should provide both the feeling and recognition of belonging. Here again, we see the limits of assimilation. Despite appearances of
structural assimilation successes, sansei and yonsei did not consistently
report a strong sense of attachment within their local neighborhood and
school-related institutions and activities. Even with such ability to participate in local organizations, sansei and yonsei often affectively spoke
of feeling a part, yet apart. As Jason, a yonsei, noted:

> I didn't feel marginal or on the outside [in my local neighborhood]. I had
> a good time hanging out with the high school folks, the white folks, but
> somehow there was a need also to connect with other Japanese Ameri-
> cans and Asian Americans. . . . Something probably was missing that I
> couldn't name.

That missing but difficult-to-name "something" was the affect of belonging. What Jason sensed was the lack of full recognition of his local
membership in the community where he grew up. It was not directly
spoken, but it was always felt. Jason's desire and effort to connect with
other Japanese Americans is the performative effect of a limited sense
of belongingness and an everyday cultural practice of a middle-class
minority. Racially driven feelings of marginalization did not allow for
the feeling and recognition of Japanese American belonging in their
local, predominantly white communities. Sansei and yonsei, like Jason,
did not note the disappearance of ethnic community bonds with other
Japanese Americans. Participation in local "clubs, cliques, and institutions" did not automatically render a full and mutual recognition of
membership and belonging within such spaces. The simultaneous maintenance of ethnic community connections speaks directly to the need
to rethink how we conceptualize successful assimilation or structural
assimilation as a tipping point for full integration. To be clear, persistent
racialized difference is a root cause of the limits of structural assimilation and persistent ethnic identity and community formation for
Japanese Americans across multiple generations.

Race scholars in sociology, particularly those studying the Black
and Latine middle class, have demonstrated how social distance and

perceived difference between racial groups can persist even in circumstances of residential integration and decreased physical distance (Bratter and Zuberi 2001; Lacy 2007; Pattillo 1999; Vallejo 2012). Looking across multiple racial groups, Bratter and Zuberi (2001) find that increased experience with racial diversity reduces the likelihood of white-minority interracial marriages. In a similar vein, Lacy (2007) demonstrates that middle-class African Americans seek co-ethnic community out of a desire for a safe place away from their daily interactions in predominantly white residential and occupational spaces but also because such communities are pleasurable in themselves. For Lacy and other scholars of the Black middle class, the reduction in physical distance and movement into predominantly white spaces does not negate persistent forms of racism or create full social acceptance and belonging but often augments feelings of racial marginalization and the seeking out of co-ethnic community (Neckerman, Carter, and Lee 1999; Pattillo 1999).

Later-generation Japanese Americans and middle-class Black and Latine people certainly have distinct experiences of race. However, these other middle-class experiences provide a frame to understand the persistent racialized experiences of ostensibly assimilated Japanese Americans. Middle-class movement of Japanese Americans into suburban Southern California placed them increasingly within predominantly white spaces and certainly added to the racial diversity of south Los Angeles and Orange Counties in the postwar period. However, the increased interaction and reduced physical distance did not allow Japanese Americans to eliminate the social distance between them and their white neighbors. The reduction in physical distance and the frequent presence in predominantly white spaces does not negate persistent forms of racism or create full social acceptance and belonging. It often augments feelings of racial marginalization. Residentially integrated sansei and yonsei do not find an affective sense of belonging within their local communities and neighborhoods as assimilation would predict.

In the face of persistent race-based marginalization in the Southern California suburbs, middle-class sansei and yonsei consistently discussed consciously seeking a sense of belonging among other Japanese Americans outside of their proximate neighborhoods. This chapter unfolds the intentional and creative strategies and practices employed by sansei and yonsei in seeking and building communities of belonging. They do so, in large part, by seeking and building community with other Japanese Americans. Even as Japanese Americans participate in semi-local community institutions, they seek out, find each other, and form Japanese American relationships in non-ethnic-specific spaces (e.g., school, athletic organizations, and places of employment). As occurs in concentrated urban areas, local ethnic institutions (e.g., ethnic clubs and religious institutions) continue to bring Japanese Americans together. However, in the suburban context, Japanese Americans must travel greater distances to participate in such institutions. As demonstrated by Deer Park employees and the allegory of the coworker from Barstow, extended travel times were a conscious effort made by later-generation Japanese Americans to find co-ethnics despite the ready access to more local, nonethnic community and institutions. These community-building practices by sansei and yonsei are a consequence of their suburban upbringing and consistent contact with white middle class peers. They exemplify a racialized minority navigation of the middle class in a way that differs from the white racial norm—a middle-class minority culture of mobility.

Southern California as Postsuburb

Making sense of the community formation practices and minority cultures of mobility of sansei and yonsei in Southern California requires a more nuanced understanding of the suburban demographic and geographic context of the region. In the postwar period, this region transitioned from its agricultural roots into a suburban paradise for urban Los Angeles white flight, reaching one million inhabitants in 1963. Today, driving north on the 405 or 5 freeways from the southern tip of Orange County toward Los Angeles, it would be difficult to tell the exact location of the county line separating these two politically distinct entities. The cityscapes of wide streets, low-rise concrete façades framed by trees, and grass-lined sidewalks throughout the Southland are slow transitions, and the traversing of city and county borders often goes unnoticed. Only minimal signage on the side of the highway marks the legal boundary between Los Angeles and Orange Counties. Even longtime residents puzzle over which cities lying along the counties' border—Cerritos, Los Alamitos, Whittier, La Habra—are part of Orange or Los Angeles.

Such visions have made coastal Southern California the model of urban sprawl, or what Kling, Olin, and Poster have described as the "postsuburb" (1991). While traditional suburban developments are characterized as "peripheral bedroom communities from which commuters travel to workplaces in the urban core," postsuburbs have a distinct business, cultural, and residential life distinct and autonomous from nearby urban centers (Kling, Olin, and Poster 1991, 5). In describing the development of Orange County in the postwar period, Kling et al. view Orange County as a traditional suburban appendage of Los Angeles during the 1960s that developed economic and cultural autonomy by the 1980s. Hallmarks of Orange County as a postsuburb came to include "distinct and separate centers: residential neighborhoods, shopping malls, and industrial parks" but also dispersed community institutions such as churches and sports leagues, often separated by drive times of fifteen to thirty minutes (Kling, Olin, and Poster 1991, ix). Postsuburban Orange County residents do not rely on the institutions and centers in urban Los Angeles but travel within their local—albeit dispersed—community to fulfill their economic, cultural, and social needs. Postsuburban decentralization and division of social spaces creates new contexts for the formation of community and fosters new practices and forms of community.

The coincidence of ethnic residential dispersal and the realities and structures of postsuburban development heavily shaped the community formation practices of sansei and yonsei across Los Angeles and Orange Counties. Distance and extended travel times became a naturalized part of participation in Japanese American community institutions. As Hansen and Ryan (1991) rightly observe about postsuburban Orange County more broadly, the greater dispersion and "reduced" social interactions do not eliminate the possibility of public life and community building. Rather, the postsuburban reality urges Orange County residents to consider alternate possibilities of connections and community. For sansei and yonsei in Southern California, the postsuburb is the landscape on which such possibilities become part of mundane everyday experiences.

Japanese American Community Possibilities in the Postsuburb

Sansei and yonsei in the postsuburbs of south Los Angeles County and Orange County explore alternate possibilities of community in a number of ways. First, similar to their urban counterparts, suburban Japanese Americans rely on local ethnic institutions to bring them together (Kurashige 2002; Matsumoto 2014). However, unlike their urban counterparts who lived in the same neighborhoods as their ethnic institutions, my respondents reported traveling rather significant distances to interact with other Japanese Americans within ethnic organizations. Second, Japanese Americans also find each other through non-ethnic-specific means. Whether through mainstream community organizations, school, or places of employment, Japanese Americans gravitated toward each other in response to perceived commonalities in experience and culture. Third and last, I find that Japanese Americans construct for themselves semi-imagined communities. I draw on the work of Benedict Anderson (1991) to demonstrate how my respondents reflected on their past, but no longer maintained, relationships to construct imagined co-ethnic communities, helping them to maintain a sense of connection, community, and belonging.

Distance to Ethnic Institutions in the Postsuburb

Reflecting their postsuburban context, middle-class Japanese Americans in south Los Angeles and Orange Counties have become accustomed to traveling significant distances and utilizing decentralized community institutions to fulfill social necessities rather than rely on their immediate vicinities. These necessities continue to include social connections, often of the ethnic variety. Many Japanese Americans traveled considerable distances across the postsuburb to join other Japanese Americans in ethnic organizations and institutions. Most prominent among respondent recollections were Japanese American religious institutions such as Anaheim Free Methodist Church, Wintersburg Presbyterian Church, and Orange County Buddhist Church, and community organizations such as the Southeast Youth Organization (SEYO) basketball league, local Japanese American Citizens League (JACL) chapters, Suburban

Optimists Club, and Orange Coast Optimists. While ethnic institutions exist within the postsuburban development of Orange and southern Los Angeles Counties, their service areas are much wider than their urban counterparts due to their more geographically dispersed memberships.

Laura, a sansei whose family moved to the suburb of Cerritos during her adolescence in the late 1960s, spoke extensively about her own coming of age exploration of her ethnic identity and community-seeking in 1970s. She related the importance of ethnic institutions and the significant distance she had to travel to find them:

> In Cerritos, there weren't too many Asians living there at that time, back in 1969. Cerritos was pretty much a rural community. So the only Japanese Americans in my junior high were myself, my cousin, and one other girl, that was it. . . . So I found myself really wondering, you know, what am I? And then, when I went into high school . . . I got involved with the JACL in Orange County. It was nice to make that connection because, you know, I was starting to wonder what my identity was. And so that kind of reaffirmed that we do have a Japanese heritage.

In her local neighborhood and school, Laura did not have access to Japanese American community or institutions. She had to wait until high school and then had to travel a significant distance to attend the meetings of the local chapter of the national JACL organization. The absence of population concentrations of Japanese Americans translates to a lower density of ethnic institutions. Ethnic institutions are spread farther apart and are required to serve Japanese Americans who reside throughout a much broader geographic region. The lower institutional density also means longer travel times to participate, such as Laura who traveled over twenty minutes to attend the nearest JACL meeting.

Laura's participation in ethnic institutions has continued throughout her life, allowing her to form relationships and community with other Japanese Americans in college and adulthood. Now a mother, Laura also expressed her eagerness to support her own daughter's community pursuits. Now living in Redondo Beach, Laura shared her participation in various churches, finally settling into a Japanese American church some thirty miles away from her home.

LAURA: The church we go to in Anaheim, Anaheim Free Methodist,
is primarily Asian. Most of our friends there are Asian. We went to
church [near our home]. Mostly those friends are a mix, Mexicans,
and I'm still very close to those friends.[1]

INTERVIEWER: And what made you interested in traveling to a church
all the way in Anaheim?

LAURA: My daughter made some friends there. She went to a church
camp; it was predominantly Asian, and she met some friends from
Anaheim. She visited the church and we just kept visiting that
church. So we ended up going there primarily, and it's because I
think she felt a part of the community more. I think, growing up
around here, she didn't think of herself as really being Asian as part
of her identity so much, except for family things. And then she
started to build that part of her identity. The next generation, they
seek to discover, and then to further that goal of identity. They still
want to feel close and feel comfortable [with Japanese Americans
rather] than with those that have some other background.

Laura's Redondo Beach neighborhood is ethnically and racially diverse,
a nod to Japanese American residential integration. However, Laura
and her daughter choose to travel the extensive distance to church
because it enables community building with Japanese and other Asian
Americans. Laura's desire to support her daughter's pursuit of ethnic
community was common among sansei parents, who often wanted their
yonsei children to enjoy the same community support they experienced
in their childhood. Laura has been willing to commute such distances
so her daughter and the rest of her family could join ethnic institutions
membered by Japanese Americans and other Asian Americans and feel
a sense of community and affect of belonging—"to feel close and
feel comfortable." The distance traveled is the performative effect of the
desire for community and belonging. Ethnic community has a continued importance for Laura's own sense of identity as well as for the sense
of identity and community for her yonsei daughter, despite other markers of assimilation.

Religious ethnic institutions serve as a common destination in
the seeking and building of community among many other yonsei

respondents as well. Jonathan, a yonsei, and his family traveled the same distance as Laura and her daughter to attend the only Japanese American Buddhist church in Orange County. He stated, "My parents commuted to Anaheim from Lake Forest, which is about thirty miles, every Friday, Saturday, and Sunday, to participate in activities with Orange County Buddhist Church." Crystal, a multiracial yonsei who grew up in La Habra, also highlighted her childhood church as a site for building Japanese American community. However, this was not her local neighborhood church. Rather, her family traveled over fifteen miles and over half an hour at least once per week to attend Christian church services with a Japanese American congregation:

> I went to church in Montebello, and our church was a historic Japanese American church. And I also played basketball, so those were my two Japanese American outlets, although, granted, I didn't appreciate that or think about it.

Similar to Laura and Jonathan, Crystal's family's commitment to attend this particular church extended beyond religion. The willingness to travel such distances is intimately attached to a desire for ethnic community housed within the religious institution. The ethnic and religious aspects of the community were physically and conceptually inseparable for its members.

Japanese American religious institutions were often pathways for involvement in other common community activities, such as the Boy and Girl Scouts and sports leagues. Amber, a yonsei from Long Beach, grew up playing basketball and attending Girl Scouts at the Orange County Buddhist Church, some twenty-five miles away. Without her realizing it, Amber's parents made this commute as part of a concerted effort to connect her with ethnic community:

> I never noticed that they [my parents] tried to when I was younger. I mean, I didn't realize it, but I was involved with the Japanese community just being involved in that Japanese league, the basketball league. That church was all Japanese. My Girl Scout troop was all Japanese. I thought that all Girl Scout troops did this. They say Namu Amida

Butsu [a Buddhist chant meaning "I follow Amida Buddha"]. I thought that was, like, a standard thing for Girl Scout troops.

For Amber, participation in these ethnic community activities was normalized in her life to the point where she did not realize she was participating in any ethnic specific community. For her, these were simply mundane after-school and weekend activities. She thought they were the same for everyone else regardless of ethnic and racial background. Japanese American community and ethnicity were a naturalized and seamless part of Amber's upbringing. This is a far cry from a twilight of ethnicity or the full assimilation allegedly achieved by later-generation Japanese Americans. For Amber and other yonsei, their spatial assimilation, represented by their residence in suburban Southern California outside of ethnic concentrations, did not lessen the presence of ethnic identity and community in their daily lives. Residential integration does not necessitate an end for the importance of ethnic identity and community.

Amber, and Crystal earlier, alluded to another major Japanese American community institution activity often attached to church affiliation—youth basketball. Japanese American basketball leagues have long been a site for community maintenance, with many stretching back to the years following World War II and the closure of the incarceration camps (Chin 2016a, 2016b; King 2002). Yonsei Henry played in a Japanese American basketball league throughout his childhood:

I grew up playing SEYO basketball. I still have friends from there when I was a teenager. . . . If you're a yonsei, you play basketball. If you grew up in Orange County, that's pretty much it.

Similar to Amber's naturalizing of her Japanese American Girl Scout troop, Henry comments on the ubiquity of basketball in the yonsei experience and goes so far as to equate playing basketball with being Japanese American. This is a sentiment shared by many of my yonsei respondents. For Henry, the decision to play in the Japanese American basketball league was not due to the lack of recreational leagues available to him closer to home. Rather, he continued to play with, and later coach, his Japanese American team out of the deep sense of community that developed, a community lacking in more local leagues. Similar to participation in various churches, Amber's, Crystal's, and Henry's basketball participation required considerable travel time within the Orange County postsuburbs. To attend games, practices, and tournaments, all their travel times ranged from fifteen to forty-five minutes, well outside the immediate neighborhoods they grew up in.

Even outside the context of Christian and Buddhist churches, sports were a common community-building mechanism among Japanese Americans. Another common ethnic sports league among sansei and yonsei in postsuburban Southern California—bowling—served as a key location for meeting other Japanese Americans. Natalie, a yonsei, shared:

> Somebody asked us, "Do you bowl? We're in the Japanese league, do you wanna bowl?" And I was like, "Okay. You know, sure, I'll try it." But then I got there like I think the first night. I already felt like I belonged there. It just seemed like I knew many people. It just felt comfortable.

While Natalie had minimal interest in bowling, she decided to join the league for the ethnic camaraderie and community. Natalie may have stumbled on the Japanese American bowling league, but once there, she felt an immediate sense of comfort and belonging.

The importance of ethnic institutions, as demonstrated by continued participation and travel effort required, was noted throughout my interviews and across sansei and yonsei who grew up in the Orange County suburbs from the late 1950s through the 2000s. While these longstanding institutions have certainly undergone internal changes across this time period, their remarkable longevity speaks to the continued interest and need for such organizations by dispersed suburban Japanese Americans. The long-term existence and continued participation by sansei and yonsei in ethnic-specific organizations with the intended purpose of cultivating ethnic community and identity further reinforces the shortcomings of their structural assimilation. Furthermore, the persistence of ethnic community and institutions also does not align with segmented assimilation's selective acculturation, given that bowling, basketball, and

Girl Scouts are not strategic holdover Japanese cultural practices. They are uniquely Japanese American. Other scholars have noted that some processes of assimilation may be delayed for some ethnic and racial minority groups but will occur eventually (Bean and Stevens 2003; Brown 2007). While this statement may be utilized to allay fears of the unassimilable minority, it remains important to recognize the structural and institutional factors that led such delays to occur along racial lines. As racial disparities are examined across multiple generations, it is equally important to question the notion of "delay" and the a priori assumption of assimilation as an end goal. Sansei and yonsei in this study make a strong case for the potential persistent and perpetual value of ethnic community, fundamentally challenging the assimilationist imperative of ethnic attenuation.

Traveling to the Urban Ethnic Enclave

While reliance on postsuburban ethnic institutions is prevalent among sansei and yonsei, respondents also noted the ethnically concentrated businesses and residential communities farther north in Los Angeles County, such as Gardena, the Crenshaw district, and Little Tokyo, as sites of ethnic connection. While these communities were too far to serve as consistent sites of ethnic community interaction, many postsuburban sansei and yonsei continued to utilize urban enclave spaces like Little Tokyo as sites for identity and community development despite the long commute times. In this way, the urban center continues to play a role in ethnic identity and community formation for postsuburban residents. Jason, a sansei in the yonsei age cohort, felt a persistent need to "connect with other Japanese Americans and Asian Americans" while growing up in Orange County. To make these connections, Jason "went up to Gardena and Torrance or the beach at Twenty-Second Street," communities and hang-out spots closer to the Los Angeles urban center where Japanese American youth were known to congregate.

Crystal, the mixed-race yonsei who grew up in La Habra and played basketball with her Japanese American church in Montebello, did not feel that she really developed an ethnic consciousness until she began to work in Little Tokyo during college, despite her heavy involvement with Japanese American institutions as a child:

Well, through basketball, but it wasn't about identity, even though it really should be. I think the leagues should work on that. It was just about basketball and snacks after basketball and playing in tournaments. You don't really discuss identity. . . . I didn't start doing Japanese American stuff until I did the Nikkei Community Internship Program [in Little Tokyo, Downtown Los Angeles].

Crystal's childhood participation in numerous Japanese American institutions put her in direct contact with many co-ethnics. However, she did not perceive the experience as directly building her ethnic identity and consciousness. She did not feel that such consciousness developed until much later in her life. Crystal's words, echoing Amber's earlier discussion of Girl Scout meetings at the Orange County Buddhist Church, demonstrate the mundanity of ethnic associations among yonsei. The concerted effort of sansei parents to connect their residentially integrated yonsei children to ethnic community was not always interpreted by yonsei as such. Such activities were naturalized as part of everyday life. While the basketball league may have been seen as little more than sports and post-game snacks to a young Crystal, the league is nonetheless part of a rich local Japanese American history and fostered the continuation of ethnic community for contemporary Japanese Americans. For Crystal, a stronger meaning and attachment to her Japanese American identity and the explicit building of ethnic community came during college, when she explored historic Little Tokyo as an intern. Ultimately, Crystal's college experience marked the beginning of her career working in Little Tokyo institutions and developing Japanese American youth programs throughout Southern California.

Community by Happenstance: Nonethnic Paths to Ethnic Community among Yonsei

While the majority of my respondents participated in Japanese American organizations or institutions in some fashion as a way to connect with co-ethnics, these spaces were by no means the only sites for ethnic community building. Alongside participation in Japanese American organizations and institutions, many yonsei were simultaneously active in mainstream, or predominantly white, organizations both within their communities and through school. However, even within these predominantly white spaces, Japanese Americans found each other. Yonsei, in particular, noted that they gravitated to the other Japanese Americans they came in contact with through happenstance. Similar to the targeted travel to ethnic institutions, these sporadic meetings with other Japanese Americans were important because of the sense of comfort and refuge from racial microaggressions they provided. Yonsei sisters Natalie and Elizabeth stated, "I think that that's kind of the theme for us, that everything kind of just happens by chance. We don't—we're never out seeking like to be part of the community." As an example of this, Elizabeth shared a story of how she was recruited to be part of a Japanese American basketball team at a birthday party for a non-Japanese American friend from school:

> I was at a birthday party, and the coach's daughter happened to be at this birthday party. I didn't know her at all. She said, "Are you Japanese?" So, I said "Yes." And so, yeah. I talked to my mom at the end of the birthday party, and I started playing basketball.

Kristina, a multiracial yonsei, also highlights this trend of happenstance:

> I played soccer in junior college, and this is where I met Tracy [another Japanese American] and played soccer with her, and I'd say we kind of hit it off right away. So just like okay you play soccer and we're like, two or three Asian girls on the team so, you know, you tend to bond right away. So she was probably one of the first Japanese American people that I stayed in touch with for most of my life, for a good amount of years. Almost eight years later, you know, she's one of the longer friends that I've had.

Ethnic background coupled with the shared interest in soccer provided Kristina and Tracy an additional layer of commonality that led to a lasting relationship originating through a nonethnic connection, a college soccer team. Kristina could relate to Tracy through their common interest in soccer and as teammates but was able to create a stronger and more lasting relationship with Tracy in comparison to other, non-Japanese American women on the team. Kristina's reflection on her friendship with Tracy demonstrates that even within participation in mainstream organizations and cliques, a hallmark of structural assimilation, race and ethnicity continues to matter for Japanese Americans.

Carrie, who also played soccer at the collegiate level, discussed whether the racial and ethnic background of her teammates impacted the type of bond she was able to build with them:

> We played soccer, so we're friends. But I think it's easier to make friends when they're the same race as you, just because there's not a lot of Japanese people, so you tend to be like, "Oh, there's another Japanese person!" You don't meet that many. Everybody's Chinese. It's like, "Oh, it's just another Chinese person." Here it's like, "Oh, it's another Japanese person," so you're actually like—and it's kind of racist or whatever you want to say, I was Lauren's [another Japanese American player] host when she came on her training trip, probably because I was Asian, they put the two Asian people together.

The obvious bond between teammates transcended race for Carrie. However, she also noted that finding other Japanese American players enabled stronger and more enduring friendships, in part because it was so rare to come across other Japanese Americans. Carrie's experience also demonstrates the ways in which the importance of ethnic bonds is also ascribed by outsiders. The coaching staff of Carrie's team housed a Japanese American recruit with her. While such placement may have been unintentional, Carrie interpreted the move as somewhat racially motivated, lumping the Asian Americans on the team together. Such an imposition highlights the ways in which Japanese Americans cannot simply fade into the American melting pot. Japanese Americans, regardless of generation, continued to be racially marked as other, far from completing the assimilation process of social whitening (Gans 2005).

While Carrie's collegiate friendships were diverse, it was also apparent that some of her relationships took on a heightened relevance due to ethnic similarities. Carrie did not participate in any Japanese American or Asian American student clubs during her college years. Nonetheless, she has a conspicuously high representation of Japanese Americans among the lasting friendships she made on campus. She did not gravitate to other Japanese American athletes simply because of practices of racial lumping by coaches. Reflecting on her interracial interactions and friendships, Carrie stated:

> I don't know that I would be in contact with anybody else that wasn't white. Jon's white, but also half Asian [Japanese]. Other than that, Dave, he's half Japanese, too. I think that's it. There's not that many Asian people in sports, so that's also a problem.

As Carrie spoke about these friendships, she did not state that such relationships were based on shared ethnic background. They were formed more through happenstance, but they also demonstrate a larger pattern of an underlying ethnic affinity. The fact that the Japanese American and Asian American student athletes found each other is especially noteworthy given their relatively small number, as noted by both Carrie and Kristina.

Because postsuburban and residentially integrated lives place considerable physical distance between co-ethnics, yonsei must often rely on happenstance and non-ethnic-specific means to find other Japanese Americans. Again and again, yonsei in this study commented on the excitement and sense of immediate connection felt with other Japanese Americans they would meet through school, local organizations, and sports teams. Such reaction to the rare find of other Japanese Americans does not point to a reduced salience of ethnicity for Japanese Americans but rather to something that is constantly being sought out even in the most unlikely of places.

Sansei at Japanese Village and Deer Park: From Happenstance to Ethnic Institution

Similar connections based on common ethnicity and interests were also built by sansei in nonethnic spaces a generation earlier. Here, I return focus to Japanese Village and Deer Park as a common place of employment for most of my sansei respondents. As previously demonstrated, Deer Park was a workplace destination and meeting place for many Southern California sansei in their high school and college years and in this way exemplifies the postsuburban distances traveled by Japanese

Americans in search of belonging through ethnic community. However, it is important to remember that despite its name and cultural theme, Japanese Village and Deer Park was not an ethnic institution in the same vein as Japanese American Christian and Buddhist churches or sports leagues. Rather, Deer Park was a capitalist venture owned and operated first by a white entrepreneur and later by the Six Flags theme parks. The primary goal of Deer Park was financial, with a business strategy that leveraged the culture of "ancient Japan." Deer Park, as an amusement park, had no intention to build community or foster ethnic identity among local sansei. Nonetheless, to maintain the park's façade, management hired hundreds of sansei youth from the communities surrounding the park's home in Buena Park in Orange County.

Certainly, the Japanese theme of the park drew sansei to the employment opportunity. As Jill shared, "I felt like there was some culture there [at Deer Park] that I would gain, just because it was, you know, Japanese." Many sansei employees, echoing this sentiment of Jill's, shared that their original attraction to working at Deer Park was at least in part to recapture some cultural knowledge they felt was not passed down by their US-born nisei parents, most of whom experienced wartime incarceration at the hands of their own government based solely on their racial and ethnic difference during the Second World War. The distance many sansei felt from Japanese culture was reinforced by their relative isolation from other Japanese Americans, a result of their assimilative residential integration and the postsuburban landscape. However, despite the connection to Japanese culture it may have provided, Deer Park's nonethnic origins mark it as a site of ethnic community by happenstance.

As discussed more fully in chapter 4, employees ultimately found much more than culture at Deer Park. The irony of Deer Park management's decision to use local Japanese American youth to augment the park's foreign façade ultimately laid the groundwork for the growth and maintenance of an explicitly American ethnic community. Despite the ambivalent intentions of management and lack of formal connection to the local Japanese American community, Deer Park became an ethnic institution, and over time, sansei youth became drawn to the employment opportunity because, as Angela stated, "there were just a lot of Japanese kids that worked there." The Japanese American community that grew at the park became self-sustaining. A former general manager recalled that the park never had a problem recruiting new workers. Someone always had a sibling or cousin who wanted the job. Judy was one of those employees who came to work at Deer Park through a sibling connection, her sister. Judy was drawn to Deer Park because of her Japanese American friends and family who already worked there but also for the opportunity to meet new Japanese Americans:

> It was comforting to know that I had friends already there. My sister was already there, and there were people I knew. But it was exciting because I made new friends immediately, and it was kind of weird to me that there are [Japanese American] high school kids that weren't related [to me] or someone you didn't know from church or anywhere else.

Such community and lasting relationships among fellow sansei were largely absent for Deer Park employees outside of the park. Darren, a former Deer Park employee, similarly spoke of Deer Park as an important site for ethnic community and relationship formation.

> [Before Deer Park,] I had never been around as many Japanese people in my life that I didn't personally know from family. And so yeah, that was—it was great. I mean, I made some very good friendships there.

What former employees found at Deer Park among their fellow sansei coworkers was much more than connection to an ancestral culture. Deer Park became a known source of ethnic community and an ethnic institution not because of its mission or origins but because of the people it brought together. The seeking of ethnic community and the realization of the importance of ethnic community by sansei working at Deer Park, regardless of initial motivations, is, again, a performative effect of the persistent marginalization Japanese Americans felt in other spaces and contexts in their residentially integrated lives.

Names in the Ether: Constructing (Semi-)Imagined Ethnic Community

The suburban-turned-postsuburban reality of the postwar Japanese American population in Southern California made community and ethnic institutions more difficult to form but no less important. The obstacles associated with residential integration and distance created the need to explore alternative possibilities and pathways to find a sense of belonging. Alongside traveling longer distances to participate in ethnic institutions and finding co-ethnics through nonethnic means, I found another peculiar phenomenon of community maintenance, particularly among sansei, within a dispersed suburbia. Ethnic community remained salient in the minds of former Deer Park employees beyond their maintained relationships and in the absence of physical, face-to-face interaction. The evidence of this salience was an unanticipated finding that frequently arose after the formal interviews about long-term friendships, community organizations, and romantic relationships had ended. Outside the standard set of interview questions, I always asked respondents, as part of my snowball sampling process, if they knew of other former employees who might also be interested in participating in the study. Almost without fail, this question would set off a litany of names of former employees, which department they worked in, whom they dated, or whom they married. However, when probed further about an email address, a phone number, or even a mailing address, respondents were unable to provide such information for the vast majority of names.

To be sure, nearly all former employees interviewed continue to maintain at least one close friendship with a former Deer Park co-worker. However, they had not maintained contact or sustained relationships with as many individuals as they were able to name as part of their extended Deer Park community. As the post-interview discussion progressed, it became apparent that my respondents continued to feel a close connection with these individuals with whom they had clearly lost touch. In their descriptions of these individuals, they clearly conceived of the life course for the individuals attached to these ethereal names as being similar to their own. They were imagining for themselves the continuation of a once real community, what might be considered a semi-imagined community. Here, I borrow the concept of imagined community from Benedict Anderson (1991), who argues that the nation is an imagined community as "the members of even the smallest nation will never know most of their fellow-members, meet them, or even hear of them, yet in the minds of each lives the image of their communion"

(6). Despite the lack of face-to-face contact, a community is constructed in the minds of individuals and conceived of as a "deep, horizontal comradeship" regardless of the actual differences that may exist in the realities of perceived community members.

Unlike the complete lack of ability to have face-to-face interaction among the vast majority of a national population within Anderson's imagined community, the community built by former Deer Park employees is not completely imagined. These communities are constructed in minds of former Deer Park employees on the basis of assumptions built on actual relationships and face-to-face interactions that existed in the past. Members of the community met at one point but are no longer in contact. The current imaginings of the community are based on the tangible commonalities observed during past periods of proximity. Additionally, the semi-imagined community among sansei continues to have some basis in reality, as some relationships have continued to be maintained through close friendships and marriages, which serve as reference points for extrapolation. Similarly, respondents often noted that they occasionally run into other former Deer Park employees in random locations such as the mall, grocery store, or their children's sporting events, where they are able to briefly catch up on each other's lives. Through various networks, they also hear about the lives of other former employees through mutual friends and relatives. As such, this semi-imagined community is not purely imagined; it has some basis in reality, both in the past and the present.

The semi-imagined community constructed by former Deer Park employees was remarkably consistent among respondents and simultaneously demonstrates the importance of Deer Park in their lives as well as the unexpected practices of community formation shaped by their residential integration in the Southern California postsuburbs. The name references made independently by respondents demonstrate how ethnic community continues to play a role in how sansei make sense of their identity and feelings of belonging in their everyday lives. As Cynthia, a former Deer Park employee stated, "The best friends I have are the friends I made at Deer Park. Even though we may not see each other very often . . . I still feel a really strong connection to everybody." Similar to the role played by the Deer Park community in their youth, there is a continued need and desire for such a community of belonging. One mechanism for obtaining, or maintaining, this community of belonging is the extrapolation from memories of past communities. The sense of local belonging felt within the context of Deer Park is maintained by imagining the continuation of this workplace community. As their lives had been so similar in their youths, respondents continued to think of other former employees as having similar ethnic, racial, generational, and postsuburban experiences throughout the rest of their lives. The semi-imagined community allows sansei to draw on their past experiences within the community of belonging found at Deer Park and to recognize their current experiences not as aberrations but as part of a racialized local and uniquely American set of lived experiences. This semi-imagined community helps to extend their sense of belonging into the present day.

Conclusion

Despite Japanese American residential integration and achievement of spatial assimilation in the postsuburb, ethnic identity and community maintain a sense of ubiquity and mundanity among sansei and yonsei in Southern California. While ethnicity is normalized, there remains an intentionality in community formation practices as sansei and yonsei travel to ethnic institutions in the postsuburb and urban ethnic enclaves and seek out other Japanese Americans in unanticipated, often nonethnic, ways. This ethnic normativity and concerted effort are a far cry from the symbolic and optional ethnicity that should be inhabited by later-generation ethnic Americans according to sociological standards (Alba 1985; Gans 2005). Within their integrated neighborhoods, Japanese Americans continue to feel an incomplete sense of belonging to their local community as they experience persistent racial othering and fall short of the promise of structural assimilation. This sense of nonbelonging, a racialized affect of citizenship, manifests itself as unique everyday community formation practices of postsuburban Japanese Americans, a performative effect of non-belonging and a minority culture of mobility.

I would like to highlight that minority cultures of mobility should not be seen simply as an extension of assimilation theory but offers an alternative way to understand how race and consequential ethnicity persists in the everyday experiences of upwardly mobile minorities (Lacy 2007; Neckerman, Carter, and Lee 1999; Pattillo 1999; Vallejo 2012). The Japanese American culture of mobility is evident in the community formation practices, which have Japanese Americans traveling significant, often inconvenient, distances to ethnic institutions or seeking out other Japanese Americans in nonethnic spaces and organizations. Ethnic and cultural practices by middle-class minorities clearly impact and structure their daily lives in meaningful ways. Residential integration does not signal the "twilight of ethnicity" for later-generation Japanese Americans, as they continue to make concerted efforts to maintain ethnic community outside of their immediate neighborhoods (Alba 1985). Japanese American community formations represent an ethnic practice and minority culture of mobility that moves beyond the symbolic for the later generations.

The community-seeking and community-building practices of later-generation Japanese Americans requires a reconsideration of how we understand the persistent impact of race on processes of integration and how we conceptualize the end points of assimilation. Rather than envision the replacement of one identity and community with another, Japanese Americans can and do hold multiple community memberships. Their formation of ethnic-specific community spaces does not diminish the fact that Japanese Americans are often active participants in other, non-ethnic-specific communities. Nonetheless, ethnic community continues to be one of these multiple communities of membership for later-generation Japanese Americans, one that has a significant impact on their lives. Connections with other later-generation Japanese Americans allow respondents to understand their personal racialized experiences with marginalization as part of a broader pattern of systemic racism rather than aberrations within a postracial, colorblind nation. In this way, ethnic community and relationships are cultural practices that pave the way for an increased sense of belonging to both broader local and national communities.

7

Ethnic History as American History

The Japanese theme of Deer Park was intentional and curated. As a tourist attraction, Deer Park drew from and helped construct the broader national popular culture's image of Japan. For all its claims of authenticity, Deer Park ultimately provided a version of Japan that selectively included and altered aspects of Japanese culture and history to present a more palatable and marketable image. Regardless of intention, Deer Park's constructed version of Japan coincided with and complemented the broader national Cold War project of reenvisioning Japan as a docile and peaceful ally. As management staffed the park with Japanese Americans, regardless of their generation, place of birth, or familiarity with Japan and Japanese culture, they reinforced the Japanese American racial uniform and its inextricable link with foreignness. While Deer Park was just a small amusement park in the emerging suburbs of Southern California, it cannot be separated from the shifting conceptions of Japan in the national imaginary that it readily consumed, repackaged, and perpetuated.

When I first tell people about Deer Park in academic circles or everyday conversations, they are often shocked that such a place could ever have existed. As an amusement park that hired the vast majority of its staff solely on the basis of race, Deer Park required staff to dress up in ways that highlighted their foreignness and at times caricatured Japanese people and culture (recall the Fuji Folk). Deer Park does seem unthinkable in the context of our present-day racial sensibilities and equal employment opportunity statutes. But Deer Park did exist, and what's more, it is recalled with great fondness and importance by sansei employees to this very day.

From our present-day vantage point, it might be easy to understand the affection of former Deer Park employees as a simple example of internalized racism—Japanese Americans happily acting out the orientalist fantasies for the sake of white middle-class tolerance. But I argue that this would be a shortsighted view. Notwithstanding any probable and inevitable presence of internalized racism, we must also understand the historical context of the 1960s and the postwar US environment, when and where these sansei lived their lives and encountered Deer Park. As discussed previously, Deer Park provides a window into the contemporary local and domestic politics of the Cold War, which included the recuperation of Japan's image from hated wartime enemy into that of a valued ally and friend (Kim 2010; Shibusawa 2006; Simpson 2002). Given their forever-foreigner status, Japanese American racialization was—and is—tied to local and national perceptions of Japan. The recuperation of Japan's image did not occur overnight, and sansei, who grew up in the 1950s and 1960s, continued to be reminded of wartime racism and national marginalization in their everyday lives and through messaging in political and popular culture.

In one recollection, Diane recalled a teenage outing to the movies with her friends, all sansei, to see the latest 1970 release *Tora! Tora! Tora!*, a World War II drama depicting the Japanese attack on Pearl Harbor. When the Pearl Harbor attack came onscreen, the predominantly white audience erupted with anti-Japan cries and racial slurs. Cheers erupted at every depiction of a Japanese bomber being shot down. Diane and her friends felt immediately conspicuous and even feared for their safety because of their racial uniform. Everyone in the theater was responding to cinematic imagery that drew on a stubbornly embedded understanding of Japan and Japanese people as the other—as the enemy—that was very much alive and visceral a quarter of a century after the end of the Second World War. This understanding made little allowance for a distinction between Japanese and Japanese American. While the fear felt by Diane and her friends was animated by their immediate surroundings and the reactions of other patrons in the movie theater, the imagery of Japan as enemy and Japanese Americans as representatives of this foreign power was not particular to the local setting and culture of suburban Southern California. Rather, it reflected a broader positioning of Japanese Americans as marginal or outside the boundaries of the imagined nation, a lack of a national sense of belonging.

It is these types of racist experiences and the accompanying understanding of their marginal and reviled position vis-à-vis the imagined national community that sansei employees brought with them to Deer

Park. Feelings of marginalization and lack of belonging within a national context served only to exacerbate the absence of local belonging sansei felt in their local neighborhoods and schools. So it is less surprising that sansei youth would so readily embrace Deer Park. For most employees, Deer Park was the first time that Japan and being Japanese were associated with something positive in a public setting. It became a means to share the positive aspects of Japan and redeem Japanese American ethnicity in the eyes of a broader national public. Former employees Debbie and Steve iterated this point:

> [Deer Park] was wonderful. It brought the cultural experience to other people, the general public. . . . To me, it just showed all the positive things about the Japanese [American] community.
> —Debbie

> Well, sometimes it made me feel good, Deer Park. I guess because at that time a lot of people had a good image of being Japanese, during the '70s. . . . The identity was no longer tarnished, but it was actually a shiny identity. Deer Park was all during that transition. The '60s seems like a transition time. It actually was a good identity to be a part of.
> —Steve

Working at Deer Park was seen as an opportunity to change park guests' opinion about Japan and by extension change the national culture. Sansei, like Debbie and Steve, readily understood the tie between Japan and the perception of Japanese Americans by a local and national audience. This assumed role of cultural ambassador at Deer Park reflects what anthropologist Takeyuki Tsuda (2016) has termed *racialized multiculturalism*. Racialized multiculturalism reflects how growing acceptance of cultural diversity in the US creates an expectation of cultural difference for racial minorities vis-à-vis the white mainstream. The sense of purpose found at Deer Park, rooted in the sansei affect of non-belonging and marginalization, was not "a voluntary and freely exercised right" (Tsuda 2016, 26) but rather "a provoked interest in either maintaining or recovering their ancestral culture" (27). Certainly, sansei complicity in Deer Park's valorization of Japan and Japanese culture did little to dismantle Japanese Americans' racialization as perpetual foreigners. Nonetheless, Deer Park was seen by former employees as a first step toward claiming a "good identity" and improve their subordinate racial position.

Thinking about Deer Park as part of a broader project of repositioning Japan in the US national imagination and how such positioning impacted Japanese Americans reveals an affective negotiation of belonging and citizenship that extends beyond the local level. In contrast to the local manifestations of citizenship as recognized membership and belonging thus far examined in this book, former employee reflections on the Japanese imagery of Deer Park were not limited or solely informed by micro-level recognitions of membership. They required an understanding of the position of Japanese Americans at the margins—or perhaps outside—of a national community. While sansei were able to achieve a form of belonging on their own terms through co-ethnic relationships and community found at Deer Park, this local belonging did not automatically translate into a sense of belonging at the national level. Conscious of this lack of recognition of their belonging as part of the nation, sansei employees and the broader Japanese American community turned to Deer Park with a sense of pride, building an affective attachment not only to each other but to one of the few positive depictions of Japaneseness in US popular culture. In this attachment, Japanese Americans accept, perhaps reluctantly, their forever-foreigner linkage to all things Japanese.[1] This acceptance reflects an understanding that an American identity tightly associated with white racial status was beyond their reach and uncontestable. Sansei employees, in choosing to see the bright side of Deer Park, chose an ethnic path to identity recuperation that did not afford a full recognition of a national belonging but moved them toward the consolation of a more positive self-image.

While a positive self-image via the persistent linkage with foreignness seemed sufficient for Deer Park sansei growing up in the immediate postwar period, it was not sustainable over time or for subsequent generations of Japanese Americans. In the context of growing community activism to recover family narratives and oral histories around World War II incarceration and the military valor of the segregated 442nd Regiment and 100th Battalion coinciding with the birth of ethnic studies in academia, Japanese Americans in the closing decades of the twentieth century were able to draw from a broader catalog of US ethnic history and positive reflections on Japanese Americans—not Japan—to find not only a positive self-image but an entitled claim on membership and belonging in the US.

This chapter explores claims on national belonging by sansei and yonsei as they are rooted in ethnic history as evidence of Japanese American participation in broader US history. Such claims are a call for a more inclusive telling of US history, which in turn challenges the narrow racial definition of US citizenship (Tsuda 2016). At its most basic, I observe that Japanese Americans' claims on citizenship rest on the long history and presence of Japanese Americans in the United States. Some claims directly reference this multigenerational presence in the abstract, but more commonly, this history is the foundation of two more specific claims that can be seen as inevitable corollaries to this long history and physical presence: the important role played by Japanese Americans in key US historical events and high levels of acculturation in comparison to other, more recently arrived immigrant-origin communities. Steve, the sansei employee referenced earlier taking pride in his participation at Deer Park, succinctly demonstrated the substantive claims on belonging and membership to the US nation beyond a positive self-image:

> I think the Japanese, basically, are more established as they have been here longer, if you compare with the Vietnamese, or whatever else, who have been here a while. Japanese Americans suffered through the camps or whatever aspect in the 1940s, and they're basically more established, where the Vietnamese are basically still, even though if it's from the 1970s, are still struggling.

Steve points to the World War II mass incarceration of Japanese Americans, through the euphemistic reference to "the camps," as evidence of Japanese American presence and entanglement within a broader US history. Steve's reference to the established status of Japanese Americans mirrors sociological notions of structural assimilation and acculturation. Such establishment is a distinct claim on national belonging that sets them apart from other more recently arrived and less established Asian American and immigrant communities. The firm grounding of the Japanese American community is seen as a consequence of the long history of Japanese Americans in the US.

In rightfully situating Japanese American ethnic history as US history, sansei and yonsei are making claims for recognition of their long-standing belonging within the boundaries of national membership. While this is distinct from the pursuit of a positive self-image by sansei through the representations of the foreign at Deer Park, there remains an important and informative parallel. Neither is an attempt to claim whiteness. Rather, the narratives leveraged by sansei and yonsei as they spoke about and around their sense of national belonging chose claims that are explicitly ethnic, reflecting a reactive ethnicity responding to a consciousness of the Japanese American racial uniform. Whereas sansei at Deer Park seemingly saw the recognition of their Americanness and membership as part of the nation as impossible because of their racial difference, these same sansei, as demonstrated by Steve, and the next-generation yonsei came to see the necessity and possibility for an expanded definition, not of whiteness but of the bounded category of the US nation and what it means to be "American." In a notable shift in just a couple of decades, Japanese Americans writ large no longer passively accepted their exclusion from the national body and no longer questioned their own belonging to the US citizenry and nation-state on the basis of their racial uniform. Yonsei Ashley exemplified this point in her upbringing:

> We were raised to be American. My mom made it a very strong point
> that we were American first and then Japanese American, to be specific.
> So we were not any less American than anyone else.

A racial and ethnic minority can also be American. In fact, being Japanese American is the means through which sansei and yonsei claim full-fledged Americanness. Claiming a Japanese American specificity does not detract from their inherent Americanness. This is a direct challenge to the racist and racialized linkage between being American and being white and pursuing a fuller actualization of the name Japanese *American*.

Belonging through Presence and Entanglement in US History

Despite the deep multiracial history of the United States and the still growing diversity of the population, the racialization of American identity to be synonymous with whiteness remains entrenched in our national imagination. Even among later-generation Japanese Americans who readily identify themselves as American, the slippage between the terms *white* and *American* is apparent, as Matthew, a thirty-something yonsei, stated:

> I know where my family is from. We have these cultural things that we do. Many Americans, they know they are white, but they can't distinguish what kind of European they are. They are just American. Whereas, for myself, I have my Japanese history.

Matthew seems to use the terms *American* and *white* interchangeably. While there is a sense of pride in Matthew's assertion of his Japanese heritage and his knowledge of the culture and history—not unlike the sansei at Deer Park—this assertion is yet another performative effect of the Japanese American racial uniform. As non-white subjects, Japanese Americans cannot be "just American" and thus assert an identity grounded in ethnicity as a source of esteem. In reading Matthew's words, it is important to remember that he is yonsei; his family has been in the United States for four generations. He has no question about his own Americanness but because of his racial uniform and the racialization of American identity, he simultaneously understands that others may not view him as such. Matthew is making a clear distinction between himself—a Japanese American—and white Americans. There is no attempt for inclusion into whiteness or an assimilationist ambition to lose his ethnic culture and history. His implicit claim on American identity is bound up in his own family history in the United States and an explicitly ethnic identity.

As my respondents are all third and fourth generation, their Japanese American families have been present in the United States since at least 1924, but most have histories extending into the late 1800s. Matthew was not alone in his discussion of the longevity of ethnic historical presence as a means to claim belonging to the broader nation and to identify himself as American. The long history of Japanese Americans becomes an integral part of how sansei and yonsei define themselves as an ethnic group and an American people. As Teresa, a sansei, stated, "I think Japanese Americans are unique because we are a community of

Japanese that had been here so many generations." The long history and resulting multiple generations make Japanese Americans unique among American ethnic groups, particularly compared to other Asian American ethnicities with whom Japanese Americans are racially lumped. However, the long history of Japanese Americans in the US is not used to distinguish them just from other Asian Americans but from other racial groups as well, even white people, who rarely have their belonging and citizenship questioned in legal, social, or racial terms. In contrast to Matthew's earlier assertion that white people can be just American and can lack a connection to their history, Carrie described her frequent interactions as a demonstration that later-generation Japanese Americans are perhaps more American than many white people: "Sometimes people are surprised. 'Oh, you're fourth generation?! Oh, wow! Some white people aren't even fourth generation.' But yeah, I get that a lot." As demonstrated in chapter 5, generational rootedness in the US is central to how Japanese Americans distinguish themselves as an ethnic group, but this is also intertwined with their claim to national belonging.[2]

Sansei and yonsei often made such matter-of-fact statements regarding the multiple generations and long history of Japanese Americans in the US without further comment or explanation. Here, simple historical presence of family and the broader ethnic group within the national boundaries of the United States allows Japanese Americans to comfortably lay claim to an American identity and belonging. Sansei and yonsei do, however, refer to major historical events to underscore their physical presence as witnesses to US history but also the centrality of Japanese Americans in important episodes in that history—often as victims of racism. Perhaps the most common historical reference is the Second World War and the mass incarceration of Japanese Americans, euphemistically known as Japanese American internment. This mass incarceration, a dark chapter in US history, serves as a touchstone for Japanese American claims of American historical participation and, hence, national belonging and citizenship.

Japanese American = WWII Mass Incarceration

The mass incarceration of Japanese Americans from the West Coast is central to the way in which Japanese Americans relay their ethnic identity and history and position themselves as longstanding members of the US nation (Nakano 2018). My respondents may not all have an in-depth or scholarly knowledge of this dark period of US history, but all readily recognized it as part of US history and the obviously central role that Japanese Americans and their families played. This history plays a strong role in how Japanese Americans define themselves as an ethnic group and, in turn, how they think about how they belong to the US nation. Elsewhere I have argued that rather than rely solely, or even heavily, on shared cultural practices, Japanese American ethnicity is more closely tied to a symbolic shared history and narrative (Nakano 2018). This historical grand narrative of Japanese American ethnicity centralizes the mass incarceration of Japanese Americans during World War II as a hallmark of the Japanese American ethnic experience and has come to define the boundaries of ethnic membership.

When asked what being Japanese American meant or what they were taught about being Japanese American, respondents generally made mention of WWII mass incarceration, but yonsei particularly centralized the experience:

> I think of Manzanar and World War II. . . . I think of—I don't know, I just keep thinking of our culture nights, we have nikkei student unions at different schools. All those Japanese American groups always emphasize—I don't know, they always emphasize the concentration camps. That's what I think of the most.
> —Emily, yonsei

> You hear a lot about camp, about the importance of the executive order and what my grandma went through going to Heart Mountain and her time there and how it changed our family dynamic. You hear a lot about the 442 and that involvement in the war.
> —Jeremy, multiracial yonsei

This ethnic narrative that centralizes the incarceration experience is familiar to sansei and yonsei because of its wide circulation within the Japanese American community but also has a deeper resonance due to a familial connection to a former incarceree, most commonly a grandparent. Another yonsei, Ryan, echoed Jeremy's reference to his grandmother's experiences, sharing his own memories of being told about "camp" by his grandfather:

> I almost feel like, if my grandfather had never told me stories about the camps, I wouldn't think about being Japanese American as much. It influences slightly in my head that there was a time when Japanese people were put in this bad situation. He is very upset about that whole era. So I kind of feel that anger within him. . . . If I had never heard that, maybe my mentality would be different.

Knowing the experience of his grandfather led Ryan to have a stronger interest and connection to his ethnic background and the history of his family and ethnic group. For sansei and yonsei, the history of incarceration and direct familial connections to it are central to their sense of being Japanese American.

Beyond claims and assertions of close familial connection to WWII mass incarceration, the centrality of this historical event is further underscored by the shock noted by some respondents that some Japanese Americans had little or no knowledge of mass incarceration. Kimi, a yonsei, relayed her interaction with a Japanese American coworker who had grown up on the East Coast:

> Joe [Kimi's coworker] didn't even know about . . . didn't know about internment until, like, really late in life. He grew up in areas where there weren't other Asian Americans, the complete opposite of me. That's so shocking to say out loud.

For Kimi and others, WWII mass incarceration is so central to the Japanese American experience that it is almost unfathomable to claim Japanese American identity without some understanding or knowledge of the historical event. Of course, this is not to say that Kimi's coworker is not Japanese American, but it nonetheless demonstrates how enmeshed this particular history has become with Japanese American identity for many, particularly on the West Coast of the US.

The WWII mass incarceration of Japanese Americans is not just a demonstration of historical presence. It is also recognized as an atrocity and victimization in an infamous period of US history during which Japanese Americans clearly bore the brunt of US racism. This serves as an additional layer in Japanese American claims to national belonging. Both historical and contemporary struggles with racism are understood by sansei and yonsei as uniquely American experiences. While such racism has the intent of ascribing a lack of belonging and of further marginalizing racial minorities, the specific American context and culture where such racism resides and is experienced also represents a means through which US racial minorities claim a place and membership in the US fabric.

While the WWII mass incarceration has tremendous historical gravity on its own, its centrality to how Japanese Americans understand their own ethnic identity also falls within a larger national narrative of assimilation and perseverance (Nakano 2018). The experience of mass incarceration is often cited as a main reason for a perceived accelerated acculturation and assimilation of Japanese Americans. William, a sansei, clearly drew this connection:

> My dad was interned. His whole family was interned, so there was a bit of an assimilationist philosophy around the language, since he was in prison for just being who he was, basically. So we didn't grow up with the language. Most of my sansei and yonsei friends, same thing. I think it's a big byproduct or negative consequence of the internment.

While William's statement is filled with lament, it illustrates the notion of assimilation as reaction to the mass incarceration and the racism experienced before, during, and after WWII. Following WWII and their release from incarceration camps, many Japanese Americans— issei and nisei—attempted to shed themselves and their families of any markers of cultural difference from the American mainstream. Nisei taught their sansei children to speak English only (Spickard 2009; Wilson and Hosokawa 1980). Interestingly, while the ethnic narrative of acculturation due to the incarceration is widespread within the Japanese American community, the process of language loss by the third generation is not unique to the Japanese American experience. As noted in chapter 2, language fluency rarely lasts beyond the second generation in any immigrant-origin community (Rumbaut 2009; also see Lopez 1978; Portes and Rumbaut 2014; Rumbaut, Massey, and Bean 2006).

Regardless of empirical findings and the theoretical inevitability of culture and language loss, Japanese Americans collectively adhere to an assimilationist telling of the incarceration experience and their postwar recuperation. In doing so, however, Japanese Americans continue to maintain a strong sense of their ethnic and racial identities—counter to assimilationist prediction. The mere fact that Japanese Americans collectively assert such a specific WWII significance demonstrates an explicitly ethnic historical claim. It is also important to acknowledge that WWII incarceration is not an event that is part of the family history of all later-generation Japanese Americans, Japanese Americans in Hawaii being the most notable exception. Nor is the narrative of perseverance through wartime adversity the only possible storyline. To adhere to the national narrative, the Japanese American narrative silences other stories of resistance and persistent hardship such as the No-No Boys who refused their draft orders from within the incarceration camps or the catastrophic economic, physical, and mental impact that mass incarceration had on the lives of incarcerees well after their release (Matsumoto 2014; Mimura 2009; Muller 2001; Nakano 2018). It is unsurprising that the most common Japanese American narrative reads as a story of the American Dream, a story of how Japanese Americans became American. The choice and proliferation of this particular narrative over other possible narratives of resistance and hardship demonstrates a strategic choice on how to recuperate the image of Japanese Americans and incorporate that image into the broader American historical narrative.

More American Than Them: History and Comparative Assimilation

Sansei and yonsei readily discussed a perceived accelerated acculturation—cultural assimilation, Americanization—as a direct result of WWII mass incarceration that underscores such mass incarceration as an American and Americanizing experience. However, sansei and yonsei also recognize and relate their acculturation to the broader multigenerational length of Japanese American presence in the United States. This acculturation, and the long history that produced it, is then leveraged as a point of differentiation between themselves and more recently arrived immigrant groups. In particular, Japanese Americans differentiate themselves from other Asian Americans, with whom they are often racially lumped as forever foreigners. While the use of any type of assimilation in this way is not without its logical holes, assimilation has become a relatable and acceptable way for Japanese Americans to understand their own distinct experiences. Japanese Americans see themselves as more Americanized—and more American—than other Asian Americans because of their longer history in the United States. Not unproblematically, such comparison equates assimilation with being deserving of local and national belonging. This logic mirrors the claims made by other immigrant groups against early Japanese and Chinese immigrants in the pursuit of an expanding boundary of whiteness (Almaguer 1994; Lew-Williams 2018; Roediger 2005). As demonstrated throughout this book, Japanese Americans recognize their racial uniform and do not directly seek entry into whiteness. Nonetheless, belongingness should not hinge on acculturation or other forms of assimilation. Notwithstanding their problematic and potentially racist logic, comparative acculturation becomes another claim on national belonging for sansei and yonsei.

Tracy, a yonsei, discussed how the long history, multiple generations, and ubiquitous WWII mass incarceration resulted in the high levels of acculturation among Japanese Americans compared to her other Asian American friends:

As a fourth generation, I was a lot more Americanized than a lot of my friends who were Korean, first- or second-generation. So there was a little bit of a difference there. I never spoke another language. I didn't speak Japanese. They were speaking different languages with their parents. But obviously once you become a fourth generation, it kind of dropped off. . . . They'll ask me why I don't speak Japanese, and I'll let them know, all these things happened. We were interned. The Japanese Americans were trying to assimilate towards American culture because they didn't want to be perceived as being different by speaking this other language. So there's a lot of history behind why a lot of people don't speak Japanese anymore. They were trying to be more American in an American's eyes. So I do sometimes go over that with people, because I get that question a lot, why I don't speak Japanese.

Language usage and fluency are common touchstones in demonstrating Japanese American acculturation. Given their racial uniform and the foreign racialization of Asian Americans, Japanese Americans are expected to speak Japanese, even by other Asian Americans. Charlene, another yonsei, also spoke of her lack of language ability in reference to meeting her Filipino American husband's family:

> When I met my husband's family—they're first generation here—his parents were like, "You don't speak your language?!" They can't wrap their head around me being full Japanese but not speaking my own language. . . . So they realized, "Oh, wow, your family has been here a long time." I'm like, "Yeah."

As an easily recognized and highly visible form of ethnic culture, it is not surprising that language was frequently commented on by sansei and yonsei respondents. Language serves as a stand-in for a broader set of cultural practices that have similarly attenuated over time or as a result of the incarceration experience. For both Tracy and Charlene, their inability to speak Japanese defied the expectation of others and sparked conversations with friends and in-laws. Here we see Japanese Americans falling victim to the forever-foreigner stigma as applied by other Asian Americans. As was common among the sansei and yonsei in this study, both Tracy and Charlene used their lack of Japanese language as a lead-in to claims about the unique history of Japanese Americans in the US and the role of WWII mass incarceration in their acculturation trajectory to dispel the forever-foreigner stigma.

Beyond relating acculturation as a historically based claim of belonging, Tracy and Charlene also demonstrated how acculturation is used to distinguish Japanese Americans from other Asian American ethnic groups. If being more acculturated is (problematically) equated with a stronger claim on national belonging, Japanese Americans leverage the example of "less" acculturated Asian Americans to help demonstrate and solidify their claims on Americanness. Interestingly, just as other Asian Americans fall into the trap of assuming Asian American foreignness when expecting Japanese Americans to speak Japanese, Japanese Americans reinforce the perpetual-foreigner racializations by using their acculturation and long history to distance themselves from other Asian Americans. Japanese Americans do not claim racial whiteness in their attempts to claim national belonging. They seek to disrupt the racial barriers to full-fledged US membership, but in doing so, they reinforce other barriers—in this case cultural—and gatekeep the membership of other Americans. In this way, Japanese American acculturation does not simply stand on its own merits but gains validation through the comparison with and subordination of others. While history and generation are provided as reasons why Tracy and Charlene no longer speak the Japanese language, these reasons are used to juxtapose the Japanese American experience with that of other Asian Americans who are first or second generation and do not have as long a history in the United States. Different levels of acculturation mark a distinct boundary between Tracy and Charlene, Japanese American yonsei, and their less acculturated—and ostensibly less American—Korean American friends and Filipino American family.

In addition to acculturation through language loss, respondents also spoke about the structural components of assimilation as impacted by the long history of Japanese Americans in the US. For instance, Megan, a multiracial yonsei, shared how she views the disappearance of Japantowns as a result of conscious assimilation following WWII mass incarceration.

> Japanese American culture . . . I would think a lot of this assimilation stuff. That's the one thing I sort of understood from after WWII. Just trying to get in and be assimilated with the group, not stay apart. You know, there are not very many Japantowns or anything like that. There are little communities here and there, but you never see—or I don't feel like I see— much of a grouping of Japanese people who aren't trying to sort of get out into the rest of the US.

The lack of ethnic enclaves, also seen as an impact of WWII, is read as a sign of Japanese American assimilation. Echoing Tracy's earlier assertion that postwar Japanese American assimilation was a reaction to experiences with racism, Megan relays that Japanese Americans assimilated through residential dispersal and integration so they could not be singled out and targeted in the future.

While the number of functioning Japantowns has certainly dwindled in the postwar period, the existent and longevity of those that remain is yet another illustration of the deep history of Japanese Americans in the US. Certainly, Chinatowns and Filipinotowns share similar long histories, but the same cannot be said for all Asian American ethnic groups. Lauren discussed the Little Tokyo infrastructure and integration of the community within Los Angeles and the broader Southern California region as a point of comparison and example for other Asian American ethnicities with shorter histories in the US. On this point, Lauren spoke of a Vietnamese American colleague who was highly involved in Little Tokyo:

> His reason for being active in all these things in Little Tokyo, even though he isn't Japanese American, is that he saw the Japanese American community as setting a precedent, and he was looking to see how the Japanese Americans have come as far as they did, and it was something that he could take and extrapolate and use in the Vietnamese American community. So as assimilation and integration and upward mobility come more into play with his own community, he had this foresight of the Japanese American community. I don't know if it was just him, but I think that might be how some people might see it. They might look to Little Tokyo, historical preservation, cultural preservation. And by looking at the Japanese American National Museum, I think other communities might look to that to see a model of how a really strong institution can be built around ethnicity.

While Lauren spoke to the way Little Tokyo serves as an example for other Asian Americans, she also described the symbolic value of Little Tokyo as an embodiment of the historical presences of Japanese Americans in Los Angeles and the United States. This presence has enabled Japanese Americans to establish this community as well as institutions, such as the Japanese American National Museum, that are dedicated to "historical preservation, cultural preservation." Juxtaposing Little Tokyo and the Japanese American community with the more recently arrived Vietnamese American community further highlights the role of a long history and presence in the United States in claims of national belonging and American identity.

Comparative assimilation also reveals itself in sansei and yonsei observations of outmarriages, both interethnic and interracial. Japanese Americans readily see this hallmark metric of sociological assimilation theories as a result of their long US historical presence. Yonsei Todd drew this direct connection:

> I think Japanese Americans have been here longer than a lot of the other Asian Americans; they're more assimilated with American culture. I see Japanese Americans marrying a lot of different types of ethnicities now, especially fourth generation, whereas other Asian Americans, like Chinese or Koreans, kind of stay within their community, which isn't good or bad or whatever. Really, it's because they're a first- or second-generation community as opposed to a fourth-generation community.

Leveraging multiple generations in the US, Todd marks the differences he sees between Japanese Americans and his first- and second-generation Asian American peers through the higher prevalence of outmarriage among Japanese Americans. Mirroring the logic of assimilation, Todd views outmarriage with other ethnic and racial groups as an expression in reduced difference and social distance (Lee and Bean 2010). In referencing outmarriage, Todd includes both interracial and interethnic unions. Todd's wife is, in fact, Chinese American. Todd reframes acculturation and generation as a reason why Japanese Americans are better able to integrate into romantic social relationships across ethnic lines. Once again, Japanese Americans are described in contrast to other Asian Americans who are somehow less "American" due to their perceived likelihood to marry within their own ethnic community.

Throughout my discussions with sansei and yonsei, the frequency of implicit and explicit references to their high level of assimilation and their comparisons to the assimilation of other Asian Americans is a manifestation—a performative effect—of an anxiety felt over a lack of recognition of Japanese American Americanness and racialization as forever foreign. Similar anxieties also exist for other Asian Americans who are also faced with the forever-foreigner stigma. Such anxieties are noted by Japanese Americans. Tammy, a sansei, commented on a Chinese American family friend:

I wonder if it's the generation . . . because we have a friend who came from Hong Kong, came here for college. Her son went to Berkeley and joined an Asian fraternity. And she told us, "I didn't raise him to join an Asian fraternity." And so she probably wants him to assimilate more with the Caucasians.

There is certainly some irony in Tammy's reflection. Tammy interpreted her friend's anger as a desire for her son to join a white fraternity, rather than an Asian one. Joining a white fraternity signals a higher degree of assimilation and acculturation, which Tammy's friend thought she had instilled in her US-raised son. In our conversation, Tammy did not seem to see the common root of assimilation-induced anxiety in her friend's irritation and her own need to assert her acculturated bona fides. Tammy, a third-generation American, is temporally and generationally further along any assimilationist path than her first-generation friend but suffers from the same anxiety and feeling a need to demonstrate her belonging and membership in the US particularly under the white gaze. Certainly, the performative effect of this anxiety takes shape differently for Tammy and her Chinese American friend, but the ironic parallel is unmistakable.

However, I assert here that it is possible to read Tammy's incredulous response to her friend in a slightly different way that illuminates the ways in which assimilationist racial assumptions permeate everyday un- derstandings of "Americanness" and reinforces the ethnic basis through which Japanese Americans claim their national belonging. In complain- ing that she did not want her son to join an Asian fraternity, Tammy's Chinese American friend drew an association between Americanization and whiteness. While participation in any collegiate fraternal organi- zation would seem to be a step toward assimilation, this friend seem- ingly dismissed this evidence because of the fraternity is predominantly Asian and not white. Assimilation into US society is valued only in its proximity—if not transition—to whiteness. It is here that Tammy saw a distinction between herself and her friend. As has been demonstrated throughout this chapter, Japanese Americans do not claim their Ameri- canness through an explicit claim on whiteness—mimicry, proximity, or otherwise. Most obviously, the focus on WWII mass incarceration positions Japanese Americans as the target of white supremacy. But even in the context of assertions of assimilation and acculturation, Japanese American claims are ethnic and cultural, not racial. In claiming to be more acculturated and assimilated, Japanese Americans are not claiming whiteness. Rather, it is relayed as an inherent part of the Japanese American experience and identity—a result of history. Inclusion or proximity with white racial status is not required for Japanese Americans to claim belonging and membership within the national imaginary.

Moments of Half-Hearted Recognition

Focusing on the words and affective sentiments of individual sansei and yonsei makes clear the ways in which national belonging is conceptualized and claimed on the individual level but tells us less about how such claims are interpreted by the national public and accepted into a national imaginary. After all, Glenn's definition of citizenship "requires the recognition of other members of the community" (2011, 3). Within episodes of a broader national historical narrative, Japanese Americans become visible, even active, participants. These moments of visible participation can be interpreted as recognition of Japanese American claims of belonging and citizenship at the national level.

As discussed in previous chapters, the shifting global politics of the Cold War era allowed for a simultaneous shift in the image of Japanese Americans from wartime enemy aliens to trusted allies and friends (Brooks 2009; Cheng 2013; Kim 2010; Shibusawa 2006; Wu 2014). This new treatment of Japanese Americans, as well as other racial minorities, was a response to increasing Soviet propaganda exposing the inherent racism within US democracy. To combat such propaganda, the US began passing anti-racist legislation in housing, voting rights, and immigration, culminating in the Civil Rights Act of 1964 and the Immigration and Naturalization Act of 1965 (Dudziak 2000). Such expansion of rights and access demonstrates a greater, if not begrudging, recognition on the part of the US government of the membership and belonging of racial minorities, including Japanese Americans, within the national imaginary.

Beyond the expansion of social rights and the shift of Japan from enemy to friend, the image of Japanese Americans also shifted as a result of Cold War politics. As a result of their high levels of postwar economic and educational success, Japanese Americans, as well as Chinese Americans, became the poster children of US anti-racism and the ability for racial minorities to find success in the US. This increasingly positive image painted Asian Americans as model minorities (Petersen 1966; Wu 2013). Notwithstanding a critical understanding of the inherent anti-Blackness and the divide-and-conquer strategy of the model minority mythology, for many Japanese Americans, who had long felt the denial of their citizenship and belonging, the model minority label seemed a recognition of their assimilation and integration into US society reflecting a successful completion of the process of becoming American. Of course, the sense of belonging and inclusion seemingly promised by the model minority mythology is deceptive at worst, conditional at best. Even within the moniker "model minority," we see the simultaneous positioning of Japanese Americans on a social pedestal but remain at the margins and distinctly othered as a permanent minority.

Whether through the expansion of social rights or model minority characterizations, recognition of Japanese American citizenship and belonging is often conditional and strategic to national goals. Even the most heralded moment of national recognition of Japanese American belonging—the achievement of redress and reparations for WWII mass incarceration in 1988—can be read as an extension of Cold War geopolitics and model minority discourse. The wartime incarceration experience was a taboo subject within the Japanese American community in the immediate postwar period, euphemistically referenced as "camp." However, as the sansei came of age and became politicized through their college experiences and the Asian American movement, they began to ask questions of their nisei parents about their wartime experiences. Such questions sparked a movement to seek redress and reparations on behalf of former incarcerees from the federal government beginning in the 1970s (Maki, Kitano, and Berthold 1999; Takezawa 1995). In response to this movement, the growing representation of Japanese Americans in the US Congress, and after two decades of struggle, a federal commission was created to investigate this dark chapter in US history. Eleven public hearings held in ten cities across the US provided a public forum for former incarcerees to share their camp experiences. The commission ultimately recommended redress and reparations to former incarcerees, which led to the passage and signing of the Civil Liberties Act of 1988

(Maki, Kitano, and Berthold 1999; Takezawa 1995). This act provided each surviving incarceree with a formal letter of apology from the president of the United States and a reparations payment of $20,000 (Maki, Kitano, and Berthold; Takezawa 1995). This bill also created an education fund to support teaching the history of WWII incarceration in K–12 curricula. Many assembly centers and incarceration camp sites are now designated as national and state historical landmarks, and a memorial to former incarcerees was built in Washington, DC (US Department of the Interior 2001; US Senate 2006). While every American may not be aware of the historical stain of WWII incarceration, the federal and state actions and attempts to preserve this history is a result of Japanese American efforts to establish this ethnic history as US history. The concerted effort by largely sansei activists to make sure this ethnic history and narrative are preserved is another demonstration of the persistent importance of ethnicity for Japanese Americans as a reaction to their racial marginalization and counter to prescribed assimilation pathways.

While the federal bill providing redress and reparation and related actions is framed as a noble righting of a wrong in US history and serves collectively as a formal federal government recognition of its violation of the rights of citizens and permanent residents, its passage cannot be disentangled from the continuing—albeit dwindling—Cold War. The twilight of the Cold War amplified the need to establish a moral superiority and American exceptionalism in terms of freedom and justice more so than righting the wrong committed against Japanese American citizens (Kozen 2012). Furthermore, the model minority positioning of Japanese Americans also made them a more palatable symbolic recipient of reparations in comparison to other racial minorities—Black and Indigenous communities, in particular—who had long sought federal reparations for past atrocities. In pointing out these considerations, I do not mean to discount the hard work or the importance of the redress and reparations movement for Japanese Americans. Beyond the formal reparations themselves, the redress movement continues to serve the Japanese American community by providing a specific turning point in the national recognition of their US belonging and citizenship (Takezawa 1995).

While the Cold War, the redress movement, and other events are important historical points marking the improved racial status and some recognition of belonging within the US, such recognition remains inconsistent and half-hearted in the lived experience of Japanese Americans. Persistent racialization as forever foreigners, daily microaggressions, and lingering prejudice and discrimination serve as a more consistent reminder for Japanese Americans of the contingent and sporadic acceptance of their national—and local—membership. Referring back to cultural studies scholars Karen Shimakawa (2002) and Anne Anlin Cheng (2000), they reference this social inbetweenness as national abjection and racial melancholy, respectively. Shimakawa's notion of national abjection conceptualizes the social position of Asian Americans, inclusive of Japanese Americans, at the periphery of the US nation demarcating the outer boundaries of national membership. Asian Americans are conditionally part of the national body and yet remain a foreign element within. While not an explicit reference, Cheng's conception of racial melancholy can be understood as an affective result of Shimakawa's national abjection. If melancholy is understood as unresolved grief, the melancholy of Asian Americans stems from a simultaneous acknowledgment of the unattainability of a "never-possible" American ideal of whiteness and the continued longing and reach for this ideal. In the end, Japanese American claims on national belonging are only claims. As they point to their history and even their assimilation, Japanese Americans clearly feel that they are deserving, and rightfully so. However, as Japanese Americans in this study continue to report that they feel racially othered as forever foreigners, it is apparent that their belonging to and within the US is still too often not recognized by others. Full belonging remains sought but unattainable.

Conclusion

Sansei and yonsei utilize their long history, their multiple generations, and the familial connection to incarceration as a way to assert their national belonging. This claim is distinct from the negotiations of local belonging described in the earlier chapters of this book. Citizenship, and the affective belonging it entails, occurs at multiple social scales and in multiple contexts. At the local level, sansei and yonsei create their own sense of belonging through the formation of ethnic and racial communities. Within these communities, their membership is mutually recognized. At the national level, there is a greater need for recognition from the national community and inclusion in the national historical record. Japanese American claims on national belonging continue to be rooted in the ethnic experience. In this way, Japanese American claims provide them with their own sense of security and belonging to the US nation and its history. This position and self-supported sense of belonging is not achieved through a relinquishing of ethnicity as posited by assimilation theorists nor a maintenance of ancestral cultural practices as seen in multiculturalist discourses (Tsuda 2016). Rather, Japanese Americans call upon an explicitly ethnic-specific history to achieve their sense of belonging within the nation.

The ethnic basis of Japanese American claims on national belonging are directly tied to racialized experiences in the US, most clearly demonstrated by WWII mass incarceration. Such racialized experiences have consistently positioned Japanese Americans at the margins or outside of the nation demonstrating the affect of non-belonging on the national stage. Claiming belonging through such a racialized and racist history is a performative effect and works against the assimilationist assumptions of ethnic attenuation alongside social whitening. In claiming their Americanness and a recognition of their national belonging, Japanese Americans are not claiming whiteness. Even in their assimilation comparisons with other Asian Americans, there is an implicit recognition of their persistent racial uniform. The comparison with other Asian Americans is rooted in their shared racialization as forever foreigners. In claiming a high level of acculturation and assimilation, Japanese American are not claiming a reduction in ethnic salience or an acceptance into whiteness. Rather, they are seeking to expand the definition of American beyond whiteness (Tsuda 2016).

Such assertions, while attempting to erase the racial boundaries around American identity and US national belonging, simultaneously create new exclusionary boundaries, albeit not necessarily along racial lines. Relying on historical presence and participation to legitimate a recognition of national belonging severely limits who can be considered an American. What is the requisite number of years or generations necessary to legitimately claim an American identity? What degree of atrocity must be committed against an ethnic group before they can be recognized as part of the nation? Furthermore, associating a higher level of acculturation and assimilation with a more legitimate claim on American identity—even if deracialized—is equally problematic. The arbitrary metrics of language spoken or culture practiced alone should not preclude recognition within the national imaginary. The other, supposedly less assimilated and acculturated Asian Americans that Japanese Americans compare themselves against are not less American and are no less deserving of recognition of their national membership. The definition of American must be rewritten to allow for recognized belonging for all regardless of difference.

Conclusion

Citizenship, Belonging, and the Racial Critique of Assimilation

I completed the full draft of this book during the COVID-19 pandemic. From the mind-boggling number of lives lost and forever changed, to the anxiety introduced into our everyday lives, to the politicization of public health efforts to curb the impact of the virus, the pandemic was tragic and enraging for many reasons. For Asian Americans—myself and other Japanese Americans included—the dangers and fears extended beyond illness.[1] While the world rushed to contain the virus, conservative US politicians seized on an opportunity to stoke the flames of racism and xenophobia by referencing the disease as the "kung flu" and "Chinavirus." While it appears that the virus originated in China, infection, of course, did not discriminate on the basis of national origin, race, or ethnicity. The racialization of this disease led to a dramatic and tragic increase in hate crimes targeting Asian American individuals, businesses, and community institutions. Despite hate crimes being notoriously underreported, 2020 and 2021 saw nearly four thousand hate incidents representing an increase of over 150 percent compared to before the pandemic (Jeung et al. 2021; Levin 2021).

Because of the pervasive popular acceptance of the model minority mythology around the Asian American experience, this tidal wave of anti-Asian hate was shocking to many in the media and to the broader public. Given their storied successes, Asian Americans were thought to be unaffected by racism and to occupy a racial status just this side of whiteness. Of course, Asian Americans have always faced racism, albeit often in ways that are less recognizable in our current racial discourse. The ease with which political and public rhetoric turned to xenophobic and racist name-calling and then quickly to ire and violence against Asian Americans is a demonstration of a particular brand of enduring anti-Asian racism—the convenient and always conditional integration of the perpetual foreigner.

The resurgence in the visibility of anti-Asian racism and violence in the wake of the COVID-19 pandemic is a magnified and physical manifestation of the everyday affect of non-belonging shared by later-generation Japanese Americans throughout this book. The lack of awareness of long-standing and ever-present anti-Asian sentiment in the US and around the world speaks to the reflections of Japanese Americans who never saw their experiences addressed in racial terms. Given the simultaneous status as a "model" and a "minority," Japanese and Asian American experiences with racism are rendered invisible. That is, until they are not. But the visibility of pandemic-fueled anti-Asian hate is also illustrative of how racism is experienced differently for Asian Americans. The rhetoric, hate, and violence levied against Asian Americans is rooted in their assumed perpetual foreignness. The fate of Asian Americans is inextricably tied to the idea of Asia in the US political and social imagination. As a result, Asian Americans are not seen as "real Americans." They are not really part of us, and therefore they are easy and acceptable targets. Of course, all this—model minority invisibility, the quick rise in anti-Asian violence, and perceived perpetual foreignness—is animated by one essential truth: Japanese and Asian Americans continue to be marked and othered by their racial uniform. In their everyday lives, race matters.

In 2014, the US Supreme Court handed down a ruling upholding a Michigan state referendum banning race-based affirmative action in public university admission decisions. While the majority's opinion focused on the right of voters to define the decision-making processes of government bodies, Justice Sotomayor penned a dissenting opinion, joined by Justice Ginsburg, reminding her colleagues of the persistent impact of race on the lived experience of minorities:

> And race matters for reasons that really are only skin deep, that cannot be discussed any other way, and that cannot be wished away. . . . Race matters to a young woman's sense of self when she states her hometown, and then is pressed, "No, where are you really from?", regardless of how many generations her family has been in the country. Race matters to a young person addressed by a stranger in a foreign language, which he does not

understand because only English was spoken at home. Race matters because of the slights, the snickers, the silent judgments that reinforce that most crippling of thoughts: "I do not belong here." (*Schuette v. Coalition to Defend Affirmative Action et al.*)

Debates over affirmative action generally place Asian Americans in opposition to other people of color, and Justice Sotomayor's quotation states no particular racial group. However, Sotomayor's vignettes of racialized experiences could very well be the everyday microaggressions shared by the later-generation Japanese American respondents in this book. In her reference to assumed foreignness in terms of origin and language, Justice Sotomayor alluded to the persistence of racialization regardless of place of birth and acculturation: race trumps assimilation. Justice Sotomayor connected race to citizenship and affect as these racialized experiences add up to a sense of non-belonging.

For sansei and yonsei, race matters as it continues to limit their ability to achieve full membership in US society. The chapters of this book share the various mundane practices and understandings employed by sansei and yonsei as performative effects stemming from the affect of non-belonging. While I argue that affect and performative effect are essential to an alternative analysis of the processes and outcomes of so-called assimilation, we cannot lose sight that the affect of non-belonging is instigated by perceptions of the Japanese American racial uniform. The story told in this book is one of persistent racialized difference producing limits on the affective dimensions of citizenship—feelings and recognitions of belonging.

Overall, *Japanese Americans and the Racial Uniform* examines the case of later-generation Japanese Americans to provide empirical proof of the limitation of contemporary assimilation theory and the impact of race on the lived experiences of immigrant-origin community members who have come to embody assimilation success. Through explorations of persistent social marginalization, the affective dimensions of citizenship, community formation practices, and self-actualized claims of belonging, this book shares its major take-away point with Justice Sotomayor's dissent: race matters. In this concluding chapter, I would like to drive this point home further through a discussion of two subjects pertaining to the future of the Japanese American racial uniform and ethnic community: symbolic ethnicity and the growing multiracial and multi-ethnic dimension of Japanese American communities, two social contexts where race still matters for later-generation Japanese Americans.

Beyond Later-Generation Symbolic Ethnicity

Also in 2014, *Ethnic and Racial Studies*, an international peer-reviewed journal committed to social science research on race and ethnicity, published a review issue on "The Coming Darkness of Late Generation European Ethnicity." Fittingly, sociologist Herbert Gans, who authored the seminal piece on symbolic ethnicity also published in *Ethnic and Racial Studies* (Gans 1979), opened the discussion among a who's-who list of immigration scholars.[2] This revisiting of the attenuation of ethnicity across successive immigrant generations generally solidified earlier findings of the increasingly nostalgic, voluntary, and "in name only" ethnicity maintained with each passing generation. What was the "twilight of ethnicity" in the 1980s was now the "coming darkness" (Alba 1985).

The symposium's focus on later-generation European Americans signals a potential recognition of the different racial trajectory of non-white later-generation Americans, such as Japanese Americans. However, Asian Americans, as well as Latines, only entered the discussion as part of the new wave of post-1965 immigrants. While their non-white racial status is recognized, their assimilatory path is all but predetermined, as authors note how their contemporary patterns of integration outpace those of European predecessors. While never directly addressed, the symposium's collection of scholars seemed to agree that with each passing generation, the salience of ethnicity, even of the symbolic variety, becomes increasingly tenuous for both white and non-white ethnics. Later-generation Japanese Americans appear in only a single sentence of Gans's final rebuttal as a largely ignored group that possibly should be studied.

Later-generation Japanese Americans are not resisting assimilation, acculturation, or a more symbolic practice of ethnicity. Within the "Coming Darkness" symposium, Kasinitz (2014) reminded us that conspicuous displays of ethnicity, often associated with a third-generation revival of ethnicity, are actually variations of symbolic ethnicity, given their weak connection to ethnic substance. It is arguable that aspects of Japanese American cultural practice have lost their ethnic significance. Many of the sansei and yonsei I interviewed were stumped when I probed them on the meaning behind cultural symbols seen in their homes or various cultural rituals they shared. They were able to provide only vague stock answers about good luck or longevity. But even if Japanese American culture has become symbolic in some ways, their ethnicity coupled with their race continues to meaningfully structure their daily lives and social behaviors.

In her contribution to the symposium, sociologist Mary Waters (2014) connected the growth of interracial marriage with an increased availability of optional and symbolic ethnicity across the color line. Intermarriage is, of course, a prominent reference by immigration and race scholars in the rapid assimilation of non-white immigrant-origin communities and the lowering of racial boundaries. Japanese Americans are often used as an example par excellence of this phenomenon. While intermarriage rates are high among Japanese Americans, this does not mean that race and ethnicity do not still shape marital choices and decision, whether to out-marry or in-marry. Several respondents spoke about intentionally wanting and seeking a white spouse so their children would look less Japanese. Such words demonstrate a reaction to a persistent racialization and othering of Japaneseness that such respondents wished to distance their children from through intermarriage and multiraciality. Conversely, respondents also spoke of wanting a Japanese American spouse because of perceived similarities in culture and experience. Such desires often expanded to potential Asian American spouses of other ethnicities. Furthermore, if we are to look at interracial marriage rates as measures of integration, what do we make of divorce rates that are also shown to be statistically higher among Asian-white couples (Bratter and King 2008)? Mere ability and achievement of intermarriage may point to diminishing ethnic distinctness and reduced racial boundaries for some individuals, but assimilation theory's focus on outcomes alone—intermarriage rates among others—overlooks the way in which race and ethnicity continue to matter in decision-making processes, lived experiences, and desires that bring about such outcomes. They are not just symbolic.

Multiracial/Multiethnic Futures of Japanese American Communities

While intermarriage itself may not be the best metric of reduced social distance between racial and ethnic groups, it is undeniable that such relationships are essential for another important trend within the Japanese American community, the nation, and the world: growing multiracial and multiethnic populations. The legitimacy of multiracial and multiethnic Japanese Americans as "real" Japanese Americans has historically been policed from within and outside the ethnic community in response to fears of diluting one population or another. During World War II, the US government excluded and ultimately incarcerated Japanese Americans on the West Coast who had as little as one-sixteenth Japanese heritage (Carbado 2005; Weglyn 1996). "Military necessity" dictated that such a minimal blood quantum was enough to turn even the most red-blooded American disloyal. Of course, it is not just external actors who are interested in policing the legitimacy of mixed-race Japanese Americans. Within the Japanese American community, blood quantum has been utilized to determine eligibility to participate in community institutions such as beauty pageants and basketball leagues (King 2002). As recently as the 1990s, the mixed-race limit for legitimate Japanese American identity was placed between 25 and 50 percent. Individuals with less Japanese American heritage would not be considered Japanese American under these rules.

Certainly, internal and external policing of mixed-race heritage are born out of different concerns. Japanese American basketball leagues and beauty pageants are focused on ethnic integrity. The basketball leagues were created to provide a safe space for ethnic community members to participate in sports when they were excluded or marginalized within mainstream leagues and clubs. Without policing the ethnic makeup of individual players and teams, there is a worry that such safety and community would be lost (Chin 2016a, 2016b; King 2002). The purpose of Japanese American beauty pageants has some overlap with basketball leagues, as Japanese American beauty queens were also excluded and marginalized in mainstream pageant circuits. However, beauty pageants and their contestants are also seen as ambassadors for the community and therefore take on an additional responsibility for representing what it means to be Japanese American (King-O'Riain 2006).

Despite the longstanding concerns over racial and cultural purity, the mixed-race segment of the Japanese American community continues to expand. In 2019, the American Community Survey estimated that nearly half of all Japanese Americans (49 percent) identified themselves as multiracial or multiethnic. These numbers demonstrate that multiraciality and multiethnicity are not just future possibilities for Japanese American communities but a contemporary reality. However, the growing multiraciality of the Japanese American population does not mean the end of ethnic community. As sociologist Rebecca Chiyoko King-O'Riain (2019) asks and answers, "With all this mixing, is it safe to say that there is a Japanese American community? Undoubtedly, yes, there is a Japanese American community, but it may look different than it did in the past" (171). Mixed-race Japanese Americans, she continues, "are not diluting Japanese Americanness or Japanese American community organizations; however, they are transforming them" (179). So in addition to the racial negotiations of community in light of suburbanization, residential integration, and ethnic demographic shifts brought on by immigration, Japanese Americans as a community must also negotiate multiethnicity and multiraciality.

The anxieties demonstrated in the historical and institutional contexts of beauty pageants and basketball leagues continue to be points of contention within the broader Japanese American community (Nakashima 1992; Williams-Leon and Nakashima 2001). Sansei and yonsei are very much aware of the shifting ethnic and racial demographics and the related tensions. Some sansei parents lament the perceived disappearance of Japanese American community as their yonsei children lack interaction with other Japanese Americans and choose spouses of other ethnic and racial backgrounds. Multiracial and multiethnic yonsei report being questioned on their Japanese American authenticity by their monoethnic peers. Such negative interaction and perceptions, however, do not stop multiracial and multiethnic Japanese Americans from claiming their membership within the Japanese American community. Japanese American ethnicity is also more than just an asserted identity for multiracial and multiethnic Japanese Americans. Their race and ethnicity also impact their experiences and practices due to external connections and perceptions. Similar to their monoethnic peers, multiracial and multiethnic Japanese Americans find commonality in terms of familial cultural practices and ethnic community participation. Many multiracial and multiethnic Japanese Americans continue to be racialized and recognized as non-white and foreign and to be seen as not belonging within predominantly white spaces.

The function of the racial uniform varies widely in the context of an increasingly multiracial Japanese America. While there may be particular physical characteristics that are more prevalent among multiracial Japanese Americans, there is no single phenotype. There is no one way to be mixed race. The racialized experience of each individual is dependent on the social perception of the individual's race (Nishime 2014). In their study of multiracial Americans, sociologists Jennifer Lee and Frank Bean (2007) include the experience of a mixed-race Japanese American man who has blonde hair and blue eyes. Given his racial uniform, this mixed-race Japanese American will live a very different racial experience from the sansei and yonsei in this study. I would venture to say that his phenotype and experiences are an outlier in terms of the mixed-race Japanese American experience. The racial uniform of multiracial and multiethnic Japanese Americans is far from consistent, but it certainly does not always produce the ability to pass for white, as argued by some assimilation scholars (Lee and Bean 2007, 2010; Waters 2014).

The majority of multiracial and multiethnic sansei and yonsei in this book reported being readily recognized as non-white although not always as Japanese American or Asian. Some multiracial yonsei reported that in their interactions with strangers, they were frequently assumed to be Latine. Of course, a more typical Asian racial uniform continues to be common and impactful for many mixed-race Japanese Americans. Take for example, the experience of my six-year-old fifth-generation (gosei) nephew. My nephew was picking out some decorative charms for his Croc shoes.[3] Usually, my nephew would choose something sports-themed or a video game character, but this time he included a charm in the shape of the US flag. Recognizing the out-of-character choice, my brother-in-law asked my nephew why he wanted that particular charm. My nephew stated matter-of-factly that he wanted his classmates to know that he was American and not from China. My nephew is mixed race. His dad, my brother-in-law, is also mixed race—white and Japanese. Despite my nephew's mixed heritage, his racial uniform is still visible and recognizably Asian to his classmates. His mixed-race identity does not save him from the same assumptions of foreignness or the affect of non-belonging seen throughout this book.

This story of my nephew's persistent racial uniform is instructive for many reasons beyond his mixed-race and fifth-generation statuses. It is also important to note the context in which this racial recognition happened. My nephew is growing up in middle-class, suburban Orange County. He attends a school that is majority-minority, but white students continue to make up the largest group at 38 percent. Nearly 30 percent of students are Asian, and 18 percent are Latine. My nephew would be part of the almost 13 percent of students who identify with two or more races. My nephew's experience captures all the major touchpoints of assimilation success. The visibility of my nephew's racial uniform persists not only into the fifth generation and his multiracial identity but in this ostensibly diverse and integrated setting—also noting the strong Asian American representation in the school. While only a single anecdote, my nephew's experience is no less real and demonstrates the enduring need to reexamine sociology's long and deeply held beliefs about race, ethnicity, and assimilation. Interracial marriage and multiraciality are not linear paths to assimilation and ethnic attenuation. Nor is residential integration. The racial uniform endures.

If we are to believe the wisdom put forth by empirical studies on assimilation, ethnic community should be of declining importance with the rise in intermarriage. As intermarriage begets racial amalgamation, race and ethnicity will fade in salience. Some sansei voiced fears over the demise of the Japanese American community brought about by the gradual dilution of ethnicity through intermarriage. But many more sansei and yonsei saw an alternative future in which multiraciality and multiethnicity are normalized as part of a growing Japanese America. As multiracial yonsei Clara succinctly put it, "It's like being mixed is part of being Japanese American for some people. . . . It's like yonsei is mixed." As an increasing proportion of the Japanese American community becomes racially and ethnically mixed with each successive generation, multiraciality and multiethnicity will become part of how the Japanese American community defines itself—perhaps, already does. Similar shifts—rather than disappearances—in ethnic boundaries have been observed in other ethnic and racial populations with substantial percentages of multiracial and multiethnic members. In particular, scholars have noted the persistence and resurgence of identity and community among Native Hawaiians (Kanaʻiaupuni and Liebler 2005), Pacific Islanders (Spickard and Fong 1995), and Native Americans (Liebler 2010).

In understanding the potential persistence of ethnic identity and community in the face of a growing multiracial and multiethnic reality among Japanese Americans, it is important to remember the critical function ethnic community continues to serve in the daily lives of sansei and yonsei. As demonstrated throughout this study, ethnic community provides a haven for Japanese Americans away from the persistent marginalization as perpetual foreigners faced in their daily interactions. Ethnic community is maintained in reaction to negative racialization in broader society that produces an affect of non-belonging. Full citizenship, inclusive of a mutual recognition of membership, is denied later-generation Japanese Americans due to race, and ethnic community becomes a space to establish their own local and national senses of belonging.

Regardless of racial or ethnic background, later-generation Japanese Americans see a reenvisioning of the boundaries of Japanese American community to be more inclusive of, or perhaps even centralize, multiracial and multiethnic Japanese Americans. Despite the growing multiracial and multiethnic segment of the Japanese American community, the continuing racial marginalization of Japanese Americans of all racial and ethnic backgrounds makes it unlikely that Japanese American ethnic community will lose its importance. The future of Japanese Americans may in fact be a multiracial and multiethnic one, but the community looks to persist for generations to come.

On Ethnic Options and Racial Options

The growing multiracial and multiethnic reality of the Japanese American community also has an important theoretical tie back to our earlier discussion of symbolic ethnicity. Recall Mary Water's assertion that the upward trend in intermarriage would produce greater opportunity for the symbolic and optional exercise of ethnicity across the racial spectrum. Notwithstanding the stated problem with using intermarriage outcomes as evidence of assimilation and ethnic attenuation, the connections between intermarriages, multiraciality, and ethnic options pose other questions about how ethnic options can be exercised among individuals who do not racially present as white.

In her seminal work, *Ethnic Options*, Waters (1990) finds white ethnicity to be optional in two ways: the option to claim any ethnic identity or just be white/American, and the option to choose among multiple ethnic ancestries given increasing multiethnic heritages. Legal scholar Devin Carbado (2005) extends this argument to all white immigrants who undergo a process of racial naturalization that provides them with a racialized American identity as white people regardless of generation (on equation of whiteness and American, also see Kim [2007], Tuan [1999], and Water [1996]). Furthermore, identification with different European ethnic groups no longer accompanies significant discrimination making the choice between them of negligible difference in terms of life chances. Given these specifications, it is unsurprising that Waters, Carbado, and other scholars saw a different trajectory for the ethnic options and racial naturalization of non-white immigrants and their successive generations (Rumbaut 2009; Tuan 1999; Waters 1996). Of course, by 2014 and the "Coming Darkness" symposium, Waters had changed her opinion.

I have argued throughout this study that the Japanese American case is ideal for tackling some of the open questions on the functions of race and ethnicity in later generations. This is true of the concept of ethnic options. The non-white case of later-generation Japanese Americans does not reveal a wholesale optional exercise of ethnicity regardless of high intermarriage rates. Rather, sansei and yonsei demonstrate a need to reconceptualize Water's original assertion to make it applicable beyond white ethnics. In chapter 5, I introduced the concept of racial replenishment of ethnicity to demonstrate how the persistent racialization of later-generation Japanese Americans as undifferentiated "Asian" and perpetual foreigners leads to a maintenance and strengthening of ethnic identity. While recognizing and finding solidarity in their shared Asian racialization, Japanese Americans maintain their ethnicity to show themselves as distinct from other Asian American ethnic groups, generally through an assertion of their later-generation status. As an asserted identity, Japanese American ethnicity can be seen as optionally exercised. The racial replenishment of ethnicity, however, demonstrates that Japanese American options are bounded by their persistent racialization. While Japanese Americans can choose whether or not to assert their ethnic identity, they will continue to be racialized as Asian and marginalized as forever foreign. Ethnic options may exist, but they are limited, as ethnic options can only occur within racial categories.

The racial limits of ethnic options are magnified as we consider the identity choices of multiethnic Japanese Americans—those Japanese Americans of mixed heritage with another Asian American ethnicity. Theoretically, increased levels of intermarriage and resulting multiracial/multiethnic population may lead to a more diverse set of ethnic and racial options. Certainly, increased diversity within one's own heritage would provide for a broader set of choices for an individual's asserted identity. But those choices are not limitless, as Jennifer, a multiethnic yonsei of Korean and Japanese background, alluded:

> I don't feel Korean at all. My mom's Japanese, and she's the one who instilled the most tradition, because she's the one who spent the most time with us as kids. On top of that, my dad being Korean, he's fourth generation, but growing up, there weren't a lot of Koreans. So he would only hang out with Japanese Americans because most Koreans were first-generation. He was fourth. The Japanese were third generation, and he felt more comfortable about it. So all of his friends are Japanese. They are Asian, and the majority of them are Japanese and Chinese. I don't think he has many Korean friends, so I don't really feel any kind of association to Korean people at all.

While Jennifer offers ample and plausible reasons as to why she feels less Korean than Japanese, the fact remains that she is able to opt out of her Korean ethnicity and claim only a Japanese American identity without notable social resistance because there is no visible racial violation. The options of multiracial and multiethnic individuals will be limited by their perceived racialized identity. Jennifer may be able to choose freely between a Japanese American and Korean American identity, but this is largely due to the similar racialized categorization of both ethnic groups. In other cases, perceived identity may or may not match one's asserted ethnic identity. As mentioned, many of my multiracial respondents often spoke of being mistaken as Latine. For Jennifer and my multiracial respondents with mistaken racial identity, their options continue to be bounded by visible race-based restrictions.

The Japanese American case draws attention to the way in which ethnic options can be understood to explain a fuller set of racial and ethnic experiences. Ethnicity is chosen not from a neutral set of options but from a set of ethnic identities with varying levels of attached stigma. For most Japanese Americans, the choice is between a default racialized identity as Asian and an ethnic specific identity. A Japanese American identity, which has come to be associated with more acculturation and assimilative success, is seen as less stigmatized than the forever-foreigner image associated with Asianness. For the white ethnics in Waters' study (1990), their ethnic identity choices seem less limited and more symbolic than those available to Japanese Americans because those choices have similarly low levels of stigma. However, even in the context of lower stigma, the ethnic options of whites are still contained within a single racial category. The difference lies in the status afforded to whiteness, the synonymous relationship between whiteness and American identity, and the minimal stigma attached to ethnicities racialized as white. The normalization of whiteness in the US racial context makes the options of white ethnics seem limitless. They are not. As white identity holds the highest status in the US racial system, it is rare for perceptually white individuals to attempt to opt into a subordinated racial or ethnic identity due to the associated loss of status. This makes is seems like white ethnics are just not *choosing* ethnic options beyond their perceived race. In fact, they would not be *allowed* that choice anyway. White ethnic options are also racially restricted. Ethnic options, then, are not racial options and ethnic options are not made simply between symbolic choices.

This reconceptualization of ethnic options that views ethnic choices as being within racial categories and between identities carrying varying levels of stigma can also be seen in other studies on racial and ethnic identities. In her subsequent work, Waters (1999) explores the ability of immigrant and second-generation West Indians in New York City to exercise their ethnicity given their similar phenotype to African Americans. The imposed racialization of Blackness makes West Indian ethnicity invisible to the mainstream public but also prompts West Indian

Americans to make their ethnicity more conspicuous through the accents, ethnic community formation, and assertion of their ethnic identity. Jimenez (2009) and Tuan (1999) note a similar phenomenon among later-generation Mexican Americans and Asian Americans, respectively. Both groups face the stigma of perpetual foreignness due to the influx of immigrants of the same ethnic and racial background. In reaction to this racialization and stigma, both groups assert their later-generation status as an integral part of their ethnic identity to distance themselves from the perception of foreignness. For Black West Indians, later-generation Mexican Americans, and later-generation Asian Americans, ethnic identity is maintained in response to broader patterns of racialization and is chosen because it carries less stigma than their respective default racial categorizations. These individuals may have a limited set of ethnic options, but they cannot escape racialization. They do not have racial options.

Assimilation, Racial Critique, and the Promise of Affect and Citizenship

While individual sociological studies have provided important and in-depth insight into the role of race in the processes of assimilation and integration (Dhingra 2020; Golash-Boza 2006; Jimenez 2009; Jung 2009; Kim 2007; Lacy 2007; Lee and Zhou 2015; Maira 2009; Romero 2008; Rudrappa 2004; Saenz and Douglas 2015; Vallejo 2012; Waters 1999; Zhou 2004), the standard texts and core tenets of this field of study remain largely race neutral. Neutrality, however, is not as impartial as it seems. In assimilation theory, race neutrality avoids and marginalizes the racialized experiences of immigrant and other communities of color. The refusal to fully account for race or to talk around race issues in processes of assimilation and integration is to deny a problem exists and be unable to offer meaningful paths towards progress and justice. Of course, race is an inescapable social force. The racial critique of assimilation theory is not just about race neutrality. It is also rooted in the metrics utilized by assimilation theorists to determine success. These simplified metrics focus on outcomes (e.g., educational attainment, language fluency, socioeconomic status, intermarriage, residential integration), which may reveal racial disparities but tell us very little about the racialized paths taken by individuals and communities to arrive at such results.

The framework of citizenship is offered throughout this text as one possible path to a reconciliation between the scholarships on race relations and immigrant integration. In considering citizenship as a framework of integration—immigrant and non-immigrant—we must look beyond the legal, economic, or other institutional aspects of citizenship. A full framework of citizenship requires researchers to consider its affective dimensions—how belonging and membership is experienced, claimed, and denied. Such affective dimensions require analysis of micro-level interactions and practices.

In this book, I have examined the community-building practices and identity formations of later-generation Japanese Americans to reveal the ways that race continues to shape the lives of an otherwise assimilated immigrant-origin community of color. Traditional assimilation theory and the more race- and class-conscious segmented assimilation theory have not observed persistent racialization as an obstacle to full integration for Japanese Americans given their quantified success story. Both theoretical frameworks look at Japanese American achievement in their standard measures and assume that race is no longer an obstacle. Through the lens of citizenship, however, race is revealed to limit Japanese Americans' abilities to find the full affect of belonging within mainstream, predominantly white spaces despite acculturative and socioeconomic successes. While the affects of belonging and non-belonging are difficult to measure or observe, Japanese American behaviors, practices, and interactions can be understood as responses to this affect rooted in marginalization based on their racial uniform. Such behaviors and practices are the performative effects of the incalculable affective dimensions of citizenship.

The lens of citizenship refocuses attention not only on the agentic success and actions of immigrants and racial minorities but also on the behaviors and shifts occurring within society itself, what Portes and Rumbaut (2014) have long referenced as contexts of reception. An analysis of citizenship and the affect of belonging requires an examination of how various status attributes are perceived by mainstream society and how immigrants and racial minorities are treated based upon those perceptions. As Glenn (2011) remarks in her definition of citizenship as a matter of belonging, it requires the recognition of membership by other community members. The lens of citizenship and the Japanese American case further reveals how contexts of reception extend beyond the immigrant and second generation and form contexts of racialization and recognized citizenship across multiple and later generations.

While this study focuses on the Japanese American case, it can also be useful to understand the integration progression of other communities that experience a racially marginalized status. As full citizenship, particularly its affective dimensions, remains elusive for many Black, Indigenous, and other people of color, the framework allows analytical space for the durability of inequality beyond socioeconomic and acculturative success. Citizenship as an analytical concept may also be useful in revealing the impact of other statuses beyond race on the integration process. Recall that the seminal work on substantive citizenship, Evelyn Nakano Glenn's *Unequal Freedom* (2002), was an intersectional study of race, gender, and class. While statuses such as gender, social class, and sexual orientation will certainly function differently from race in processes of integration, future research should examine how each impacts a sense of belonging individually and intersectionally.

In Closing

In a dusty box in my parents' garage, a photograph from the Deer Park days lay untouched for decades (figure C.1). There is no signage in the photo. What is visible in the photograph is around fifty young men and women, mostly Japanese Americans, wearing happi coats, yukata, or work shirts standing under torii gates and paper lanterns framed by bamboo with non-descript rooftops and powerlines in the background. To the casual observer, the fading colors and blurry lines of the photograph might correctly point to late 1960s. The content, however, might incorrectly place the photograph in Japan.

Of course, I am not a casual observer. I heard stories and grew up among family and friendships that began at Deer Park. I am a product of Deer Park. I know that this photograph was taken in Buena Park, an Orange County suburb in Southern California. I know that the Japanese Americans in this photograph are third generation (sansei). I see the American popular culture and fashion in their faces, hairstyles, and

Figure C.1. Deer Park employees gather for a group photograph at the bridge entrance to the park circa 1968. Courtesy of Gary and Sheri Nakano.

color choices. I am told that this photograph was taken in the early days of Deer Park and that these young men and women are standing at the foot of a bridge leading into the entrance of the amusement park. The moment and location of this photograph are emblematic of the hopes of sansei employees of what might be found at the park and the potential for community and belonging that lay just inside the gates. This hope and potential—these affects—are deeply shaped by race. The imagery represented in this photograph—both the readily apparent and that requiring additional insight—is an ideal metaphor to close this book.

This book began by introducing Deer Park as a microcosm of the processes and impacts of race on the lives of later-generation Japanese Americans in the affluent Southern California suburbs. The nuanced themes of local invisibility and racial visibility through foreignness, the negotiated and visual claims of citizenship, and the importance of ethnic community as a source of belonging are all present in this image. In illuminating these themes, the words in this book are a call to reimagine sociological prescriptions of assimilation by placing race at the center of our analyses as it is a central organizing force in every aspect of society. Race is not only impactful in the designated outcomes of assimilation but fundamentally shapes the processes and lived experiences that produce such outcomes. Such an examination of race also illuminates an understanding of unseen impacts—affect and its performative effects. As the hopeful photographed faces foreshadow the friends and community waiting for them at Deer Park—feeling that race has brought them together but perhaps without the language to describe it—*Japanese Americans and the Racial Uniform* seeks to add to the critical language that will enable us to discuss race in constructive and progressive ways and works toward a growth in scholarship that continues to clarify how much race matters.

ACKNOWLEDGMENTS

In completing this monograph, the acknowledgments section both excited and terrified me. I looked forward to the public opportunity to express my deepest gratitude to the multitude of people who have helped to bring this book to fruition. I worried about the names and impacts I might neglect to mention. I apologize now for the inevitably incomplete nature of these acknowledgments.

First and foremost, this book would be nothing without all the sansei and yonsei who generously shared their time, memories, and keepsakes with me to produce the data at the heart of this project. I have done my best to stay true to their words and sentiments. I hope I have done their stories justice. All images throughout the book are used for the purposes of scholarly discussion and analysis, but a special thank you to Gary and Sheri Nakano, Karen Yoshikawa, and Vicki Ohira Yoshikawa for providing the images in these pages.

This book capped off my doctoral studies at the University of California, Irvine (UCI), and was completed as a faculty member at California State University, Stanislaus (Stan State). At UCI, Rubén Rumbaut (co-chair), Glenn Mimura, and Francesca Polletta provided invaluable direction and support early in this process as members of my dissertation committee. I must make special mention of two other committee members—Linda Trinh Vo (co-chair) and Eiichiro Azuma. Both Linda and Eiichiro have gone above and beyond as mentors during my graduate work—Eiichiro since my first year as an undergraduate at Penn—and my faculty career. Both were instrumental in introducing me to the book publication process. Linda has been a staunch supporter of this project since my first clumsy proposal. I hope that Eiichiro does not hold it against me that I proceeded with a Japanese American project despite his early advice. After all, he played a huge role in shaping my interest and understanding in the subject. Ann Hironaka and Catherine Bolzendahl also provided meaningful guidance and support for this project at every stage. At Stan State, my colleagues in the Department of Sociology, Gerontology, and Gender Studies provided encouragement and a home for the development of this book. My college dean, Jim Tuedio, has provided support for this project in various forms throughout my time at Stan State.

At NYU Press, I am grateful to my editor, Ilene Kalish, for her savvy advice and for shepherding this project through the daunting publishing process. Thank you also to Yasemin Torfilli for her care for this project and her patience with me. Anthony Ocampo, my friend and series editor, has been a long-time supporter of my work and has been a strong advocate and sounding board for me at countless moments throughout my academic career. I also thank the anonymous reviewers whose comments helped strengthen this book.

Throughout my career, I have been fortunate to connect with and build a generous community of scholars across sociology and Asian American studies who have challenged me to think ever more critically and intersectionally about how race functions in our complex world. This book has benefited from the helpful critiques of Edelina Burciaga, Kelly Ward, Paul Morgan, Jessica Kizer, Yader Lanuza, Matt Rafalow, Mark Villegas, Margaret Rhee, James Zarsadiaz, Vincent Laus, Todd Honma, and Christen Sasaki at various stages in the writing process. Sara Jo Cohen was an early supporter of this project and made important comments on early chapter drafts that changed the shape of this book. Tanya Golash-Boza, Pawan Dhingra, Wendy Cheng, and Yaejoon Kwon served as informal reviewers of the full manuscript and provided instrumental feedback at a crucial moment in this project. Michael Omi has been a kind and selfless mentor to me ever since I randomly requested a meeting as a wayward graduate student living in the Bay Area on fellowship. Thank you for all the guidance—and lunches.

This book has also benefited tremendously by community and friendship beyond academia—with some overlap. Edelina Burciaga and Kelly Ward have been my academic ride-or-dies since grad school, but our friendship and group chat have grown to be so much more than that. My Stan Gays—Rachel Grimshaw, Matthew Moberly, and Paul Morgan— have been my homebase at Stan State and an important repository of personal complaints and judgements.

Thank you Katie Furuyama, Warren Chung, and Stephanie Liu for your friendship. The San Francisco Spikes Soccer Club has been an essential escape and reset for me time and again as my enthusiasm for writing this book ebbed and flowed. The individual and group friendships made there are too many to name, but I hope that you know who you are and how important you have been to this process on and off the pitch.

Last, but certainly not least, thank you to my family. I dedicate this book to my parents, Gary and Sheri Nakano, because of their unending love and support. My father fought and lost his battle with cancer as I completed the first full draft of this manuscript. My only regret for this book is that he will never hold a copy in his hands and see how central he has always been to my work. To my sisters Liane and Blaire and brothers-in-law Anthony and Bobby, thank you for always being there and providing the scaffolding of my support system. To Tyson, Dominic, Tre, and Nicholas, my nephews and the next generation of Japanese Americans, this book is also for you in the hope that it will help you know a bit about your history and prepare you for your future.

NOTES

1. RACE, BELONGING, AND THE AFFECTIVE DIMENSIONS OF CITIZENSHIP

1 Robert Ezra Park looms large in a US brand of sociology that championed scientific positivism and emphasized the role of social contact known as the Chicago school (Yu 2001). Invoking Park's words for the title of this book, however, is not as straightforward as simply citing a renowned sociologist. To say the least, Park and his scholarship are divisive within sociology and beyond. Park's formulation of the race-relations cycle is responsible for centering assimilation in social science analyses of immigration and race. This cycle has been critiqued for its blind eye to structural impediments and its prescriptive—rather than descriptive—orientation (Steinberg 2007). Aldon Morris levied strong critiques of Park's racial analyses as not only overly reliant on biological determinism but explicitly anti-Black (2015). Henry Yu (2001) demonstrates that Park built many of his ideas and writings on the work of graduate students and local informants who were ethnic insiders, often without proper credit. Contrast these critiques with the glowing biography of Park that appears on the American Sociological Association's website as one of the association's former presidents; note that Aldon Morris is also a past president of this academic body. In leveraging the concept of the racial uniform, I do not intend to recuperate Park's image. I do not believe building directly on a useful concept is condoning the entire body of work or the life of any scholar. It is worth noting that I am also not the first Asian Americanist to leverage Park's racial uniform. Ronald Takaki is often noted as using this concept in his lectures and included it in his essay "The Centrality of Racism in Asian American History" (2003, 12). Sucheng Chan (2004) also used the concept.

2 Tsuda's *Japanese American Ethnicity* is one of the few (and recent) book-length studies on the contemporary Japanese American community and covers many of the same themes as this book. In exploring how Japanese Americans navigate and claim their "racial citizenship," Tsuda focuses on the extent to which Japanese Americans "remain connected to their ancestral cultural heritage" (Tsuda 2016, 5). This heritage "consists of their traditional culture, which originates in and is derived from their ethnic/ancestral homeland. . . . In contrast, cultural forms adopted from the natal homeland by ethnic minorities are usually understood to be part of the assimilative process" (13). Tsuda finds compelling examples of how racialization and multiculturalism impact how Japanese Americans explore and

practice their ethnic heritage. This focus, however, differs from my own in this book. In exploring the impact of race on ethnicity, I am less concerned with the maintenance of ancestral cultural practices than I am with the maintenance of community ties. Community formation is certainly impacted by race and engenders new cultural practices that are not simply derived from an ancestral cultural heritage nor adopted cultural forms of the host society.

3 On the benefits of persistent ethnic community, also see Lacy (2007) and Portes and Rumbaut (2006).

4 Some scholars have claimed that the processes of assimilation for some ethnic groups, particularly non-whites, may be delayed by a generation or two but are nonetheless progressing in the same manner as early waves of European immigrants (Brown 2007). While such assertions remain open questions, calling attention to the delay itself also marks a racial difference in the assimilation process as defined by the canon. But how long can we claim that something is delayed when it has not yet arrived? Is it just to tell a certain type of immigrant to wait, it gets better? The question should not be when will assimilation happen, but does assimilation happen in the same way for all groups? If so, why do processes or timelines differ?

5 Studies making explicit examination of the intersection of race and middle-class status have largely overlooked Asian American experiences, particularly surprising given their ascribed model minority status. However, and perhaps because of the model minority label and their positioning as "honorary white," it is assumed that the Asian American middle class is the same as the white middle class and therefore unworthy of further investigation. Lee and Zhou (2015) offer an application of the minority cultures of mobility framework to the Asian American case, focusing on second and 1.5 generation Chinese and Vietnamese Americans. Lee and Zhou demonstrate a persistent reliance on cross-class ethnic resources and knowledge and co-ethnic role models and mobility prototypes in aiding upward mobility and middle-class attainment rather than convergence and mimicry of native-born white norms. This book focuses on a middle-class and suburban segment of the Japanese American population to add to the dearth of literature on Asian American cultures of mobility, furthering our understanding of how differential racialization impacts middle-class experiences.

6 The recruitment from former Deer Park employees also followed this strategy. Deer Park is not a Japanese American institution. It was an amusement park owned and operated by white capitalists that leveraged Japanese culture and Japanese faces. It was not intended to be a space for Japanese American identity and community formation, regardless of its ultimate impact.

7 Multiracial individuals are those who self-identify as Japanese American and one or more other races. Multiethnic individuals are those who self-identify as Japanese American and one or more other Asian ethnicities, but not any other racial category.

8 In only one case, a former Deer Park employee explicitly declined participation in the study because of social proximity. However, that participant's spouse agreed to be interviewed and is included in the sample.

9 My apologies to journalists. These words—not my own—reflect academic elitism and not the realities of journalistic rigor and training. I do not mean to offend or demean the important field of journalism.

2. CONTEXTUALIZING JAPANESE AMERICA

1 The Page Act of 1875 was the first federal immigration law and banned the entry of immigrants from Asia who did not come voluntarily and/or came for "lewd and immoral purposes." This law was intended to end the entry of Asian contract laborers and Asian women, who were thought to come to the United States solely for the purpose of prostitution. The impact of this law was to effectively thwart the immigration of Chinese women into the United States (Chan 1991; Takaki 1998).

2 Many Japanese American men were bachelors when they left Japan for the United States. As these bachelors sought Japanese wives, many relied on family members or matchmakers back in Japan to find suitable spouses, giving rise to the picture bride phenomenon. Picture brides were so named because their marriages and voyages to the United States were often based only on (often outdated or even fraudulent) photographs of their future spouses. This may have been the first instance of "catfishing."

3 While bans on Asian immigration into the United States are generally bookended by the Chinese Exclusion Act of 1882 and the National-Origins Quota Act of 1924, it is important to note that the Asiatic Barred Zone was created in 1917 and extended from the Middle East, through South and Southeast Asia, and into the Pacific Islands. The Page Act of 1875, which euphemistically targeted immigrant women from China, and the Tydings McDuffie Act of 1934, which prohibited the free movement of colonial Filipino nationals into the United States, are also part of this history of exclusion (Takaki 1998).

4 During the exclusion period, a loophole was created in 1947 in the Soldier Brides Act. The Soldier Brides Act allowed for the entry of wives of US servicemen returning from overseas deployment, including Japan and other parts of Asia, regardless of race and outside national-origin quotas (Chan 1991; Simpson 2002; Spickard 2009; Takaki 1998).

5 With the rise of the Japanese economy in the 1970s and 1980s, many migrants from Japan to the United States came on temporary business assignments on rotation in the US offices of Japanese companies. This practice brought a revolving door of Japanese businessmen and their families as temporary residents in the US (Kurotani 2005; Nakano 2014).

6 The time period of immigration from Japan is highly gendered. Because of the specificities of the Gentleman's Agreement, nearly all Issei men arrived prior to 1908. Women represented a very small proportion of immigrants prior to 1908

but represented the majority of immigrants from 1908 to 1924 (Glenn 1988; Takaki 1998).

7 In 1960, the US census also included "Hawaiian" and "Part Hawaiian" under the "Asian" race category (Pew Research Center 2020, https://www.pewresearch.org /interactives/what-census-calls-us/).

8 See *Los Angeles Almanac*; *Orange County Almanac*; 2010 United States census.

9 While imprecise, generational cohorts are estimated based on accepted conventions of the birth year ranges for nisei and sansei and the birth years of my own research subjects (Glenn 1988; Nakano 2014; Petersen 1971). I estimate that sansei were born between 1940 and 1964. Yonsei are estimated to be born between 1965 and 2004.

10 Estimates for nativity and multiethnicity/multiraciality are based on IPUMS ACS data.

11 The available American Community Survey data from 2015 and 2019 showed marginal growth of the multiracial and multiethnic Japanese American population compared to 2010.

3. THE FALSE PROMISE OF ASSIMILATION

1 All data are from the five-year aggregate of the American Community Survey of the US census. Also see Alba and Nee (2003), Fugita and O'Brien (1994), King-O'Riain (2006), Spickard (2009), and Teranishi (2010).

2 Examining a similar issue and location, Kurashige (2008) focuses Brooks's argument to show that Japanese American racial positioning within the US landscape had been dependent on geopolitics and US-Japan relations long before the Cold War and even before World War II. In addition, Kurashige highlights the triangulation and coalition building with African Americans. Japanese American oppositional placement vis-à-vis African Americans in Los Angeles resulted in numerous shifts in residential acceptance of these two groups, where Japanese Americans were not always the beneficiaries.

4. HOW TO BE COOL AT DEER PARK

1 The Fuji Folk, costumed characters with their green skin and slanted eyes, added to the park's repertoire of attractions in the early 1970s further caricatured Japanese people and culture. The Fuji Folk were added to the park's entertainment amid much controversy and some protest by groups such as the Japanese American Citizens League due to their racist portrayal of Japanese people. The park stood by their new mascots claiming that the Fuji Folk were not intended to be representations of Japanese people but rather fantasy creatures who descended from Mount Fuji.

5. THE RACIAL REPLENISHMENT OF ETHNICITY

1 In discussing Asian American racialization, it is also important to clarify my usage of race rather than panethnicity. Panethnic collectivities do not rely on similar

physical markers as seen in racial groupings. Panethnicity connects individuals and groups across and beyond ethnic boundaries based on a sense of linked history, fate, and structural position (Espiritu 1992; Okamoto 2014). When used panethnically, the term *Asian American* encompasses a broader set of people and ethnic groups compared to a racial definition. Notwithstanding power differences among constituent ethnic groups, Asian American panethnicity as a political identity is generally intended to include people of East Asian, Southeast Asian, and South Asian descent (Espiritu 1992; Nakano 2013; Okamoto 2014). In contrast, popular racial understandings of South Asian Americans—generally people of Indian, Pakistani, Sri Lankan, Bangladeshi, Nepali, or Bhutanese descent—do not confuse their phenotypical markers with those of Americans of East and Southeast Asian ancestry (Okamoto 2014; Schacther 2014; Shankar and Srikanth 1998). South Asians are racially distinct from East and Southeast Asians. I recognize that the distinction drawn here diverges from the definitions and categorizations of race imposed by the US census. On the US census, Asian Indian and other South Asian groups are categorized as part of the Asian race. This current configuration has existed since the 1980 census (Okamoto 2014). Nonetheless, given how sansei and yonsei participating in this study discuss their identities and community affiliations, they are clearly functioning off a racial understanding of Asian American identity and community rather than a panethnic one.

2   See *Los Angeles Almanac*; *Orange County Almanac*; 2010 US census.

3   While some have argued that clothing and mannerisms may be visible cultural markers of generation and acculturation (Louie 2004; Tuan 1999;), chapter 3 of this book demonstrates how the racial body can often obscure such markers in the example of sansei Deer Park employees.

4   In another example of acculturation and hybridity, many Buddhist religious institutions within the Japanese American community are officially named "churches" rather than "temples." This unique Japanese American formation sets Japanese American Buddhist churches apart from the Buddhist temples associated with other Asian American ethnicities.

5   In using the nomenclature *Japanese Americans* and *Japanese immigrants* to distinguish these two groups, I do not mean to insinuate that immigrants are not or cannot be Americans. They most certainly are and can be.

6   Political commentary was largely confined to yonsei respondents. While Deer Park (1967–1974) was open for operation during a tumultuous political moment in US history and formative years of the Asian American and redress movements and employed a highly politicized age demographic, former sansei employees surprisingly made little to no mention of contemporary politics and social movements. When I began this project, I thought Deer Park might be a site for the burgeoning racial justice and anti-war movements, as I had found an anti-war sticker in one of the old boxes that held my parents' Deer Park memorabilia. Neither of my parents could recall where the sticker was from or why it was in the box. Similar reactions came up across my interviews. Even when directly

asked about politics, respondents had no recollection of overtly political activities or discussions at Deer Park. Most said Deer Park was an apolitical space because many of the employees were "too young" (high school) to be interested in politics. But sansei employees were a mix of high school and college ages. Some sansei respondents would eventually become involved in community organizations with political missions, such as the Japanese American Citizens League, but these activities were oddly separate from their Deer Park social lives and were not discussed in political terms. While I did not get to interview him for this project, former California state assemblymember and noted civil rights activist Warren Furutani was mentioned by several sansei respondents as a Deer Park alumnus. But even if he had attempted to bring a political consciousness to Deer Park, it seems that the vast majority of employees did not want to engage in politics. The reasons for this remain unclear.

6. HAVE ETHNICITY, WILL TRAVEL

1 While Laura references the church membership as generically "Asian," Anaheim Free Methodist Church is historically Japanese American, and the majority of its members continue to be Japanese American.

7. ETHNIC HISTORY AS AMERICAN HISTORY

1 Attachment to a non-US culture or national identity should not preclude any claim on a US-based identity and membership.

2 While the number of generations in the US is how Japanese Americans lay claim to an American identity, I am aware—and agree—that this is a problematic and inaccurate metric.

CONCLUSION

1 My usage of *Asian* here references a racial marker, as I hope has been clear throughout the book. Individuals who are racialized as Asian in the context of the COVID-19 pandemic have largely been of East and Southeast Asian descent and not of South Asian descent. This is not meant to exclude South Asian Americans from Asian American formations—particularly panethnic ones—or to say that issues facing South Asian communities are not inherently Asian American concerns. They are.

2 Participants in this symposium included Herbert J. Gans, Mary C. Waters, Philip Kasinitz, Peter Kivisto, Werner Sollors, Richard Alba, Nancy Foner, Stephen Steinberg, and John Mollenkopf.

3 Around the time of this book's publication, Crocs were a popular, functional slip-on shoe that could be adorned with charms, known as Jibbitz. Charm designs ranged from cartoon and video game characters, sports teams, emojis, and other objects allowing wearers to display their personalities, identities, interests, and style.

BIBLIOGRAPHY

Alba, Richard D. 1985. *Italian Americans: Into the Twilight of Ethnicity*. New York: Prentice Hall.

Alba, Richard D., John Logan, Amy Lutz, and Brian Stults. 2002. "Only English by the Third Generation? Loss and Prevention of the Mother Tongue among the Grandchildren of Contemporary Immigrants." *Demography* 39:467–84.

Alba, Richard D., and Victor Nee. 2003. *Remaking the American Mainstream: Assimilation and Contemporary Immigration*. Cambridge, MA: Harvard University Press.

Almaguer, Tomas. 1994. *Racial Fault Lines: The Historical Origins of White Supremacy in California*. Berkeley: University of California Press.

Anderson, Benedict. 1991. *Imagined Communities: Reflections on the Origin and Spread of Nationalism*. New York: Verso.

Barthes, Roland. 1977. *Image-Music-Text*. New York: Hill and Wang.

Bean, Frank D., and Gillian Stevens. 2003. *America's Newcomers and the Dynamics of Diversity*. New York: Russell Sage Foundation.

Bratter, Jenifer, and Rosalind B. King. 2008. "'But Will It Last?': Marital Instability among Interracial and Same-Race Couples." *Family Relations: An Interdisciplinary Journal of Applied Family Studies* 57 (2): 160–71.

Bratter, Jenifer, and Tufuku Zuberi. 2008. "As Racial Boundaries 'Fade': Racial Stratification and Interracial Marriage." In *White Logic, White Methods: Racism and Methodology*, edited by Tufuku Zuberi and Eduardo Bonilla-Silva, 251–70. Lanham, MD: Rowman & Littlefield.

Brooks, Charlotte. 2009. *Alien Neighbors, Foreign Friends: Asian Americans, Housing, and the Transformation of Urban California*. Chicago: University Of Chicago Press.

Brown, Susan K. 2007. "Delayed Spatial Assimilation: Multigenerational Incorporation of the Mexican-Origin Population in Los Angeles." *City & Community* 6:193–209.

Carbado, Devon W. 2005. "Racial Naturalization." *American Quarterly* 57:633–58.

Caulfield, Jon. 1996. "Visual Sociology and Sociological Vision, Revisited." *American Sociologist* 27 (3): 56–68.

Chan, Sucheng. 1991. *Asian Americans: An Interpretive History*. Woodbridge, CT: Twayne.

———. 2004. *Survivors: Cambodian Refugees in the United States*. Urbana: University of Illinois Press.

Charles, Camille Zubrinsky. 2007. "Comfort Zones: Immigration, Acculturation, and the Neighborhood Racial-Composition Preferences of Latinos and Asians." *Du Bois Review* 4:41–77.

Chavez, Leo R. 2001. *Covering Immigration: Popular Images and the Politics of the Nation*. Berkeley: University of California Press.

Cheng, Anne Anlin. 2000. *The Melancholy of Race: Psychoanalysis, Assimilation, and Hidden Grief*. New York: Oxford University Press.

Cheng, Cindy I-Fen. 2013. *Citizens of Asian America: Democracy and Race during the Cold War*. New York: New York University Press.

Chin, Christina B. 2016a. "The Continued Legacy of Japanese American Youth Basketball Leagues." In *Asian American Sporting Cultures*, edited by Stanley I. Thangaraj, Constancio Arnaldo, and Christina B. Chin, 180–95. New York: New York University Press.

———. 2016b. "'We've Got Team Spirit!': Ethnic Community Building and Japanese American Youth Basketball Leagues." *Ethnic and Racial Studies* 39 (6): 1070–88. https://doi.org/10.1080/01419870.2015.1103878.

Clough, Patricia Ticineto. 2007. Introduction to *The Affective Turn: Theorizing the Social*, edited by Patricia Ticineto Clough and Jean Halley, 1–33. Durham, NC: Duke University Press.

Cohen, Elizabeth F. 2009. *Semi-Citizenship in Democratic Politics*. New York: Cambridge University Press.

Cornell, Stephen, and Douglas Hartmann. 2006. *Ethnicity and Race: Making Identities in a Changing World*. Thousand Oaks, CA: Sage.

Daniels, Roger. 1962. *Politics of Prejudice: The Anti-Japanese Movement in California and the Struggle for Japanese Exclusion*. Berkeley: University of California Press.

Dear, Michael. 2002. "Los Angeles and the Chicago School: Invitation to a Debate." *City & Community* 1 (1): 5–32.

Dhingra, Pawan. 2020. *Hyper Education: Why Good Schools, Good Grades, and Good Behavior Are Not Enough*. New York: New York University Press.

Du Bois, W. E. B. ([1903] 1997). *The Souls of Black Folk*. Boston: Bedford Books.

Dudziak, Mary L. 2000. *Cold War Civil Rights: Race and the Image of American Democracy*. Princeton, NJ: Princeton University Press.

España-Maram, Linda. 2006. *Creating Masculinity in Los Angeles's Little Manila: Working-Class Filipinos and Popular Culture, 1920s–1950s*. New York: Columbia University Press.

Espiritu, Yen Le. 1992. *Asian American Panethnicity: Bridging Institutions and Identities*. Philadelphia: Temple University Press.

———. 2008. *Asian American Women and Men: Labors, Law, and Love*. Lanham, MD: Rowman & Littlefield.

Ewing, Eve. 2018. *Ghost in the Schoolyard: Racism and School Closings on Chicago's South Side*. Chicago: University of Chicago Press.

Forstall, Richard L. 1995. *California Population of Counties by Decennial Census: 1790 to 1990*. Washington, DC: US Bureau of the Census. http://www2.census.gov.

Fugita, Stephen S., and David J. O'Brien. 1994. *Japanese American Ethnicity: The Persistence of Community*. Seattle: University of Washington Press.

Gans, Herbert J. 1979. "Symbolic Ethnicity: The Future of Ethnic Groups and Cultures in America." *Ethnic and Racial Studies* 2:1–20.

———. 2005. "Race as Class." *Contexts* 4 (4): 17–21.

Glenn, Evelyn Nakano. 1988. *Issei, Nisei, War Bride: Three Generations of Japanese American Women in Domestic Service.* Philadelphia: Temple University Press.

———. 2002. *Unequal Freedom: How Race and Gender Shaped American Citizenship and Labor.* Cambridge, MA: Harvard University Press.

———. 2011. "Constructing Citizenship: Exclusion, Subordination, and Resistance." *American Sociological Review* 76:1–24.

Golash-Boza, Tanya. 2006. "Dropping the Hyphen: Latino(a)-American through Racialized Assimilation." *Social Forces* 85 (1): 27–55.

Gordon, Milton M. 1964. *Assimilation in American Life: The Role of Race, Religion and National Origins.* New York: Oxford University Press.

Gotanda, Neil. 1996. "Towards Repeal of Asian Exclusion." In *Asian Americans and Congress: A Documentary History,* 309–36. Westport, CT: Greenwood.

Gutiérrez, David G. 1995. *Walls and Mirrors: Mexican Americans, Mexican Immigrants, and the Politics of Ethnicity.* Berkeley: University of California Press.

Hall, Stuart. 1993. "Encoding, Decoding" In *The Cultural Studies Reader,* edited by Simon During, 90–103. New York: Routledge.

Hansen, Debra Gold, and Mary P. Ryan. 1991. "Public Ceremony in a Private Culture: Orange County Celebrates the Fourth of July." In *Postsuburban California: The Transformation of Orange County since World War II,* 165–89. Berkeley: University of California Press.

Harper, Douglas. 1998. "Visual Sociology: Expanding Sociological Vision." *American Sociologist* 19 (1): 54–70.

Hoefell, Elizabeth M., Sonya Rastogi, Myoung Ouk Kim, and Hasan Shahid. 2012. *The Asian Population: 2010* (C2010BR-11). Suitland, MD: US Census Bureau.

Ichioka, Yuji. 1988. *The Issei: The World of the First Generation Japanese Immigrants, 1885–1924.* New York: Free Press.

Itzigsohn, José, and Karida Brown. 2015. "Sociology and the Theory of Double Consciousness: W. E. B. Du Bois's Phenomenology of Racialized Subjectivity." *Du Bois Review* 12 (2): 231–48.

Jeung, Russell, Aggie Yellow Horse, Tara Popovic, and Richard Lim. 2021. *Stop AAPI Hate National Report.* StopAAPIHate.org.

Jimenez, Tomas. 2009. *Replenished Ethnicity: Mexican Americans, Immigration, and Identity.* Berkeley: University of California Press.

Jung, Moon-Kie. 2009. "The Racial Unconscious of Assimilation Theory." *Du Bois Review* 6:375–95.

Kana'iaupuni, Shawn Malia, and Carolyn A. Liebler. 2005. "Pondering Poi Dog: Place and Racial Identification of Multiracial Native Hawaiians." *Ethnic and Racial Studies* 28:687–721.

Kang, Laura Hyun Yu. 2002. *Compositional Subjects: Enfiguring Asian/American Women.* Durham, NC: Duke University Press.

Kasinitz, Philip. 2014. "Herbert Gans and the Death of Miss Norway." *Ethnic and Racial Studies Review* 37:770–73.

Kikumura, Akemi, and Harry H. L. Kitano. 1973. "Interracial Marriage: A Picture of the Japanese Americans." *Journal of Social Issues* 29:67–81.

Kim, Jodi. 2010. *Ends of Empire: Asian American Critique and the Cold War*. Minneapolis: University of Minnesota Press.

Kim, Nadia Y. 2007. "Critical Thoughts on Asian American Assimilation in the Whitening Literature." *Social Forces* 86:561–74.

King, Rebecca Chiyoko. 2002. "'Eligible' to be Japanese American: Multiraciality in Basketball Leagues and Beauty Pageants." In *Contemporary Asian American Communities: Intersections and Divergences*, edited by Linda Trinh Vo and Rick Bonus, 120–33. Philadelphia: Temple University Press.

King-O'Riain, Rebecca Chiyoko. 2006. *Pure Beauty: Judging Race in Japanese American Beauty Pageants*. Minneapolis: University of Minnesota Press.

———. 2019. "Mixed-Race Japanese Americans Millennials: Millennials or Japanese Americans?" In *Japanese American Millennials: Rethinking Generation, Community, and Diversity*, edited by Michael Omi, Dana Y. Nakano, and Jeffrey T. Yamashita, 171–89. Philadelphia: Temple University Press.

Klein, Christina. 2003. *Cold War Orientalism: Asia in the Middlebrow Imagination, 1945–1961*. Berkeley: University of California Press.

Kling, Rob, Spencer C. Olin, and Mark Poster. 1991. *Postsuburban California: The Transformation of Orange County since World War II*. Berkeley: University of California Press.

Knowles, Carolina. 2006. "Seeing Race through the Lens." *Ethnic and Racial Studies* 29:512–29.

Kozen, Cathleen K. 2012. "Redress as American-Style Justice: Congressional Narratives of Japanese American Redress at the End of the Cold War." *Time & Society* 21:104–20.

Krug, Gary J. 2001. "At the Feet of the Master: Three Stages in the Appropriation of Okinawan Karate into Angle-American Culture." *Cultural Studies ↔ Critical Methodologies* 1 (4): 395–410.

Kruse, Kevin M. 2005. *White Flight: Atlanta and the Making of Modern Conservatism*. Princeton, NJ: Princeton University Press.

Kurashige, Lon. 2002. *Japanese American Celebration and Conflict: A History of Ethnic Identity and Festival, 1934–1990*. Berkeley: University of California Press.

Kurashige, Scott. 2007. *The Shifting Grounds of Race: Black and Japanese Americans in the Making of Multiethnic Los Angeles*. Princeton, NJ: Princeton University Press.

Kurotani, Sawa. 2005. *Home Away from Home: Japanese Corporate Wives in the United States*. Durham, NC: Duke University Press.

Lacy, Karyn R. 2007. *Blue-Chip Black: Race, Class, and Status in the New Black Middle Class*. Berkeley: University of California Press.

Lee, Erika. 2016. *The Making of Asian America: A History*. New York: Simon & Schuster.

Lee, Jennifer, and Frank D. Bean. 2007. "Reinventing the Color Line: Immigration and America's New Racial/Ethnic Divide." *Social Forces* 86:561–86.

———. 2010. *The Diversity Paradox: Immigration and the Color Line in 21st Century America*. New York: Russell Sage Foundation.

Lee, Jennifer, and Min Zhou. 2015. *The Asian American Achievement Paradox*. New York: Russell Sage Foundation.

Lee, Robert G. 1999. *Orientals: Asian Americans in Popular Culture*. Philadelphia: Temple University Press.

Leong, Andrew Way. 2019. "Critique Is Not That Old, Composition Is Not That New: Sadakichi Hartmann's Conversations with Walt Whitman." In *The New Walt Whitman Studies*, edited by Matt Cohen, 185–202. Cambridge, UK: Cambridge University Press.

Levin, Brian. 2021. *Report to the Nation: Anti-Asian Prejudice & Hate Crime*. San Bernardino: California State University, San Bernardino Center for the Study of Hate & Extremism.

Levine, Gene Norman, and Colbert Rhodes. 1981. *Japanese-American Community: A Three-Generation Study*. New York: Praeger.

Lew-Williams, Beth. 2018. *The Chinese Must Go: Violence, Exclusion, and the Making of the Alien in America*. Cambridge, MA: Harvard University Press.

Liebler, Carolyn A. 2010. "Homelands and Indigenous Identities in a Multiracial Era." *Social Science Research* 39:596–609.

Lim, Shirley Jennifer. 2005. *A Feeling of Belonging: Asian American Women's Public Culture, 1930–1960*. New York: New York University Press.

Lopez, David. 1978. "Chicano Language Loyalty in an Urban Setting." *Sociology and Social Research* 62:267–78.

Lopez, Ian Haney. 1996. *White by Law: The Legal Construction of Race*. New York: New York University Press.

Lorde, Audre. 1984. *Sister Outsider: Essays and Speeches*. Berkeley, CA: Ten Speed Press.

Los Angeles Almanac. 1998–2014. "Historical Census Records of Ethnic Groups in Los Angeles County 1850 to 1960." http://www.laalmanac.com/.

Los Angeles Historical Resources Survey. 2018. *Los Angeles Citywide Historic Context Statement—Context: Japanese Americans in Los Angeles, 1869–1970*. Los Angeles, CA: Department of City Planning—Office of Historic Resources.

Louie, Andrea. 2004. *Chineseness across Borders: Renegotiating Chinese Identities in China and the United States*. Durham, NC: Duke University Press.

Maira, Sunaina Marr. 2009. *Missing: Youth, Citizenship, and Empire after 9/11*. Durham, NC: Duke University Press.

Maki, Mitchell T., Harry H. Kitano, and S. Megan Berthold. 1999. *Achieving the Impossible Dream: How Japanese Americans Obtained Redress*. Champaign: University of Illinois Press.

Massey, Douglas S., and Nancy A. Denton. 1993. *American Apartheid: Segregation and the Making of the Underclass*. Cambridge, MA: Harvard University Press.

Matsumoto, Valerie J. 2014. *City Girls: The Nisei Social World in Los Angeles, 1920–1950*. New York: Oxford University Press.

McGirr, Lisa. 2001. *Suburban Warriors: The Origins of the New American Right*. Princeton, NJ: Princeton University Press.

Mettler, Meghan Warner. 2018. *How to Reach Japan by Subway: America's Fascination with Japanese Culture, 1945–1965*. Lincoln: University of Nebraska Press.

Mimura, Glen. 2009. *Ghostlife of Third Cinema: Asian American Film and Video*. Minneapolis: University of Minnesota Press.

Montero, Darrel. 1980. *Japanese Americans: Changing Patterns of Ethnic Affiliation over Three Generations*. Boulder, CO: Westview.

Morris, Aldon. 2017. *The Scholar Denied: W. E. B. Du Bois and the Birth of Modern Sociology*. Berkeley: University of California Press.

Muller, Eric L. 2001. *Free to Die for Their Country: The Story of the Japanese American Draft Resisters in World War II*. Chicago: University of Chicago Press.

Nakagawa, Gordon. 1995. "Deformed Subjects, Docile Bodies: Disciplinary Practices and Subject-Constitution in Stories of Japanese-American Internment." In *Narrative and Social Control: Critical Perspectives*, edited by Dennis K. Mumby, 143–62. Newbury Park, CA: Sage.

Nakano, Dana Y. 2013. "An Interlocking Panethnicity: The Negotiation of Multiple Identities among Asian American Social Movement Leaders." *Sociological Perspectives* 56:569–95.

———. 2014. "Japanese Immigration." In *Asian American Society: An Encyclopedia*. Edited by Mary Yu Danico and J. Geoffrey Golson. Thousand Oaks, CA: Sage.

———. 2018. "Telling the Right Story: Narrative as a Mechanism for Japanese American Ethnic Boundary Maintenance." *Sociological Inquiry* 88 (2): 216–44.

Nakashima, Cynthia L. 1992. "An Invisible Monster: The Creation and Denial of Mixed Race People in America." In *Racially Mixed People in America*, edited by Maria P. P. Root, 162–78. Newbury Park, CA: Sage.

National Park Service. 2001. *Report to the President on Japanese-American Internment Sites Preservation*. Washington, DC: US Department of the Interior.

Neckerman, Kathryn M., Prudence Carter, and Jennifer Lee. 1999. "Segmented Assimilation and Minority Cultures of Mobility." *Ethnic and Racial Studies* 22:945–65.

Nishi, Midori. 1958. "Japanese Settlement in the Los Angeles Area." *Yearbook of the Association of Pacific Coast Geographers* 20:35–48.

Nishime, Leilani. 2014. *Undercover Asian: Multiracial Asian Americans in Visual Culture*. Champaign: University of Illinois Press.

Nye, Russell B. "Eight Ways of Looking at an Amusement Park." *Journal of Popular Culture* 15 (1): 63–75.

Obasogie, Osagie K. 2013. *Blinded by Sight: Seeing Race through the Eyes of the Blind*. Stanford, CA: Stanford University Press.

Ochoa, Gilda L. 2004. *Becoming Neighbors in a Mexican American Community: Power, Conflict, and Solidarity*. Austin: University of Texas Press.

Okamoto, Dina G. 2014. *Redefining Race: Asian American Panethnicity and Shifting Ethnic Boundaries*. New York: Russell Sage Foundation.

Omi, Michael, Dana Y. Nakano, and Jeffrey T. Yamashita. 2019. Introduction to *Japanese American Millennials: Rethinking Generation, Community, and Diversity*, edited by Michael Omi, Dana Y. Nakano, and Jeffrey T. Yamashita, 1–19. Philadelphia: Temple University Press.

Omi, Michael, and Howard Winant. 2014. *Racial Formation in the United States*. 3rd ed. New York: Routledge.

Orange County Almanac. 2004–2006. "Historical Resident Population Orange County, 1890 to 2000." http://www.ocalmanac.com/.

Park, Robert E. 1914. "Racial Assimilation in Secondary Groups with Particular Reference to the Negro." *American Journal of Sociology* 19:606–23.

Pattillo, Mary. 1999. *Black Picket Fences: Privilege and Peril Among the Black Middle Class*. Chicago: University of Chicago Press.

Petersen, William. 1966. "Success Story: Japanese American Style." *New York Times Magazine*, 22–26.

———. 1971. *Japanese Americans: Oppression and Success*. New York: Random House.

Portes, Alejandro, and Rubén G. Rumbaut. 2014. *Immigrant America: A Portrait*. Berkeley: University of California Press.

Portes, Alejandro, and Min Zhou. 1993. "The New Second Generation: Segmented Assimilation and Its Variants." *Annals of the American Academy of Political and Social Science* 530:74–96.

Pulido, Laura. 2006. *Black, Brown, Yellow, and Left: Radical Activism in Los Angeles*. Berkeley: University of California Press.

Roediger, David R. 2005. *Working towards Whiteness: How America's Immigrants Became White: The Strange Journey from Ellis Island to the Suburbs*. New York: Basic Books.

Romero, Mary. 2008. "Crossing the Immigration and Race Border: A Critical Race Theory Approach to Immigration Studies." *Contemporary Justice Review* 11 (1): 23–37.

Rudrappa, Sharmila. 2004. *Ethnic Routes to Becoming American: Indian Immigrants and the Cultures of Citizenship*. New Brunswick, NJ: Rutgers University Press.

Ruggles, Steven, J. Trent Alexander, Katie Genadek, Ronald Goeken, Matthew B. Schroeder, and Matthew Sobek. *Integrated Public Use Microdata Series: Version 5.0* [Machine-readable database]. Minneapolis: University of Minnesota, 2010.

Rumbaut, Rubén G. 2009. "A Language Graveyard? The Evolution of Language Competencies, Preferences, and Use among Young Adult Children of Immigrants." In *The Education of Language Minority Immigrants in the United States*, edited by Terrance G. Wiley, Jin Sook Lee, and Russell W. Rumberger, 35–71. Tonawanda, NY: Multilingual Matters.

Rumbaut, Rubén G., Douglas S. Massey, and Frank D. Bean. 2006. "Linguistic Life Expectancies: Immigrant Language Retention in Southern California." *Population and Development Review* 32:447–60.

Saenz, Rogelio, and Karen Manges Douglas. 2015. "A Call for the Racialization of Immigration Studies: On the Transition from Ethnic Immigrants to Racialized Immigrants." *Sociology of Race and Ethnicity* 1 (1): 166–80.

Sakamoto, Arthur, Isao Takei, and Hyeyoung Woo. 2011. "Socioeconomic Differentials among Single-Race and Multi-Race Japanese Americans." *Ethnic and Racial Studies* 34:1445–65.

Schuette v. Coalition to Defend Affirmative Action et al., 572 U.S. 291 (2014).

Sedgwick, Eve Kosofsky. 2003. *Touching Feeling: Affect, Pedagogy, and Performativity.* Durham, NC: Duke University Press.

Seigworth, Gregory J., and Melissa Gregg. 2010. "An Inventory that Shimmers." In *The Affect Theory Reader*, 1–28. Durham, NC: Duke University Press.

Shibusawa, Naoko. 2006. *America's Geisha Ally: Reimagining the Japanese Enemy.* Cambridge, MA: Harvard University Press.

Shimakawa, Karen. 2002. *National Abjection: The Asian American Body Onstage.* Durham, NC: Duke University Press.

Simpson, Caroline Chung. 2002. *An Absent Presence: Japanese Americans in Postwar American Culture, 1945–1960.* Durham, NC: Duke University Press.

Skidmore, Max J. 1991. "Oriental Contributions to Western Popular Culture: The Martial Arts." *Journal of Popular Culture* 25 (1): 129–48.

Slater, Don. 1995. "Photography and Modern Vision: The Spectacle of 'Natural Magic.'" In *Visual Culture*, edited by Chris Jenks, 218–37. New York: Routledge.

Smith, Rogers M. 1997. *Civic Ideals: Conflicting Visions of Citizenship in U.S. History.* New Haven, CT: Yale University Press.

Spickard, Paul R. 2009. *Japanese Americans: The Formation and Transformations of an Ethnic Group.* Rev. ed. New Brunswick, NJ: Rutgers University Press.

Spickard, Paul R., and Rowena Fong. 1995. "Pacific Islander Americans and Multiethnicity: A Vision of America's Future?" *Social Forces* 73:1365–83.

Steinberg, Stephen. 2007. *Race Relations: A Critique.* Palo Alto, CA: Stanford University Press.

Sturken, Marita, and Lisa Cartwright. 2009. *Practices of Looking: An Introduction to Visual Culture.* New York: Oxford University Press.

Sue, Derald Wing, Christina M. Capodilupo, Gina C. Torino, Jennifer M. Bucceri, Aisha M. B. Holder, Kevin L. Nadal, and Marta Esquilin. 2007. "Racial Microaggressions in Everyday Life: Implications for Clinical Practice." *American Psychologist* 62 (4): 271–86.

Sumida, Stephen H. 1998. "East of California: Points of Origin in Asian American Studies." *Journal of Asian American Studies* 1 (1): 83–100.

Takahashi, Jere. 1997. *Nisei/Sansei: Shifting Japanese American Identities and Politics.* Philadelphia, PA: Temple University Press.

Takaki, Ronald. 1998. *Strangers from a Different Shore: A History of Asian Americans.* New York: Back Bay.

———. 2003. "The Centrality of Racism in Asian American History." In *Major Problems in Asian American History: Documents and Essays*, edited by Lon Kurashige and Alice Yang Murray, 9–15. Boston: Houghton Mifflin.

Takezawa, Yasuko. 1995. *Breaking the Silence: Redress and Japanese American Ethnicity.* Ithaca, NY: Cornell University Press.

Tan, Kevin S. Y. "Constructing a Martial Tradition: Rethinking the Popular History of Karate-Dou." *Journal of Sport & Social Issues* 28 (2): 169–92.

Teranishi, Robert T. 2010. *Asians in the Ivory Tower: Dilemmas of Racial Inequality in American Higher Education.* New York: Teachers College Press.

Tsuda, Takeyuki. 2016. *Japanese American Ethnicity: In Search of Heritage and Homeland across Generations.* New York: New York University Press.

Tuan, Mia. 1999. *Forever Foreigners or Honorary Whites?: The Asian Ethnic Experience Today.* New Brunswick, NJ: Rutgers University Press.

United States Department of Homeland Security. 2010. *Yearbook of Immigration Statistics 1969–2009.* https://www.dhs.gov.

United States Department of Interior, *Report to the President on Japanese-American Internment Sites Preservation.* Washington, DC: US Department of the Interior. http://npshistory.com.

United States Senate. 2006. *Senate Report 109–314: Preservation of Japanese American World War II Confinement Sites.* Washington, DC: US Government Publishing Office. www.govinfo.gov.

Vallejo, Jody Agius. 2012. *Barrio to Burbs: The Making of the Mexican American Middle Class.* Stanford, CA: Stanford University Press.

Volpp, Leti. 2012. "American Mestizo: Filipinos and Anti-Miscegenation Laws in California." *University of California, Davis Law Review* 33:795–835.

Warren, Jonathan W., and France Winddance Twine. 1997. "White Americans, the New Minority?: Non-Blacks and the Ever-Expanding Boundaries of Whiteness." *Journal of Black Studies* 28:200–18.

Waters, Mary C. 1990. *Ethnic Options: Choosing Identities in America.* Berkeley: University of California Press.

———. 1996. "Optional Ethnicities: For Whites Only?" In *Origins and Destinies: Immigration, Race, and Ethnicity in America,* edited by Sylvia Pedraza and Rubén G. Rumbaut, 444–54. Belmont, CA: Wadsworth.

———. 1999. *Black Identities: West Indian Immigrant Dreams and American Realities.* Cambridge, MA: Harvard University Press.

———. 2014. "Ethnic Identities in the Future: The Possible Effects of Mass Immigration and Genetic Testing." *Ethnic and Racial Studies Review* 37:766–69.

Weglyn, Michi. 1996. *Years of Infamy: The Untold Story of America's Concentration Camps.* Seattle: University of Washington Press.

Williams-Leon, Teresa, and Cynthia L. Nakashima, eds. 2001. *The Sum of Our Parts: Mixed-Heritage Asian Americans.* Philadelphia: Temple University Press.

Wilson, Robert A., and Bill Hosokawa. 1980. *East to America: A History of the Japanese in the United States.* New York: Morrow.

Wu, Ellen D. 2014. *Color of Success: Asian Americans and the Origins of the Model Minority.* Princeton, NJ: Princeton University Press.

Yanagisako, Sylvia. 1992. *Transforming the Past: Tradition and Kinship among Japanese Americans*. Stanford, CA: Stanford University Press.

Yancey, George. 2003. *Who Is White?: Latinos, Asians, and the New Black/Nonblack Divide*. Boulder, CO: Lynne Rienner.

Zarsadiaz, James. 2022. *Resisting Change in Suburbia: Asian Immigrants and Frontier Nostalgia in L. A.* Berkeley, CA: University of California Press.

Zhou, Min. 2004. "Are Asian Americans Becoming 'White?'" *Contexts* 3:29–37.

Zhou, Min, and Jennifer Lee. 2007. "Becoming Ethnic or Becoming American? Reflecting on the Divergent Pathways to Social Mobility and Assimilation among the New Second Generation." *Du Bois Review* 4:189–205.

Zhou, Min, Jennifer Lee, Jody Agius-Vallejo, Rosaura Tafoya-Estrada, and Yang Sao Xiong. 2008. "Success Attained, Deterred, and Denied: Divergent Pathways to Social Mobility in Los Angeles's New Second Generation." *ANNALS of the American Academy of Political and Social Science* 620 (1): 37–61.

INDEX

Page numbers in *italics* indicate Figures and Tables

ABOUT THE AUTHOR

DANA Y. NAKANO is Associate Professor in the Department of Sociology, Gerontology, and Gender Studies at California State University, Stanislaus, and co-editor of *Japanese American Millennials: Rethinking Generation, Community, and Diversity.*